River City

River City

A HISTORY OF
CAMPBELL RIVER
AND THE
DISCOVERY ISLANDS

For my lovely friend and neighbour, Jo-Anne,

Jeanette Taylor
December 1999

Jeanette Taylor

HARBOUR PUBLISHING

Published by

HARBOUR PUBLISHING
P.O. Box 219, Madeira Park, BC Canada V0N 2H0

Cover design by Martin Nichols
Page design and composition by Martin Nichols
Edited by Brian Brett

Printed and bound in Canada

Photo credits: BCARS = British Columbia Archives & Records Service; IWA = International Woodworkers of America; MCR = Museum at Campbell River.

Harbour Publishing acknowledges the financial support of the Government of Canada through the Book Publishing Industry Development Program (BPIDP) and the Canada Council for the Arts, and the Province of British Columbia through the British Columbia Arts Council, for its publishing activities.

THE CANADA COUNCIL | LE CONSEIL DES ARTS
FOR THE ARTS | DU CANADA
SINCE 1957 | DEPUIS 1957

Canadä

Canadian Cataloguing in Publication Data

Taylor, Jeanette, 1953-
  River city

Includes index.
ISBN 1-55017-211-5

1. Campbell River (B.C.)—History. 2. Discovery Island (B.C.)—History. I. Title.
FC3849.C35T39 1999   971.1'2   C99-910911-1
F1089.5.C35T39 1999

"We cannot question seriously or effectively without reference to the past. Without the past there is no future for man, nor even a present being. All he is is the sum of his past, and all he can hope to become is written somewhere in this experience. To know the past is not necessarily to be bound by it, but some degree of knowledge can save a lot of wasted effort and set a frame for performance that gives life the meaning of shared human endeavour."

—Roderick Haig-Brown, 1970

Contents

Preface

The town of Campbell River stretches along the benchland of Discovery Passage on the east coast of Vancouver Island. The snow-clad mountains of the Vancouver Island Range lie behind the town, while at its feet is the tightly packed archipelago of the Discovery Islands, backed by the mountains of the mainland. People have lived in this dramatic setting for thousand of years. They came to extract the wealth of natural resources in the forests, mountains and sea, braving the rapid tides that surge between the islands and the lashing rains and winds of winter. For some the place was too raw and bold; they made their stake and moved on. Others were (and continue to be) captivated by the drama of the setting, its boundless opportunity and the beauty of its wilderness.

Campbell River serves as a hub for north Vancouver Island. In just over a century it has grown from an unpretentious sport fishing and logging village to a substantial town serving over 30,000 people.

New highways and electronic communication links have made the region more accessible, and the rough edges and transient lifestyle that once characterized Campbell River have been smoothed, but the place still retains its quirky charm and working-class appeal. Its people carry on a tradition of speaking out on civic affairs, with a certain "spit in your eye hardihood" identified by Arthur Mayse, a writer who worked in Campbell River logging camps when he was a young man.

I began writing River City in 1997, after a well-timed phone call from Howard White of Harbour Publishing. I was completing the last day of a long and challenging contract as interim director at the Museum at Campbell River, and Howard called to say he had read that Campbell River was celebrating its 50th anniversary (marking the start of local government in 1947). He thought it was time for a new book on the history of the town. Could I suggest anyone to write it? I instantly recommended myself. I had lived in the district since 1977 and had worked at the Museum for more than twenty years, so I thought I would just have to brush up on a few topics and then fly at the writing. I was entirely wrong—researching and writing the book has been far more complex and demanding than I imagined. It has also been the most stimulating and rewarding project I have ever undertaken.

Some distinctive patterns emerged as I wrote the book. The Campbell River area has experienced continuous boom-and-bust cycles, starting with the recession of the 1890s, followed by the hard times of World War I (which proved more difficult for coast residents than the Great Depression of the 1930s), and so on through the recessions of the 1980s and 1990s. People who enjoyed high-end wages during the good times have been hit particularly hard by the economic downturns, but each recession has been followed by a period of unprecedented growth. And while Campbell Riverites have always enthusiastically embraced economic and technological progress, they have not accepted it at all costs. Many have chosen to live here because of their love of the natural world, and they have not been willing to witness heedless destruction of waterways and wilderness areas. We have a proud history of standing up to business and government in order to preserve key aspects of the natural environment of northern Vancouver Island.

An enjoyable aspect of researching and writing River City was selecting cameo portraits of a sampling of the many residents who have put their distinctive stamp on the region—in both its development and the preservation of its wilderness areas. Quotes from their yarns, diaries, letters and books, and many photographs, have been extracted from the treasure trove of material available in the Museum at Campbell River Archives. The museum has played a major role in bringing this book to fruition. The staff have shared in the excitement of fleshing out the stories of our history. Sandra Parrish and Linda Hogarth in particular have provided unstinting assistance, advice and in-kind support throughout. Irene Ross, a museum volunteer and former archivist, has been a diligent and enthusiastic partner in the research and writing of the book, selecting photos, hunting for elusive facts and assisting with editing. The staff of the BC Archives and Records Service and Vancouver Island Regional Library have also provided much-appreciated assistance.

Many others have made important contributions. Annette Yourk, a Quadra Island writer, provided helpful editorial feedback, as did Colin Gabelmann, Dr. Bob Gordon, Dr. Richard Mackie and Ken Drushka. My family—Gerry Coté, Etienne Coté and Elise Coté—were my first reviewers, providing critiques throughout the writing and rewriting of each chapter. Peter Macnair, Dr. Richard (Dick) Murphy, Bob Duncan and Leona Taylor (my sister and fellow research fanatic) have reviewed the text, sharing valuable information and insights.

And most importantly I am indebted to the hundreds of long-time residents of the Campbell River area who have shared their photos and memories. Their gift gives us a deeper sense of connection, continuity and belonging. The storytellers and writers who have made the past live and breathe are Captain George Vancouver, Archibald Menzies, Roderick Haig-Brown, Eustace and Cecil Smith, Katie (Walker) Clarke, Eve (Willson) Eade, Bill and Tom Hall, Bill Law, Jim Henderson, Ruth (Pidcock) Barnett, Wallace Baikie, Darrell Smith, Sir John Rogers, Arthur Mayse, Mike Manson, Moses Ireland, Bruce Saunders, By-God Stafford and George Verdier, to name but a few.

Thanks are also due to those who have written histories of the district. Helen Mitchell's book Diamond in the Rough: The Campbell River Story, Doris Andersen's Evergreen Islands: The Islands of the Inside Passage: Quadra to Malcolm and Edge of Discovery: A History of the Campbell River District, co-authored by D.E. Isenor, E.G. Stephens and D.E. Watson, have been important references.

CHAPTER 1

The First People

The transformer, Kumsno'otl, descended from the sky and wandered all over the earth...[Near Campbell River he found that] a monster in the shape of an octopus lived in a lake and devoured anyone coming down to get water. Nobody dared to go down any more and the village's inhabitants died of thirst. Only one old man was resourceful. He went across to Mitlenatch Island every day and caught red snapper. He melted down the fat and drank it. Thus it came about that he and his grandchild survived while everyone around died.

[The transformer] told his companions to heat big flat stones [which] he put on as a hat and with the others covered his body. [When the octopus-like creature attacked Kumsno'otl the searing stones killed it.] Then Kumsno'otl cut the [monster] up and flung the parts in all directions into the sea. He said, "You shall change into an octopus and in future serve as food for people." He threw the stomach onto the land, where it was transformed into a huge stone—[now known as Big Rock]. He plunged the head into the sea close to Cape Mudge, where it creates the dangerous whirlpools and current even today.[1]

The First People spent much of their lives upon the sea, canoeing with the tides through a myriad of channels narrowly separating the islands of the northern Strait of Georgia and Johnstone Strait. Everything in their lush homeland was bold, from the grandeur of the forests, enriched by the endless runoff from towering mountains, to the wild tidal race squeezing between the islands. With experience developed over centuries they harvested salmon, seals and sea lions, shellfish and seaweed. In the forest they hunted elk and deer, dug the bulbs of fawn lilies and gathered salal berries, huckleberries and salmonberries. On the rocky islets they picked strawberries and gathered nodding onions. This was the place the Transformer enriched for the original inhabitants of the inner coast. But thousands of years before the arrival of the Transformer, in a past so very distant that its secrets are confined to the rocks and earth, there were no people, cedar trees or salmon.

Eighty million years ago the climate and vegetation of this coast were entirely different; in fact its location lay hundreds of miles to the south. The Vancouver Island mountain ranges were not yet formed and creatures of massive proportions, giant sea turtles, crocodile-like mosasaurs and long-necked elasmosaurs chased fish and ammonites through the warm ocean waters that covered much of Vancouver Island. Over the millennia the plates lying beneath the earth's surface slid the island northward and mountains were squeezed out at the meeting point of two tectonic plates. As the temperature changed, the flowering tropical plants and dinosaurs died, leaving their remains embedded within the earth and stones of the Trent and Puntledge Rivers, in the mountains of Strathcona Park and on the Willow Point reef.[2]

By 40,000 years ago much of coastal BC lay frozen beneath perpetually retreating and advancing glaciers, scraping and dragging a new landscape into place. In their final retreat, nearly 12,000 years ago, the glaciers deposited deep piles of sand at the south tip of Quadra Island and dropped erratic boulders (including Big Rock) in their melting paths, leaving only scattered remnants of ice in the mountain peaks of Strathcona Park and Bute Inlet.

Into this transformed landscape with its moist, temperate climate, came new plant and animal colonies suited to the post-glacier environment. Pollen samples found alongside the remains of black bears that fell to their deaths 10,000 years ago in caves at White Ridge, near Gold River, show tree species such as Douglas fir and western hemlock had already taken root.[3]

People also migrated down the coast in the wake of the melting glaciers, following herds of woolly mammoth and bison across a land bridge that once connected Alaska to Russia. How and when these people arrived in BC is an ongoing subject of scientific debate. The earliest evidence of human occupation in this region is an 8,000-year-old site at Bear Cove, near Port Hardy.[4]

According to the rich oral history of the First Nations people they have lived on this coast since the beginning of time when magic ancestors transformed from supernatural birds and animals into humans, who founded clans at various locales. Thus it was that an Island-Comox family once living at Gowlland Harbour are said to have descended from a whale, while a Lekwiltok family of Topaze Harbour (on the mainland across from Sayward), trace their descent from kolus, a supernatural bird:

> Yakayalitnuhl was walking near Tekya [in Topaze Harbour], when he saw sitting on a rock a very large bird covered with soft down of dazzling whiteness. The tip of its hooked beak could just be seen in the midst of the thick down. He cried out, "Whatever you are, I tlugwala you [claim your special powers]!" The bird threw back the feathers and skin from its head, revealing the head of a man, and spoke: "I am kolus, yet I am man. My name is Toqatlasaqiaq [born to be admired]." His face was steaming with heat, because of the thick covering of feathers. Soon the entire coat fell away and he stood forth with the full figure of a man.[5]

Few archaeological digs and surveys have been conducted in the Campbell River area. The oldest discoveries to date have been chance finds. A skeleton uncovered during the construction of the Campbell River Fishing Pier and another unearthed in the Cape Mudge village on Quadra Island were, coincidentally, both dated to approximately 2,000 years ago.

The Fishing Pier skeleton was that of a man in his mid-thirties whose existence of hard work

Petroglyph found at a former First Nations site on the beach at Campbell River, below 5th and 6th Avenue, now in the Museum at Campbell River collection. *MCR 17950*

had already taken a toll on his health. His left arm was highly developed, as indeed was his whole upper torso, yet he suffered from a crippling back problem, all likely the result of a lifetime of paddling against the strong tides in Discovery Passage.[6] Where this man may have lived is not known but there is evidence of ancient food gathering and village sites at Willow Point, on the bluffs at Sequoia Tree Park, along the former shoreline of what is now Shoppers Row and at various places in the Campbell River estuary. The remains of clamshell middens (refuse heaps) and salmon weirs (woven fences used to trap fish) can be seen on the shore near Tyee Plaza, and in the mouth of the river at the lowest tides.

Archaeological surveys conducted in the 1950s and '60s show relatively few villages in Johnstone Strait, compared with areas to the north and south. The dense pockets of population were generally confined to protected bays like Gowlland Harbour, Kanish Bay, Waiatt Bay and Heriot Bay on Quadra Island; at Thurston Bay on Sonora Island; and on the west coast of Cortes Island. The navigational challenges of the waters surrounding the Discovery Islands may have been a limiting factor, while at the same time forming a defensive barrier.

The Johnstone Strait and upper Georgia Strait region, the geographical meeting point of three different First Nations groups (the Island-Comox, Mainland-Comox and the Lekwiltok), has had a complex territorial history. The Discovery Passage region formerly belonged to Salish people, the Island-Comox, but in the nineteenth century their northern neighbours, the Lekwiltok (who have cultural and linguistic ties with the Kwakwaka'wakw of north Vancouver Island), gradually took control of the area through intermarriage and warfare. The mainland shores and inlets remain within the territory of yet another Salish group, the Mainland-Comox.

The First People lived in close rhythm with the natural world. Their knowledge of plant cycles and the migrations and habits of birds, fish and animals was highly complex. Salmon and other fish were taken with nets, hooks, harpoons and traps. Thick robes were woven from the wool of mountain goats, while the inner bark of the yellow cedar tree was processed into finely wrought rainproof clothing. House planks were split from standing cedars and giant red cedars were felled and hollowed out for canoes, some upwards of 60 feet (18 m) in length. In this abundant environment the spiritual and cultural life of the First Nations people was dramatically expressed in ritual and art.

All matters in life from food gathering to status and power revolved around extended family groups, who pooled their efforts and resources. Each kin group had a head man, charged with ensuring the success of his family and followers. Such a man might have greater say within the village as a whole, but no one held absolute authority:

> He must be an unassuming man and "quiet," by which is meant that he spoke little, and that little only after mature consideration. He maintained his dignity but without hauteur, for it was bred into him and was genuine. He was careful to avoid trouble but led the way when trouble was imminent. And, whatever his temper might be, a chief had to be generous. He gave frequent feasts and entertainments to the members of his family group to maintain their good will. In fact, the ability to do so was one of the criteria... A miserly person was simply not a chief, no matter what his wealth or ancestry."[7]

In winter, kin groups congregated in villages sheltered from the driving wind and rain of southeast storms. Their massive post-and-beam houses were large enough to accommodate extended families of twenty people or more, with each family having its own hearth in a partitioned corner of the house. The smoke from their cooking fires escaped through a central opening in the roof. Boxes of food and goods were stacked in the corners upon the benches and sleeping platforms that hugged the walls.

Village houses were tightly packed along curved pebble beaches or on hillsides and clifftops. Elaborate painted and carved house fronts and doorways proclaimed family privileges to visitors, who approached with formality, exchanging speeches before stepping onto shore.

The singing of the pond frogs in spring signalled the start of the food-gathering season. Individual family groups left their winter villages and moved to a variety of sites to harvest herring roe, berries, fish, shellfish, ungulates and birds. The wall boards of their great houses were straddled across their canoes to be re-erected at three or more food-gathering locations from early spring to late fall.

To enhance their skill as hunters and fishers, men sought supernatural encounters and performed elaborate purification rituals. Some Salish groups believed they possessed two souls, one in their heart and the other in their head. Either or both sometimes roamed at night, as the body slept, enlarging the prowess of a hunter or artisan through contacts in a spirit world ruled by wondrous beings, some of which transformed easily between animal and human form. A man could also attain new powers through prolonged periods of fasting and isolation, as in the case of a Mainland-Salish youth who was chided for his laziness:

> After his father had berated him one morning for lying in bed later than anyone else, he left the house and remained away for one year at a lake on Cortes Island. Each day he made a circuit of the lake, swimming, diving, and scouring himself with cedar and hemlock branches at stations only a few feet apart. He had several opportunities to accept supernatural helpers. A female wolf wanted him to marry her and each day she brought deer to please him. He, however, was not to be satisfied with anything less than power from a certain star. One day in April this star fell and he found a piece of it. Thus he gained the sanction he craved. Before entering his village, he sent word that his parents should have the house cleaned out and purified and that all the villagers should get their canoes and sealing harpoons ready. This they did, and, upon his return, the young man took one canoe after another out a short distance, and, simply by plunging a harpoon into the water, was able to strike a seal.[8]

Men who had such experiences owned songs, masks and dances that enhanced the success and prestige of their families. An ancient family of Gowlland Harbour who claimed descent from a whale regularly re-enacted a ceremony in which numbers of young men climbed inside a carved whale, controlled by concealed towlines. Drifting out into the harbour the whale bobbed up and down, spouting feathers from its blowhole.[9]

All the major events of life were marked with ceremony, from birth and puberty to marriage and death. Families arranged marriages through a formal interchange of gifts and privileges, exchanged over a period of years. Death rites were carefully observed, from the pitch and energy of the wailing by the mourners to the burning of the deceased's worldly goods.

Slavery was known among coastal people, who captured the women and children of rival tribes. Unless ransomed by their families, the captives remained slaves throughout their lives, performing menial household tasks.

From this highly complex world of wealth and magic a man of noble ancestry and high standing set off down the steep path of his clifftop village at Cape Mudge, to welcome strangers from a distant land. Everything about these visitors was foreign, including the size and appearance of their ships, the absence of women and children among them, and the fact that they spoke none of the languages of the inner coast. They did not observe the proper protocol for disembarking on the beach in front of the village, but the chief nonetheless stepped forward alone, as his position required, without any apparent fear.

CHAPTER 2

A Moment in Time
1792

My grandmother [Lucy Homiskinis] often told me the story of a young woman, a prophetess who lived long, long ago at the Salmon River village of Hkusam. She said there would be strange people coming around that didn't know how to talk Indian, they were going to be "iniecinootl," people who don't know anything. She said that some of them were going to have hair the colour of the grass at the back of the village in late summer and some would have fire in their hair. They were going to come in huge canoes, not like ours, and she predicted that one day there would be nobody left at the village. A lot of people didn't believe that because Salmon River was one of the biggest villages on the coast at that time; the biggest and strongest. Everything she said came true. The white man came and the village is lost.[1]

—Ruby (Hovell) Wilson

Two separate expeditions of British and Spanish explorers sailed into this region of mountainous inlets, massed islands and turbulent waters in 1792. Without maps, the sailors relied upon the solar system, tidal action, kelp beds and water discoloration for navigation. They also received advice, conducted in sign language and a superficial exchange of basic words, from First Nations people. The journals of these explorers, the first written record of this coastline, provide a fascinating glimpse into not only their own experiences but the lives of the First Nations people at a pivotal point of change.

Captain George Vancouver, commander of the British expedition, was certain he and his Spanish cohorts were the first non-Native people to enter the upper reaches of the Strait of Georgia, though he noted in his journal that the Native groups encountered showed little or no surprise at their arrival. Vancouver and Galiano may well have been the first of their kind to fully explore the inner coast of Vancouver Island, but the aboriginal people had no doubt heard tales of these "mamałni" (people who float around on the water) from their trading partners, the

Nuu-chah-nulth, on the west coast of Vancouver Island. By 1792 Russian, American and European explorers and traders had been bartering furs with the Nuu-chah-nulth people for nearly two decades.[2] From the west coast European goods and information were exchanged throughout the inner coast.

The aboriginal people of Georgia Strait seemed to view contact with Spanish and British sailors as a useful opportunity for direct trade. Their welcoming response may have been entirely different had they been aware of the Europeans' weighty political and territorial goals for exploring the Pacific Northwest.

The British expedition was charged with multiple orders. They were to meet with Spain's representatives to resolve a dispute over property ownership in Nootka Sound, which a few years prior had brought the two countries to the brink of war. They were also to collect plant specimens and ethnographic information, and to explore and chart the Pacific Northwest coast to aid British colonial and economic interests. In this latter task Vancouver was required to pay "particular attention to the supposed Straits of Juan de Fuca" in the vain hope that this uncharted waterway might open into the Northwest Passage—the fabled sea route connecting Europe to the Orient.

George Vancouver was a competent choice for this important mission. He was a seasoned veteran of years of exploration and mapping in uncharted waters, including previous trips to the Pacific Northwest under the late Captain James Cook. At thirty-four Vancouver was one of the oldest men aboard ship. Zachary Mudge, a second lieutenant with years of experience, was twenty-one and William Sykes, the artist who created many of the sketches for Vancouver's published journals, was just sixteen years old.

Vancouver sailed from London on April 1, 1791 in the newly built *Discovery*, with a crew of 101 men. William Broughton had command of the consort ship, the *Chatham*, with a crew of 45. Vancouver and his officers were served their meals and wine in some degree of comfort, but the tars (who kept their hair stiffly groomed with liberal quantities of tar) were separated into small groups called messes. Each mess assigned a cook for the duration of the voyage, who prepared the food for the ship's ovens. Three square meals a day were served on trenchers, square wood boards fitted together upon hanging tables. Their rations were doled out in fixed proportions and, to the disgust of many, those who did not eat their quota of sauerkraut were flogged. Vancouver had learned by hard experience that the high vitamin C content of preserved cabbage kept his men from contracting scurvy. Where captains of previous expeditions lost as many as a third of their crew to such dietary illnesses, only two men died by chance accidents on Vancouver's voyage. Oddly, despite his precautions, Vancouver himself was suffering a disease (not now identifiable) that his ship's surgeon treated throughout the voyage.

Spain's survey expedition to the Pacific Northwest was headed by Captain Dionîsio Alcalá Galiano, who was likewise well-suited to the task of exploring and mapping a challenging coastline. His ships, however, proved inadequate. The *Mexicana* and *Sutil* were built in the Spanish colony of Mexico, where a crew of seventeen men and officers was assigned to each ship. These relatively small ships, at just over 50 feet long, were a constant source of difficulty for Galiano, who found them slow and unwieldy.

Vancouver and Galiano met by chance at the outset of their exploration of Juan de Fuca Strait and agreed to work in tandem. Their survey methods were laborious. The *Discovery*, *Chatham*, *Sutil* and *Mexicana* were anchored in safe waters near what is now the City of Vancouver, and small

Captain Cayetano Valdés, from a posthumous portrait by José Roldan. Typical of most eighteenth-century European explorers, Valdés was only twenty-five years old when he served as captain of the *Mexicana*. *Museo Naval, Madrid, A-676*

Captain Dionîsio Alcalá Galiano, from an anonymous portrait. Galiano was captain of the *Sutil*, exploring the Inside Passage between the mainland and Vancouver Island in 1792 with his consort ship, the *Mexicana*. *Museo Naval, Madrid, A-421*

parties of men were provisioned for up to eight days of northward exploration by small boats. Upon their surveyors' advice, Vancouver and Galiano proceeded to the next safe anchorage, at Desolation Sound, from which the process of exploration and charting by small boat was continued. According to one historian Vancouver's ships sailed 65,000 miles (104,000 km) during his four-and-a-half-year voyage, while his surveyors covered about 75,000 miles (120,000 km), mostly under oar.[3]

Waiting through weeks of summer rain, Vancouver made "fair" copies of his surveyors' maps and described his surroundings in a journal, which formed the basis of his books on the voyage. Desolation Sound didn't match Vancouver's European taste for rolling fields and villages. He found the dense forest and cliffs of what is now a favoured marine park to be "desolate, gloomy and impenetrable."

Three parties of British and Spanish surveyors explored the confusing tangle of inlets and channels to the northwest and northeast of Desolation Sound. The British surveyors Peter Puget and Joseph Whidbey were struck by the fertile appearance of the benchland of Vancouver Island, as they rowed into what Vancouver later named Discovery Passage. North of their overnight camp was a "rivulet" of fresh water—perhaps the first written record of Campbell River. Where Desolation Sound seemed destitute of people, there were large numbers of Native people in Discovery Passage, who eagerly surrounded the small survey party. Fearing for their safety the sailors fired a swivel gun over their heads, and the Natives withdrew "peaceably."

Before returning to Desolation Sound the surveyors noted a suitable anchorage at Menzies Bay and, more important, that the tides from the north and south meet in the Passage. This meeting of the tides was a clear indication that they were headed back toward the Pacific Ocean, meaning the land mass on their western horizon was an island.

The other survey parties, under the British sailor James Johnstone and two Spaniards, Vernaci and Salamanca, also noted the significance of the meeting of the tides before turning back to their ships in Desolation Sound.

A Klahoose child watched these Europeans with fascination. As a very old man, "a wizened chap, bent with age," he told the Mansons (Cortes Island settlers of the 1880s) about observing the European surveyors at work exploring the inlets in their small boats. His people had, along with the Native people in Juan de Fuca Strait, continually pointed out to the Europeans that their

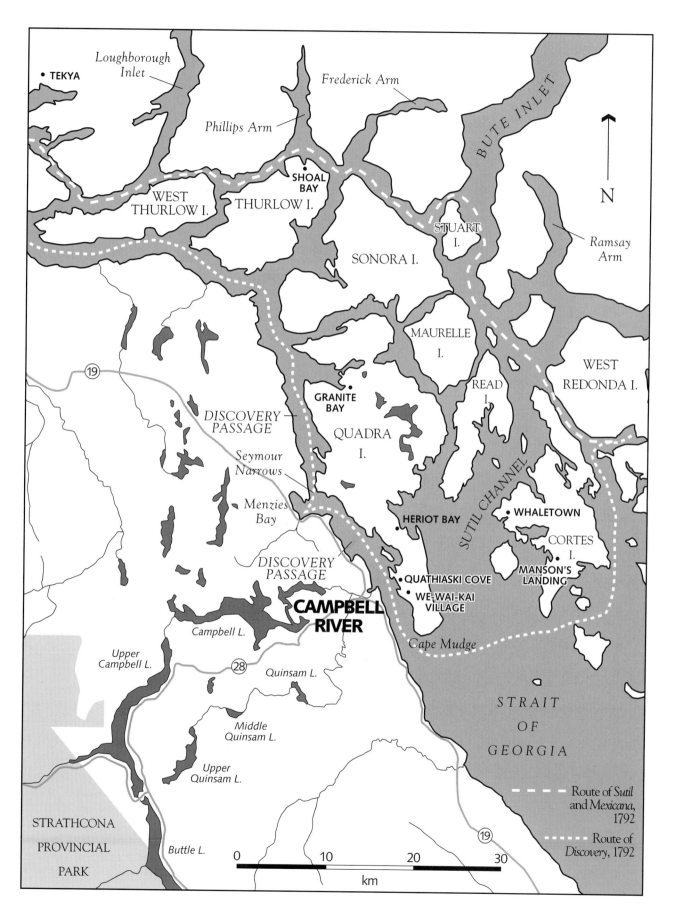

TEKYA

Loughborough Inlet

Frederick Arm

Phillips Arm

BUTE INLET

SHOAL BAY

N

WEST THURLOW I.

THURLOW I.

STUART I.

Ramsay Arm

SONORA I.

MAURELLE I.

WEST REDONDA I.

READ I.

DISCOVERY PASSAGE

GRANITE BAY

QUADRA I.

Seymour Narrows

SUTIL CHANNEL

Menzies Bay

WHALETOWN

HERIOT BAY

CORTES I.

DISCOVERY PASSAGE

QUATHIASKI COVE

MANSON'S LANDING

WE-WAI-KAI VILLAGE

CAMPBELL RIVER

Campbell L.

Cape Mudge

Upper Campbell L.

Quinsam L.

S T R A I T

O F

G E O R G I A

Middle Quinsam L.

Upper Quinsam L.

- - - Route of *Sutil* and *Mexicana*, 1792

STRATHCONA

PROVINCIAL

PARK

Buttle L.

······ Route of *Discovery*, 1792

0   10   20   30

km

The *Discovery* and the *Chatham*, from a drawing by Zachary Mudge, 1792. While travelling in heavy fog in Queen Charlotte Sound, the *Discovery* was grounded on sunken rocks. She was lightened and propped up with spars to await the changing of the tide, when she was refloated with no further mishap.
MCR 11399, *from* A Voyage of Discovery to the North Pacific Ocean and Round the World, *by George Vancouver, printed for G.G. & I. Robinson, London, 1798*

Captain Vancouver captioned this illustration "Village of the Friendly Indians," from a sketch by T. Heddington (engraved by J. Landner), in his published account of his voyage through to the Pacific Northwest, *A Voyage of Discovery to the North Pacific Ocean and Round the World*, published in 1798. The Native people guided both British and Spanish explorers through the dangerous rapids beyond their village, while warning them against proceeding northward where there were "evil men; murderers." *Courtesy MCR*

route would soon take them back into open waters.

Based upon the reports of their surveyors, Vancouver and Galiano decided to proceed north via different routes. Galiano favoured the mainland passages for his smaller ships, while Vancouver opted for the larger watercourses beyond Discovery Passage.

The anonymous author of the published account of Galiano's voyage said their passage through the rapids and overfalls beyond Bute Inlet was the most awe-inspiring event of their travels. The Native people advised them to wait for the sun to line up against a particular mountain peak in order to pass through in safety, but their boats proved too sluggish to get through quickly enough to escape the changing tide: "We endeavoured constantly to follow the right shore, with the aid of oars, but the current carried us forward, bringing us sometimes to this shore and at others driving us to mid-channel, without our being able with all our efforts to avoid these variations of course. The *Sutil* was caught by a rush of the current…and sailing more than three cables nearer the shore was almost caught on the rocks which jutted out from it, allowed herself to be carried by the violence of the waters."[4]

Just as the ship seemed free of immediate danger, it was caught by the force of a strong eddy and swung around three times "with such violence that it made those who were in her giddy." The crew rowed the ship with all their might but were caught up yet again in a violent whirlpool which snapped loose a cable tied from the ship to shore. It was only by luck and hard work that both of the ships missed being dashed against the rocky shore.

The British had better luck in Discovery Passage, where they stopped on the fair summer day of July 13, 1792 for a much needed shore walk at the large village on the bluffs of Cape Mudge (named for Vancouver's first lieutenant, Zachary Mudge). The village excited the men's curiosity. Both Vancouver and the expedition's botanist, Archibald Menzies, described it in some detail.

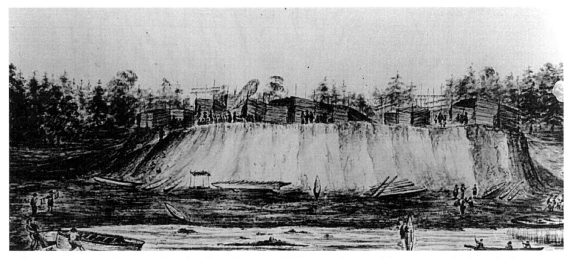

Village at Cape Mudge, Quadra Island, as drawn by William Sykes, midshipman on the British ship *Discovery*, in 1792. *MCR 18089, British Naval Records, London*

Vancouver was impressed by the chief's greeting. "He approached us alone, seemingly with a degree of formality, though with the utmost confidence of his own security, whilst the rest of the society, apparently numerous, were arranged and seated in the most peaceable manner before their houses." Menzies gave a more detailed description of the people of Cape Mudge:

I landed with Capt. Vancouver & some of the officers on the North Point of the Entrance which was afterwards named Cape Mudge. It forms a steep elevated naked bank on the edge of which we found a considerable village consisting of about 12 houses or Huts plankd over with large boards some of which were ornamented with rude paintings particularly those on the fronts of the houses. They were flat roofed & of a quadrangular figure & each house contain several families to the number of about 350 Inhabitants [Vancouver estimated the population at 300].

Like the generality of Natives we met with in this Country these were of a middling stature & rather slender bodied, of a light copper colour: they were awkward in their motions & ill formd in their limbs which no doubt in some measure proceeded from their constant practice of squatting down on their heels in their posture of setting either on Shore or in their Canoes: They have flat broad faces with small starting eyes:—Their Teeth are small & dirty; their Ears are perforated for appending Ornaments either of Copper or pearly Shells; the Septum of their Nose they also pierce & sometimes wear a quill or piece of tooth-shell in it; their Hair is streight black & long, but mixd with such quantity of red-ocre grease & dirt puffed over at times with white down that its real colour is not easily distinguishable; they have long black Beards with long hair about their privates, but none on their Breasts or on the Arm pits.—Some had ornamented their faces by painting it with red-ocre sprinkled over with black Glimmer that helped not a little to heighten their ferocious appearance.

The women & children did not appear any wise shy or timerous tho we were pretty certain our party were the first Europeans they had ever seen or had direct intercourse with, nor did they seem to regard us or the Vessels with any particular degree of curiosity.

The women were decently coverd with Garments made either of the Skins of wild Animals or wove from the Wool or the prepared bark of the American Arber Vitae Tree [cedar], but many of the Men went entirely naked without giving the least offence to the other Sex or shewing any apparent shame at their situation.

We saw but few Sea Otter Skins amongst them which shews that these Animals do not much frequent the interior Channels & perhaps only straggling ones at particular Seasons, for the Fur of the few pieces we saw was of a very inferior quality to those found along the exterior edge of the Coast.

Some Fish & curiosities were purchasd from them for Beads & small Trinkets, & in these little dealings they appeard to be guided by the strictest honesty, indeed their whole conduct during our short stay was quite friendly & hospitable, pressing us often to partake of their entertainment such as Fish Berries & Water, & we in return endeavored to make them sensible of our approbation by distributing among the Women & Children some small presents, which made them appear highly gratified.

We afterwards walkd to the Westward along the side of the Channel on a pleasant clear level pasture for near two Miles, where we observed in the verge of the wood their manner of disposing of their dead which was putting them either in small square boxes or wrapping them well up in Mats or old garments into square bundles & placing them above ground in small Tombs erected for the purpose & closely boarded on every side, but as we saw only two or three of these places they might probably belong to the Chiefs or some Families of distinction.—After enjoying this walk we returned on board in the dusk of the evening."[5]

With a fresh breeze from the northwest and a continuation of pleasant weather, the *Discovery* and *Chatham* proceeded to an anchorage at Nymphe Cove in Menzies Bay to await reports from survey parties exploring to the north of Seymour Narrows. While there they visited a small village, "whose inhabitants had little to dispose of, though they were very civil and friendly." From this safe haven Vancouver watched the movement of the tide in the Narrows, which he said rushed "with such immense impetuosity as to produce the appearance of falls considerably high."

The British surveyors made no mention of villages in the Campbell River estuary or in other places known to have been occupied far back into antiquity, such as Quathiaski Cove, Gowlland Harbour and Kanish Bay on Quadra Island. Either they had fallen into disuse, or the surveyors simply missed seeing them, as they did Okisollo Channel, which separates the islands of Quadra, Sonora and Maurelle.

Beyond Seymour Narrows the British sailors met with an increasing number of people, including a flotilla of twenty canoes somewhere near Elk Bay. They noted a number of villages, one just beyond Chatham Point (probably at Rock Bay), another in the vicinity of the Amor de Cosmos River,[6] one at Salmon River and one near St. Vincent's Bight, opposite Port Neville. At this latter place they met with two canoeloads of people whose character and circumstances showed a marked contrast with the shy friendliness of the people of Georgia Strait. According to Vancouver these people were a "daring and insolent" group whose chief showed "uncommon audacity" in his dealings. Furthermore they were armed with guns. "These were the first fire-arms we had seen from the ships, but, from the number Mr. Johnstone had seen in his late excursion [during the initial survey of Johnstone Strait] it would appear, that the inhabitants of this particular part are amply provided with these formidable weapons."[7]

Some historians and geographers speculate that St. Vincent's Bight was, in 1792, the boundary between Salish and Kwakwa̱ka'wakw territories.[8] Menzies, who conducted simple language tests throughout the voyage, said the people living north of Menzies Bay spoke a different language from the people of Georgia Strait. These northern people were also fluent in the language of the Nuu-chah-nulth people (living on the west coast of Vancouver Island) and could "blab smatterings of English."

Vancouver was surprised by the number of canoes that passed back and forth in front of his ship as he sailed beyond St. Vincent's Bight. One of these canoes escorted him to a large village of about 500 people at the Nimpkish River, known as Whulk. Unlike the people of the south, who had few sea otter pelts to trade, these people had an abundant supply of high-quality skins. They also had an exacting notion of the value of their goods, for which they preferred sheet copper and blue cloth in trade.

Cheslakees, as Vancouver interpreted the name of the chief, invited Vancouver to visit his village on the western shore of the Nimpkish River. Standing on the beach were several chiefs, while the rest remained quietly seated in front of their houses. Vancouver counted thirty-four houses

Kwakwaka'wakw chief of northern Vancouver Island, as drawn by José Cardero of the Spanish expedition, 1792. The British encountered people at the entrance to Johnstone Strait who, as George Vancouver wrote, were "more variously painted than any of the natives our gentlemen had before seen . . . and the generality had their hair decorated with the down of young sea-fowl."
Museo de América, Spain, 2-282, Palau 78, Sotos 650

arranged in rows on a hillside and flanked by "regular streets." As he walked about he observed the daily occupations of the women, who were weaving garments from bark and other materials, mats for a variety of purposes, and "a kind of basket, wrought so curiously close, as to contain water like an earthen vessel without the least leakage or drip."

When Galiano entered these same waters some weeks later, following his charting of the mainland passages, he too noted that the people of the Nimpkish River were well supplied with sea otter pelts, guns and all the necessary "appurtenances." Their primary trade access to Nuu-chah-nulth territory had formerly been an overland route, but in recent years trading ships had ventured into the rough waters off the north tip of Vancouver Island and into Queen Charlotte Strait. While Galiano was at the Nimpkish River village a well-armed British trading vessel—*Venus*, with a small crew of "black" men from the Philippines—arrived to trade, even though they were soon complaining bitterly about the high prices demanded by the Namgis people.

The chronicler of Galiano's expedition noted that sexual favours were offered as an item of barter. While the Spanish were on the west coast of Vancouver Island earlier in the season they were offered boys and women (which they felt were slaves). In Queen Charlotte Strait a chief made them a similar offer: "He asked us to pass by his villages, where we could sleep; he said that he would make presents to us, and told us that his women would serve us as they had served other travellers, these travellers being, as he explained by signs, English merchants and traders, who paid the women for this kind attention by giving them a quantity of copper."[9]

After concluding their exploratory work on northern Vancouver Island, Galiano and his crew followed the British down the west coast of Vancouver Island to the Spanish settlement at Yuquot, in Nootka Sound. There they found Captains Vancouver and Bodega y Quadra, the commandant of the Spanish, engaged in an elaborate interchange of dinner parties, gun salutes and firework displays. In spite of these friendly relations Vancouver and Quadra were unable to settle upon the terms of an accord. Vancouver sent Zachary Mudge aboard a Portuguese trading brig to Canton, and from there to London, to seek further instructions from the Admiralty. It was a year before Vancouver received a response, as he continued his detailed mapping of the Pacific Northwest; and yet several more years before the two nations arrived at an agreement in which Spain agreed to withdraw her northernmost post to California.

As a mark of respect for his Spanish colleague, Vancouver named what they now knew to be a massive island, the Island of Vancouver and Quadra. Within a few years this cumbersome name was simplified to Vancouver's Island and eventually to Vancouver Island.

Reflecting upon his exploration of the inside coast Vancouver puzzled over how few people they had met in Georgia Strait, which he said was "nearly destitute of inhabitants." The numerous abandoned villages, many of them in strategic defensive locations, and a few sightings of people scarred by smallpox led Vancouver to speculate that the inhabitants had "migrated, fallen by conquest, or been destroyed by disease."

While some of the abandoned villages were simply not used in mid-summer, historians now believe that Georgia Strait was struck by a devastating smallpox epidemic a decade prior to the arrival of Europeans.[10] The northern limit of this first epidemic is thought to have been Cape Mudge. There is no way of estimating the number of people who died, but judging by the horrendous effects of later epidemics the death toll must have been extreme.

In their weakened state the Salish people were preyed upon by their neighbours to the north, who had the tremendous advantage of firearms. By the time the Hudson's Bay Company set up trading posts along the coast starting in the 1820s the Lekwiltok people (living directly to the north of the Island-Comox people) were poised to take control of the Discovery Islands and Campbell River.

CHAPTER 3

Power Shifts
1800–1880

I had the pleasure of making the acquaintance of a chief of the Yougletas [Lekwiltok], who by a recent alliance was found among the different nations whom I instructed. The man is of remarkable stature and outstanding because of his stately bearing. He had a forehead high and wide, and hair long and thrown back.

—Father Demers of the Catholic Mission, Fort Langley, 1841

Few, if any, traders or explorers from the outside world entered the Strait of Georgia following the Spanish and British expeditions of 1792. But to the north, in Kwakwaka'wakw territory, a general trade in furs expanded as the market for sea otter furs declined. From about 1800, an area known as Nahwitti, off the northeast tip of Vancouver Island, became a trading mecca. This gave the Lekwiltok people prior access to metal tools, blankets, guns and whiskey—and a tremendous economic and military advantage over their Salish neighbours, the Mainland-Comox and Island-Comox. But a few decades later, when the Hudson's Bay Company opened a fort in 1827 on the Fraser River at Langley, the balance of power shifted yet again, intensifying and complicating relations between the Lekwiltok and Coast Salish people of Georgia and Johnstone Straits.[1]

In the early nineteenth century the Lekwiltok were living in upper Johnstone Strait, centred around Loughborough Inlet. Directly below them, from Kelsey Bay to Campbell River and the surrounding islands, lived a Coast Salish group, the Island-Comox. And to the east of the Island-Comox, living within the relative safety of the deep inlets of Bute, Toba and Jervis, lived another Coast Salish group, the Mainland-Comox.

The Lekwiltok made slave raids among the Coast Salish, trading their captives at Nahwitti for European goods. With their increasing prosperity and firearms, the Lekwiltok began moving southward into Island-Comox territory, taking control through both friendly means and warfare. Early in the nineteenth century they merged with the Island-Comox of Hkusam, an important

Hkusam, on the banks of the Salmon River near Kelsey Bay, 1881. The former occupants of this territory, the Island-Comox people, were among the first to merge with the Lekwiltok, in the 1820s. The prediction of a legendary prophetess that one day this powerful centre would be no more, came to pass early in the twentieth century. *L.A. Davidson Collection, MCR 4908*

village on the Salmon River, at Kelsey Bay. When the Hudson's Bay posts opened to the south, the Lekwiltok expanded their influence and control farther south. By the 1820s they were using seasonal villages on some of the Discovery Islands, and were poised to infiltrate the Island-Comox heartland, Discovery Passage.

How and when this southward movement began remains a puzzle of tangled accounts. Some have speculated that Lekwiltok tribes wanted to control trade with the HBC by maintaining a presence at the bottleneck created by Seymour Narrows, which was called Yuculta Rapids (an early spelling of Lekwiltok) until 1846. Others say they moved south to gain access to better fishing grounds, and at least one Lekwiltok family[2] claim their people have always lived at Campbell River.

Any one or all of these views may have a basis in fact, for the Lekwiltok once comprised seven or more large kin groups, the Wewaikai, Weiwaikum, Tlaaluis, Walitsma, Hahamatsees, Kwiakah and Komenox, each with their own distinct history and territory.

Long ago the Wewaikai (now of Cape Mudge and Quinsam) lived near the Nimpkish River and at Beware Pass.[3] About 1800 they moved to Tekya, in Topaze Harbour[4]—a village of great significance to the Wewaikai. An elder, the late Harry Assu, described the reasons for his band's move into Discovery Passage: "We were many years coming. All the Indian people moved around a lot with the seasons at the time when we still lived in our village beside Jackson Bay...We were

Many generations ago We-Kai, the figure holding a stick, predicted a great flood. The mountains backing his village rang with laughter, but when the flood water rose, We-Kai and his followers set off for new territories in the canoes they had prepared on a mountaintop. *E.F. Meade Collection, MCR 8411*

moving around in Johnstone Strait too and came all the way down to this area around the Campbell River at certain times of year. We came for the blueback salmon off Cape Mudge in spring. We wanted this place because we could get all five species of salmon twelve months of the year. The reason our people moved from the mainland villages to the Campbell River was to secure the fishing grounds here."[5]

The takeover was not a simple matter of warfare and displacement. The earliest anthropological records, based on interviews with elders, demonstrate there were also mergers. One Lekwiltok tribe, the Komenox, had a name that suggests Island-Comox origin. Likewise, Island-Comox families at Quathiaski Cove, the "YayaqwiLtah" (a name that sounds similar to Lekwiltok), all had Kwakwaka'wakw names.[6]

The Weiwaikum (now at Campbell River) and the Wewaikai are said to have separated in about 1835. The latter were centred around Loughborough Inlet until the mid-1880s when chief "Kwak-sees-tahla" moved to "Tlamatook," Campbell River, where his wife had ancestral ties.[7] As time passed they were joined by other Lekwiltok tribes, including the Kwiakah.

Early Hudson's Bay Company records give a vague sense of the movements of the Lekwiltok in Discovery Passage. When Aemilius Simpson visited Hkusam, at Kelsey Bay, in 1827, he said the area was under Lekwiltok control. In 1839 J.M. Yale visited Cape Mudge and described it as being Island-Comox country and added that the "Comox" people brought few skins to Fort Langley because they were trading with the "Lay Cultas."[8]

In 1840, Hudson's Bay Company Chief Factor James Douglas stopped to trade at Cape Mudge. He also identified it as Comox territory and said their population was 300 adult males (which would suggest a total population of about 1,000 people):

> At Point Mudge...we anchored in the Comoks country near their three most populous towns, one of which is fortified with a stockade, while the others are open on all sides, being in fact mere clusters of low moveable huts.
>
> Their intercourse with the whites has been confined to a few visits to Frasers and the greater number have probably never had any direct dealings with us; so

The *Beaver*, a paddlewheel vessel, was used by the Hudson's Bay Company to trade with the Native people of the coast starting in 1836. She was later revamped, as seen here in the 1880s at Camp O on Thurlow Island, as a towboat. *Doris Andersen Collection, MCR 18053*

> that they are still in a state of unmitigated barbarism and decidedly the most daredevil, forward and saucy Indians that ever came under my observation. We traded 50 Beaver skins from them, almost exclusively for woolens...[9]

On his return trip, with a pall of smoke from a massive forest fire hanging over Johnstone Strait and Discovery Passage, Douglas noted seeing "several strong camps of Neekultaws" on the Vancouver Island side of the Passage, where they were curing salmon for winter use. "Nature has made a bountiful provision for these people, they have only to cast their nets into the waters and withdraw them full, as the strait appeared after sunset literally to swarm with salmon."

The Hudson's Bay Company journals imply that the takeover of Discovery Passage by Lekwiltok people was complete by the early winter of 1853 when Douglas wrote: "Ran and anchored at Point Mudge. A number of Laycultas exceeding one hundred hung about the vessel all day..."[10]

These journals are not clear on the fate of the original inhabitants, the Island-Comox people, though oral history accounts say the remaining people relocated to Comox to live near the Pentlatch, who had been reduced to a few families. A Lekwiltok version of the takeover of Discovery Passage was published by the ethnographer and photographer Edward Curtis in 1915:

About the year 1850, a large party of Lekwiltok with a few Comox suffered a disastrous defeat at the hands of the allied Salish tribes, and the handful of survivors
were forced to take to the woods and make their way northward along the coast
of Vancouver Island. A few Lekwiltok, arriving at the Campbell River, sought
shelter with Hekwutn, of the [Island]-Comox [who was of mixed Lekwiltok and
Island-Comox descent]. They were well received, but some mistakenly entered
the house of Ketsis, a ruffian who stationed a man outside his house to entice
them in. As soon as one entered, he struck down the unfortunate guest, dragged
the body aside, and waited for the next victim.

Grieved and incensed by the act of Ketsis, Hekwutn sent a messenger to the
Lekwiltok at Tekya, inviting them to come and kill all the Comox.[11]

According to Curtis's informant, the Comox-Salish of Campbell River, anticipating retaliation,
moved their house boards to Qequakyulis, "a small, rocky, elevated islet not far north of
Quathiaski cove." In his message to the Lekwiltok, Hekwutn said they would know his house from
the others because he would be singing at dawn. The Lekwiltok approached as instructed, killing
all but the family of Hekwutn and a Lekwiltok woman who hid her Comox-Salish husband inside
her large food storage basket.

Hekwutn and his relatives then moved to Kawitsn, a beach at Seymour Narrows, where they
were joined by another Salish group who had been living farther upstream on the Campbell River.
They decided it was unsafe to remain near the Lekwiltok so they moved to Comox. "Since that
time," wrote Curtis, "the Lekwiltok have possessed the territory southward to Cape Mudge."[12]

The Island-Comox and Lekwiltok people continued their changeable relations following this
territorial shift. Marriage ties gave Lekwiltok families the right to fish at Comox, Qualicum and
Nanoose, as well as in Discovery Passage and at their northern villages. The late Mary Clifton of
the Comox Reserve described the interdependence of the two groups:

I think the people have been living here [Comox] a long time. The way I was told
they were moving around, you see, all the way down from Salmon River they were
moving around. All the way down they have Comox names [for] Campbell River,
Cape Mudge, Quinsam, Mitlenatch. They were moving around looking for a nice
place to live where it was easy to get food. [My] people had two languages, Comox
and Kwakiutl [a tribe name formerly used for all Kwakwaka'wakw people] because
I guess they were quite mixed and were really almost one. Everybody spoke both
languages in Comox.

It was not just the Island- and Mainland-Comox who kept a wary eye on the Lekwiltok. They
were feared throughout Georgia Strait, Juan de Fuca Strait and up the Fraser River as far as Yale
where they made slave raids. In Hudson's Bay Company journals and in early colonial records the
Lekwiltok were referred to in damning terms, as "fierce and bloodthirsty men"; "the fear inspiring
Youkiltas"; and "the Ishmaelites of the coast." In 1829 Archibald McDonald of Fort Langley wrote
with annoyance that all business with other Native groups stopped when the Lekwiltok were
rumoured to be at hand. "At the very risk of Starving they will not appear in the main river in

any Shape when the Yewkaltas are reported to be near, & that is not Seldom."[13] The Mainland-Comox (the Homalco, Klahoose and Sliammon) also kept watch for their old enemies, the Lekwiltoks.

Attacks and counterattacks continually figure in the Fort Langley journals, including a rumour of an attempt to take the fort (which did not transpire). In the spring of 1829 the Hudson's Bay Company drove off a force of 240 Lekwiltok men who were set to assault Salish people at the mouth of the river, but a month later the Lekwiltok were back in even greater numbers, preying upon the Kwantlens, Cowichans and Skagits.

Women and children were the prime targets for the slave market, bringing profit through ransom or through trade with northern groups. A slave might be ransomed for seven to eight blankets plus "trifles"; or a gun, a blanket and two yards of collar wire. A Musqueam chief, Shientin, went north into Lekwiltok territory in 1828 to try and recover his wife and daughter, but he was too late; they had already been sold to the north.

Dr. Tolmie of Fort McLoughlin (near Bella Bella) described the barter system for slaves in a journal entry of 1834: "Have received an account of a tribe called the Leequeeltanoch ... whose predatory habits accord with those ascribed by the natives of Puget's Sound to the fear inspiring Youkiltas—they are in all likelihood the same people. Boston says they barter their prisoners directly with the Quaghcuils & Nawity, who again dispose of the slaves to the Haeeltzook from whence they spread over all parts of the coast."[14]

The assertive self-determination of the Lekwiltok and their noble bearing also brought them grudging admiration from some of their non-Native contemporaries:

> A large canoe came to our anchorage [south of Cape Mudge] yesterday with 12 men on board; one of these a decent looking man, with a high forehead and mild expression of countenance. [He] informed us, in reply to our inquiries that his name was Nickayazi and that he was chief of one of the strongest gangs of the La cul tah tribe, and that the people of his canoe are his followers, in part freemen and others slaves. They were all more or less dressed either in English woolens or stuffs made by themselves ... [they] carried no weapons of any description ...
>
> The hair of the forehead and temples is combed back towards the crown of the head from infancy leaving their features fully exposed. The chief had [painted his forehead down to the eyelids] with red ocre, the eyes are black and of moderate size, nose strait, and small, mouth and chin well formed cheekbones slightly prominent. They [have] generally strong bushy beards and appear to take some pains in trimming a good looking moustache which they wear on the upper lip.[15]

The next era of monumental change in the lives of the First Nations came about with the discovery of gold on the Fraser River in 1858, which brought a flood of miners. From the 1850s colonial settlement began in what is now the province of BC.

Britain shored up its claim to the territory by expanding upon the 1792 marine surveys of Vancouver and Galiano. Captains George Richards and Daniel Pender, using the *Plumper*, *Beaver* and *Hecate* from 1857 to 1863, scattered the names of their shipmates, friends and patrons around Georgia and Johnstone Straits. Discovery Passage was surveyed by Captain Richards aboard the

Plumper in the spring of 1860 and though no official record was kept, it is thought he named Campbell River for the expedition's Irish surgeon, Dr. Samuel Campbell. Beyond Campbell River, Richards's men (like Vancouver and Galiano before them) entirely missed Okisollo Channel—so the islands of Maurelle, Sonora and Quadra remained as one on the charts, under the name Valdes Island.

The increasing non-Native population was disastrous for the First Nations. With the miners and settlers came another spate of diseases, for which the Native people had little or no inherited resistance. The combined effects of waves of disease, and the negative impact of alcohol abuse and prostitution, wiped out one third of the aboriginal population of BC within a few decades.[16] The Lekwiltok declined from a proud group amassing increasing wealth and territory in the 1830s to a dwindling population confined to reserves by the 1880s.

The most destructive epidemic in the colonial era was an outbreak of smallpox in 1862 at Victoria, a mecca for newcomers and First Nations groups from all parts of the coast. After an infected man disembarked from San Francisco the disease spread rapidly through the aboriginal population. Local residents, including some Natives, were inoculated but those from elsewhere, many of them now carriers of the disease, were simply ordered home and their temporary camps destroyed.

Lekwiltok people contracted the disease when they attacked a canoeload of Haidas, their old enemies, as they passed Cape Mudge village on their way home from Victoria. "The Euculets—This late powerful and war-like tribe," wrote the *Colonist* of July 1862, "residing...near Cape Mudge...are dying from smallpox in scores." It is not known how many Lekwiltok people died, but estimates for the province as a whole run as high as 20,000 people. Before this epidemic there were an estimated 4,002 Lekwiltok people. By 1881 only 381 people remained and three of the original seven tribal groups had been wiped out.[17]

Campbell River is thought to have been named in 1863 for an Irish surgeon, Dr. Samuel Campbell, aboard the British survey ship *Plumper. E.F. Meade Collection, MCR 9383*

A Klahoose boy, of the Mainland-Comox, was spared from the disease. As an old man he recalled watching his fever-ridden relatives make their way to the ocean shore, where they collapsed and died. He remembered a time when his people were so numerous "the beach was black with indians," but after the smallpox epidemic of 1862–63 only a small number remained.[18]

As with coastal groups in general, a disproportionate number of the survivors were elderly or middle aged, and the few surviving women of child-bearing age had an alarmingly low fertility rate. The glum prediction of many was that the First Nations were bound for extinction.

Smallpox figured in another gold rush story of the 1860s, an attempt to build a wagon road from the head of Bute Inlet to the goldfields. On a map the long inlet looked like the perfect route into the Interior, creating an easy shipping route from Victoria. But Alfred Waddington and his partners, the entrepreneurs who undertook to build the road, had not factored into their plans the rugged terrain of the inlet with its towering mountains, rushing water and high winds.

The project was a failure from the outset. Waddington's crew built sixty-six bridges in the first two summer seasons, only to find much of their work destroyed by winter storms. By the summer of 1864 the crew was on slim rations, which they were loath to share with their First Nations co-workers. When the crew boss attempted to get the Chilcotins to work harder by threatening to infect them with smallpox, it was the final straw. In an early morning attack the Chilcotins killed fourteen of the seventeen white crewmen. The survivors made their way to Victoria, where colonial officials assumed the attack was a full-scale Indian uprising. Troops were sent in from various directions and those supposed to have been the perpetrators of the crime were rounded up and hanged.

Bute Inlet, from a painting by Edward Bedwell, 1862. A group of Victoria entrepreneurs proposed Bute Inlet as the ideal route into the Cariboo goldfields, but the poorly financed project resulted in the maltreatment of the Chilcotin members of the road construction crew, who revolted, killing fourteen members of the non-Native crew. *BCARS PDP 02615*

Though the "Chilcotin War," or "Bute Inlet Massacre," ended Waddington's immediate plans for a wagon road, he nevertheless continued his schemes for Bute Inlet. Waddington was among the first to suggest a transcontinental rail link as part of BC's entry into Canadian Confederation. According to him, Bute Inlet was the natural location for the western terminus. But in supreme irony, while Waddington was in Ottawa in 1872 to promote this concept, he contracted smallpox and died.

The gold rush was waning by 1862, but immigrants were still pouring into the province. James Douglas, formerly the Hudson's Bay Company chief factor for the region and now colonial governor, rounded up would-be miners from the tent camps surrounding Victoria and provided them with basic supplies to start a farming settlement in the Comox Valley. Port Augusta, as they called their small centre, brought the first non-Native settlers into north Georgia Strait.

By the 1860s alcohol had become a serious problem for the First Nations. A law prohibited the sale of alcohol to them, but an illegal traffic in adulterated "rotgut" whiskey was impossible to police. Sailing ships with their hulls painted black slipped in and out of First Nations villages, and crimes involving Native people were more often than not the direct result of a visit from a whiskey peddler.

With colonial settlement came the "provisional" allocation of reserves in Johnstone Strait in 1879. Twenty plots of land were initially set aside for the Lekwiltok people but in 1886, when reserve agreements were formalized, ten of these were disallowed, including the Wewaikai people's principal village, Tekya, at Topaze Harbour. A few years later, in 1888, two reserves on the Campbell River were added, bringing the total to twelve, scattered amongst the islands and inlets from Cape Mudge to Loughborough Inlet.[19]

The Lekwiltok people, like the Kwakwa̱ka'wakw, did not take an interest in Christianity until the latter part of the nineteenth century. Catholic missionaries visited throughout the region by canoe and are said to have planted unusual medicinal herbs on Campbell River Spit. They established a mission at Fort Rupert in 1863, but after a decade they pulled out and were not replaced until 1877 when the Anglican Church set up a mission. In the late 1880s the Wewaikai people of Cape Mudge invited the Methodist Church to send them a teacher, as they attempted to gain an advantage in the new society unfolding around them.

Catholic missions were established in Mainland-Comox territories starting in the 1860s. A large, self-sufficient Oblate mission was set up in Sechelt in the 1890s to serve people from Bute Inlet south, complete with brass bands and a boarding school. Traditional ceremonies and languages were discouraged as Sechelt became the religious centre for the Mainland-Comox people.

The Klahoose people moved their principal village to Squirrel Cove on Cortes Island in the 1890s, relocating from isolated villages in Ramsay Arm, East Redonda Island, West Redonda Island and Toba Inlet. *MCR 17143*

Other than the settlement at Port Augusta (Comox) in 1862 and a short-lived sawmill at Port Neville, non-Native settlers and industrialists passed over northern Georgia Strait and Johnstone Strait until the early 1880s. The rocky landscape had marginal appeal to farmers, and the rapids and overfalls between the islands made navigation difficult.

Seymour Narrows was known by coastal mariners as one of the trickiest pieces of water on the inner coast route. When the USS *Saranac* approached the Narrows in the summer of 1875, most of the 300-man crew came on deck to watch the infamous "tidal race." Their expectations for amazement were amply fulfilled.

The US steamer *Saranac* struck Ripple Rock in 1875, as depicted in *Harper's Weekly* magazine. All 300 men aboard, on a mission to collect Indian "curios" for a centennial exposition, escaped before the ship broke apart and sank. *Ruth and Herbert Hardin Collection, MCR 7813*

The ship's pilot is said to have warned the captain against running the Narrows at low tide, when the peaks of Ripple Rock lay just 6 feet (2 m) below the surface. However, overruled by the captain and ordered to dash through at all possible speed, the pilot called for a full head of steam. The instant the ship hit the whirlpools it was snatched up and slammed against Ripple Rock, which ripped a gaping hole in her side. One of the shipboard spectators, Charles Sadilek, described the action of the water: "the contending currents take a vessel by the nose and swing her from port to starboard and from starboard to port as a terrier shakes a rat."

Fortunately the *Saranac* drifted shoreward, making it possible to fasten the ship to a tree. Men and provisions, including bread, meat, the ship's records and cash, were hurried into the lifeboats. Some of the boats were caught in the current, but all eventually made it to shore, where they watched the ship's decks "burst open with a noise like thunder," as the *Saranac* slid into the ocean, stern first.

The only wreckage that drifted ashore were four geese, three chickens and a duck—along with a steam launch, which they used to relocate to Valdes (Quadra) Island. An officer was dispatched to Victoria for help, while the remainder of the large party took what comfort they could in roughly contrived shelters. The crew lived on meagre rations, augmented by the exchange of pieces of ship's silver (a covered dish and a fruit bowl) for venison, provided by the Lekwiltok.

After seven days and nights in relentless rain the sailors set up a deafening huzzah as their Victoria rescuers rounded into view, to take them away from a scene they were never to forget. The ship's silver took on a life of its own. After being sold to a Comox settler named Rodello, it moved through various hands by exchange and bequest until 1990, when it was donated to the Vancouver Maritime Museum.

The loss of the *Saranac* was followed within a few years by the tragic wreck of the *Grappler* in 1883. Ironically this decommissioned British naval vessel, which had seen years of service on the coast, ran into trouble as it approached Seymour Narrows at slack tide.

The ship, carrying freight and work crews to canneries at Alert Bay and Rivers Inlet, had an unofficial roster of about 100 passengers. They were just bedding down for the night as the *Grappler* reached Seymour Narrows when fire was discovered around the ship's aged boilers. According to *Lewis and Dryden's Marine History of the Pacific Northwest*, smoke was curling up from the forward end of the boiler, "and before the pumps were started the flames belched forth from under the main deck and spread rapidly toward the engine-room. As soon as it became evident that the fire was beyond control, Captain Jagers ordered the vessel headed for shore, which was but a short distance away. The helm was put to starboard, but, when an attempt was made to steady her it was found that the wheel ropes had been destroyed by the flames, and the vessel swung round in a circle, uncontrollable and helpless in the roaring tide."

Since the majority of passengers were Chinese, language barriers led to panic alone guiding the lowering of lifeboats, which all capsized, overburdened with passengers and needless freight.

With the flaming engines propelling the boat forward at full speed, a cannery operator named John McAllister ripped free one of his own skiffs, heaved it overboard and leapt in. Using a bamboo pole and a broom as oars, McAllister headed for the Quadra Island shore, picking up survivors along the way. When they neared the beach one of McAllister's passengers sent out a warning cry. The *Grappler*—now a torch, echoing with the screams of those remaining on board—bore down on the loaded skiff, barely missing it as the ship careened back into the passage.

Leaving his first boatload of survivors to warm themselves at a fire on shore, McAllister made several more trips, pulling people from the water until the increasing velocity of the tide and his bleeding hands forced him to stop. The story of his rescue efforts appeared in Nanaimo and Victoria newspapers, along with several other harrowing accounts. One man failed in his attempt to swim a line from the ship to shore; another burst open a hatch with his head to break free from the hold; two others managed to cling to an overturned skiff for eight hours in the whirlpools and rapids. The captain, true to the traditions of his profession, stayed with the ship until the last possible moment. He was picked up on the rocky Vancouver Island shore by Duncan Bay loggers. Only 37 of the 100 or more passengers survived.

Kenneth Henderson was among the survivors who spent the night on the Quadra Island shore. In the morning this small cadre of cold and downcast men accepted the Wewaikai people's offer to await a rescue ship at the Cape Mudge village. Some of the Native people had salvaged a keg of whiskey which, according to Henderson, had worked a terrible effect upon them: "The nervous [men] were worried that they had survived a death by drowning only to meet a violent end by another means. One of the Indians from the Cape found the body of a Chinese washed up on shore. His pocket contained $1,100. The lucky finder was able to throw a potlatch with this windfall and he became a chief."[20]

By 1883 the first halting attempts at farming and logging on the mid-coast had begun. The loggers who came to the aid of Captain Jagers at Duncan Bay, and the ranchers who settled on the benchland to the south of Campbell River were a bold and determined lot, having much in common with the Lekwiltok people in their unquenchable spirit. In spite of the incursion of farming, mining and logging into their homeland, the Lekwiltok and the Mainland-Comox people were to survive and flourish—against all odds and predictions.

CHAPTER 4

Stump Ranchers and Loggers

1880–1900

They are talking of extending the Island Railroad up here, it has been surveyed right through our land. We have been offered $4800 for our land (£960), not bad considering we have only been here a year. I am certain there is coal on our land and certain people know of it, hence the offers.

—Fred Nunns, from a letter to his brother Ernest, March 1889[1]

Nunns Creek, quietly following its marshy course through the rapidly growing town of Campbell River, is a lasting reminder of the Nunns family, who were among the town's first non-Native settlers. Fred Nunns had the foresight to keep a journal of his pioneer experiences, leaving us a poignant insider's view of a transition point in the history of this coast.

The Nunnses had the privilege of seeing the landscape in all its wild beauty, not yet touched by the dreams of development they shared with their generation. Fred was an unusual man. He was intelligent, sober, fastidious and sometimes cranky. Alone for much of his life, Fred yearned for good conversation and would row many miles in an open boat to visit friends and borrow books.

Nunns, of an Anglo-Irish family, was raised in Dublin and educated in England. He left Ireland in 1878 and joined his elder brother Jack in South Africa, where they served together as military police troopers. Fred later made a futile attempt at diamond and gold mining. With their parents gone, Fred's main contact at home was his brother Ernest, to whom he wrote in 1887: "Jack's and my plan about going to [British] Columbia is to start farming and if we do any good, get the rest of you to join us...We so long to see the sea again."

The Nunns family were part of a general northward expansion of settlement from the Comox Valley to the river and creek mouths between the Oyster and Campbell Rivers in the 1880s. The powerful Dunsmuir family provided the stimulus for this growth when they took over the Union/Cumberland coal mines and made plans for railway development. In exchange for 2 million acres (800,000 ha) of land on the east coast of Vancouver Island the Dunsmuirs agreed to fulfill the federal government's promise to build a rail line from Victoria to Duncan Bay, just north of Campbell River.

The logging camps that sprang up along the shores of Discovery Passage in the early 1880s provided a more immediate stimulus for growth. Hungry loggers, with no time for growing crops and chasing cattle along the coast, created work for farmers and ranchers. Loggers scorned these "stump farmers," especially when the light-headed fools tried their hand at logging, but the two were inextricably linked. Logging produced our first and foremost cash economy but ranchers and farmers, especially those with families, supported the industry and created communities.

To attract settlers the government pumped out alluring propaganda loosely based on fact. According to a provincial directory of 1893, Quadra Island was an agricultural paradise: "...the soil is a beautiful brown loam, well adapted for raising good crops. The resources of the Island are stock raising and vegetables. The cattle and hogs roam at large on the fine pasture lands and become fat and good for market." In fact the thin mineral soil on the island proved, after much labour, to be best suited for growing timber, not hogs and cattle.

Aspiring farmers were offered 160-acre (64 ha) tracts at the incredible price of $1.00 an acre for "pre-emptions" or timber leases. Who could resist? The requirements were relatively simple. Applicants must be British subjects (men or widows), and they must make improvements valued at $2.50 per acre in chopping, clearing, fencing, ditching and housing. To "prove" his homestead the settler must hire a surveyor such as George Drabble, who typically appraised log houses at between $50 and $150 (the higher amount applying to squared logs) and cleared and seeded fields at between $50 and $90 an acre. The generosity of this arrangement spawned a land grab, but many weren't able to pay even these meagre fees for several decades or more of hard work.

By the 1891 Dominion census there were roughly 244 non-Native people living between the

Fred Nunns, left, was one of Campbell River's first non-Native settlers. His diaries and letters provide a peephole glimpse into the joys and travails of pioneer life. On May 25, 1890, he wrote: "Blowing southeaster. Walked down the coast for 8 miles and in the woods. Arrived at Knights at noon. He told us our cattle were down at Oyster River, 7 miles, so I made up my mind to go and fetch them, arriving home just before dark. My feet completely worn out and no wonder, after 35 miles beach walking."
Ruth (Pidcock) Barnett Collection, MCR 6910

Horace and Amelia Smith and family, before leaving England to immigrate to British Columbia in 1887. The Smiths left the comforts of English middle-class life in search of new opportunities for their large family. Their sons and daughters became well-known sport fishing guides, big-game hunters and timber cruisers. *Pidcock Collection, MCR 14352*

Oyster and Salmon Rivers and on the adjacent islands. Thirty-seven were ranchers, farmers, fishermen and tradespeople and their families. The whopping majority, 207 men, were loggers.

Farming had particular appeal for British immigrants like the Smith family of Black Creek, who left a decided mark upon the social and economic development of the mid-coast, though not through their attempts at farming.

Amelia Smith, a gently bred Englishwoman with a continental education, packed up her large family in 1887 to follow her eldest son to the wilds of British Columbia. Her recalcitrant husband, Horace Sr., was unconvinced of the wisdom of the move and didn't join them for nearly a year. With their English fortune strained, the Smiths hoped to establish a country estate in Black Creek, on land purchased in haste from a man named Whiskey Jones. The place turned out to be a determined swamp, more suited to growing cedar, which in the end provided them a modest income as shake cutters. In spite of the farm's failure, some of Amelia and Horace's children went on to pursue the agrarian dream as they came into maturity.

One of their sons, Eustace Smith, began his married life at a homestead on the Nimpkish River, where he learned by hard experience (which included flooding, loneliness and the death of a child) to let go of the English dream: "I wanted a farm as I remembered farms to be in England. Many here worked hard at making an England out of Vancouver Island—making these the British Isles of the West. I guess we all had that idea, 'gentleman farmers'. In the old country a big farm would make you landed gentry; land was associated with wealth. Here it meant toil. You became a serf to your own land...[We were] trying to make a little England here, 'a green and pleasant

Eustace Smith started work as a farm labourer at age eleven, following the English dream, but later gave this up to become one of BC's foremost timber cruisers. "There's hardly a piece of timber on the coast that I can't tell you something about," Smith told an interviewer in 1948.
Pidcock Collection, MCR 10610

land.' Well it's green here all right, but by God it's fierce. It was [with] axes and saws and oxen and horses [that we] carved out our life in this country."[2]

This same lust for land prompted the Nunns family to pre-empt hundreds of acres of flood plain a mile up from the mouth of the Campbell River. Though government requirements specified that land claimed must not be in use by other settlers or First Nations people, the Nunns trespassed upon the Weiwaikum Reserve. When a dispute erupted with the Quack-sus-tu-la family (later Anglicized to Quocksister), Fred Nunns hoped a friendly game of whist with the government surveyor would quickly settle the matter in his favour: "Mr. Green has full power to deal with our case so in a week's time we will start putting our house and store up." However, many days later Nunns grumbled over the results of the survey: "We have nothing to be thankful for...[we will] lose about five chains...In place of Quack-sus-tu-la we have to plough a piece the same size on his own land and also pay him $5 for some clearing he has done. At the finish the old chief was highly pleased and said we were all the same now as his five sons, intending to pay us a high compliment."[3]

John Kwaksistala was an important chief among the Lekwiltok people, having connections at both Campbell River and Cape Mudge. In the 1880s Kwaksistala invited a Cortes Island trader, Michael Manson, to a theatrical performance at the Cape Mudge Reserve. The "play" turned out to be a lighthearted parody of white settlers, which Manson said was arranged by a man named "Chekite," who had seen a theatre performance in San Francisco. "He got the idea that the Indians could make a better play than the whites," wrote Manson in his memoirs.

Kwaksistala's people dressed Manson to join the chief in his place of rank on a raised platform. Manson's face was painted and he wore a button blanket adorned with nearly $100 worth of pearl buttons and headgear made from eagle feathers and bear claws. "[Chekite] had [the actors] all dressed up like ducks, with long tin bills and wings fixed to their arms which they kept flapping around, and quacking like ducks."

The ducks continued around and around the big house, gathering together a tremendous flock as they spread the news of their discovery

Captain John Kwaksistala, a high-ranking Lekwiltok chief, was among the first of his people to take up permanent residence at Campbell River Spit in the 1880s. *Russell Kwaksistala Collection, MCR 16713*

of a plentiful feeding ground. At the end of the performance their tin beaks were knocked off and the performers slapped with small cheesecloth bags filled with flour that stuck to their greased faces, completing their transformation into white people. "Chekite interpreted the play as it went along and the Indians almost lifted the roof from the house in their glee."[4]

Fred Nunns noted in his diary the occasional stormy periods in his friendship with Captain John Kwaksistala, who continued to assert that Nunns was on his land. Smoothing over such troubles was in Nunns' best interest, for it was the First Nations people who helped these early settlers, who clung to their impractical European ideals and experience, to learn the ways of the coast.

The Nunns brothers' initial plan had been to wait until they'd proved their new home a success before sending for their siblings, but things must have seemed immediately promising because within a year they were joined by Annie, Frank and Larry. The fivesome built a two-storey, seven-room "log chateau" which they called Padeswood. Among its remarkable furnishings was a piano, the Victorian icon for superior society. The piano, on planks straddling two canoes, was paddled up coast from Comox to the Nunns' new home.

Fred Nunns and a neighbour, c. 1912. Nunns was among the first non-Native people to settle at Campbell River, in 1887–88. He made a basic living from mixed farming, and although he complained about the weather and the lack of "congenial society," the independence of pioneer life suited Nunns. "I am my own boss," he wrote in a letter to a brother in Ireland, "and have all the shooting and fishing I want. I make my own butter, bake my own bread, wash my clothes, kill and cure my bacon."
Ruth (Pidcock) Barnett Collection, MCR 6911

Though their start seemed promising, all but Fred moved on within two years. "So I will be here alone" was his sorrowful entry in his journal. Fred continued to farm on the banks of the Campbell River, raising chickens and pigs and growing turnips, cabbages by the hundreds, cucumbers, tomatoes, lettuce, strawberries, hay, potatoes, carrots, squash and pumpkins. The task of selling his crops must have often made Fred rue the day he took up farming in such a sparsely settled region, like the time he got caught by the tides in Seymour Narrows.

Weighed down with a canoeload of pumpkins and squash to sell at Grant's camp at Granite Point, on north Quadra Island, Fred Nunns reached the Narrows as the tide was beginning to race. He made camp on the beach and was aroused from a thin sleep just before dawn to find his canoe capsized and his precious cargo floating around the bay. Retrieving what he could the tired homesteader took up his paddle under rainy skies and continued his journey: "Got through the Narrows at daybreak and had a hard pull up to Grant's where I arrived 11 a.m. wet through. Found Grant was not there but expected in afternoon." To add to the sober man's annoyance a steamship arrived that night "and the men got a lot of liquor and had a regular drunken night of it. I never got a wink of sleep." The next morning Fred sold his pumpkins at 37 cents each and the squash at 12 cents, using his earnings to buy five bags of crushed barley for his hogs, one dozen cartridges and three large bottles of sauce (to flavour meat). He also borrowed twenty books.

Fred made regular trips across Discovery Passage to get his mail and replenish basic supplies at King and Casey's logging camp commissary in Quathiaski Cove. For major provisioning he paddled down to Comox, a trip requiring anywhere from three to five days.

September 29, 1890: Raining all morning. 12 noon cleared up in NW so I started. Pulled [rowed] to Oyster River where I arrived 5 p.m. without stopping. Stayed there 5 minutes, had a cracker and then went on to Kitty Coleman Creek where I arrived about 7:00 and as it was getting rough camped there. Put up a bear, could hear him going through brush.

September 30: Very rough this morning but got canoe out all right. Went to Millers where I had breakfast and then walked in to Comox.

Oct. 1: Blowing hard and raining. Have got all my things ready for a start tomorrow.

Oct. 2: Started out to Millers 10 a.m., McPhee [storekeeper] sending my things out in cart. The tires got coming off every hundred yards and it took us over 2 hours to get out. I have 2 men coming up with me ... When we loaded canoe found we had too much so [one man] stayed behind. Left Miller's 1:30 p.m. and pulled to Joe Stewart's. Arrived there 10 p.m. and slept.

Oct. 3: Fine. Left Joe's 7 a.m., arrived home 10 a.m. Found everything all right.

Oct. 4: Blowing hard and raining all day. Busy making a sail for canoe.[5]

Access to the growing markets, mail and supply centres at both Comox and the Union Mines (later called Cumberland), was crucial for the settlers. The "Colonization Road" was extended as far as Oyster River (22 miles/35 km south of Campbell River) in 1887, where a massive fallen log served as a bridge until a frame structure was erected in 1892.[6] A trail was hacked through to Campbell River in 1890, but it was little more than a cattle path, barely fit for livestock.

In the 1880s passenger and freight ships running up the coast from Victoria and Vancouver were prevailed upon to make occasional stops in Discovery Passage. At the sound of the whistle the shoreward settlers and First Nations people paddled out to the waiting ship to retrieve mail and supplies or pick up passengers. Coastal steamers operated by the Union Steamship Company of Vancouver are the most fondly remembered of these. They began making regular stops at docks built on Cortes Island and Quadra Island in the early 1890s.

The powerful rush of tide through the constriction of Seymour Narrows and along the shallow reefs on either side of Discovery Passage, at Cape Mudge and Shelter Point, was a constant threat for coastal mariners. In 1898 a lighthouse was constructed at Cape Mudge—just in time for a rush of boats heading north in search of Yukon gold.

The Nunns brothers were touted as the "vanguard of settlement in the north" but in fact there were a number of non-Native people who preceded their arrival in 1887–88, including Edward Barton Hill, whose homestead covered much of what is now downtown Campbell River.

Cape Mudge Lighthouse, on the southern tip of Quadra Island, as sketched by Sybil Andrews Morgan, a Campbell River artist, in 1962. The lighthouse was installed in 1898 to warn mariners away from the dangerous reef at Cape Mudge.
MCR 993.12.45, courtesy Glenbow Museum

Fred Nunns' diary provides a little information about "old Hill," whom Nunns described as a difficult neighbour, though it should be noted this was a characteristic he freely ascribed to many of his fellow settlers. Hill's place was something of a social centre and news-swapping hub for a surprisingly active transient population of trappers, would-be settlers, prospectors, road construction crews, whiskey peddlers and sportsmen; each arrival and departure being carefully noted by Nunns.

The pioneer population was dominated by single men like Hill and Nunns, who lived by a patchy assortment of means, supporting their attempts at farming by dabbling in prospecting, logging, and guiding visiting game hunters and fishers.

Hill appears to have worked as a logger in association with Hugh Grant, who ran small logging camps in Discovery Passage from 1887 onward. With no descendants in the area to remember them, our only record of these bachelors is through their fleeting appearance in community records, from which they eventually retreat into obscurity.

The shape of the land has changed since "old Hill's" day. Shoppers Row curves around what was originally the foreshore of a tidal bay, filled in later years to create Tyee Plaza. Hill's shack sat upon rising ground at the water's edge, near what is now the north corner of 10th Avenue.

Hill remained a squatter on District Lot 69 for a number of years until he took a notion to move in 1890, making it necessary to register his pre-emption claim. Nunns cheerfully noted the pending change: "Old Hill talks of leasing his place to a man with a family who wants to start a store. I hope he does as he is not a very good neighbour." This lease arrangement did not transpire, but in the spring of 1892 Hill sold out to John and Annie Peacey of the Comox Valley. With his abiding interest in pecuniary matters, Nunns noted the sale price at $1,500, a substantial sum at a time when the country was sliding into a serious economic recession. Hill invested the proceeds into a pre-emption and logging operation with Hugh Grant in a protected bay on Quadra Island, across the Seymour Narrows.

Annie Peacey was pregnant when she and John settled at Campbell River in 1892. Setting a white cloth fluttering atop a pole outside their log home in the dim light of a November day, the Peaceys gave notice to Alice Pidcock, a midwife living 2 miles (3 km) across Discovery Passage in Quathiaski Cove, to come to their assistance. With the solid reassurance of Alice at her side

Annie gave birth to Campbell River's first non-Native child, John Campbell Peacey, whose second name marked his birthplace. In later years Annie captivated her grandchildren with tales of this pioneer birthing and the gifts of salmon the First Nations people brought in specially woven baskets.

Young Katie Walker (later Clarke), child of the Methodist lay missionary at the Wewaikai village at Cape Mudge, was struck by the grandeur of the Peaceys' four-room house. It had the marvel of a squared stone chimney and fireplace, a luxury afforded by Peacey's English training as a plasterer and mason. John and Annie expanded Hill's clearing to bring 7 or 8 acres (3 ha) under cultivation, planted an orchard and raised cattle, pigs and a few sheep.

The Peaceys' story is typical of many. Following five or six years of hard labour they moved on, discouraged by the lack of a steady market for their produce, the ceaseless battle to save their stock from predatory cougars and bears, and the loneliness of isolation.

A new opportunity presented itself to John in the form of the Yukon Gold Rush of 1898. Eight-year-old Katie Walker watched in awe from her home at Cape Mudge as boats of every size and description transformed Discovery Passage overnight into a busy shipping lane, carrying men and women to the Yukon. On board one such boat went John Peacey, while Annie packed up the children and returned to her extended family in Comox.

James Curtis's paintings of himself and his brother at his cabin at Bates Beach, south of the Oyster River. The majority of non-Native settlers were bachelors; in the years before World War I the male-to-female ratio was about fifteen to one. *Courtesy MCR*

The Peaceys didn't sell their Campbell River property until 1904, taking a substantial loss if reports of the Thulin family's purchase price of $800[7] are accurate. The Euro-Canadian settlement's first-born, John Campbell Peacey, went on to become a decorated World War I hero.

There were about ten families and single men living on large-scale cattle ranches between Campbell River and Oyster River before 1900. While the names of some of these people are familiar today in place names such as McGimpsey Road, Stories Beach, Galerno Road and Erickson Road very little is otherwise known of them. Snippets of family tales, local folklore and terse notations in Nunns' diary provide fleeting glimpses into their lives.

James McIver owned a cattle ranch at Oyster River, at what is now the University of British Columbia Experimental Farm. The McKeever, as he called himself, was a Nova Scotian of Scottish ancestry. He fired the imagination of young Arthur Mayse, a budding writer, who fly-

The Peacey family bought a ranch in what is now downtown Campbell River, from E.B. Hill in 1892. After six years of struggling against cougars, bears and isolation, John Peacey decided the Yukon gold rush was a better gamble. He went north, leaving Annie and the children with her family in Comox. *Mardy Cross Collection, MCR 20016*

fished the Oyster River starting in the 1920s. Though McIver was in his seventies when Mayse first met him, the Gaelic-speaking ancient was still remarkably strong. "He was a man of legends; the definitive old-timer for my money," recalled Mayse in later years. He had a "big barrel of a chest and craggy rugged features [with] beetling white eyebrows and fierce blue eyes. He would have looked good with a claymore in his fist."

McIver came up from Victoria to look over the

Annie Peacey had just settled into her log cabin on the beach when she gave birth to John Campbell Peacey in what is now downtown Campbell River, November 1892. John went on to become a much-decorated World War I hero. A few years after he returned from overseas, he died of injuries he had sustained when hurling an enemy bomb from the trenches. *Mardy Cross Collection, MCR 20149*

Katie Walker (later Clarke), left, at the Wewaikai Reserve at Cape Mudge, c. 1897. She retained detailed memories of her childhood on Quadra Island, where her father and mother, Robert J. and Agnes Walker, were Methodist lay missionaries. *Joy (Walker) Huntley Collection, MCR 7555*

Oyster River property in 1887. Smitten by the beautiful delta land, he bought it and outfitted himself for homesteading. He might have spared himself the trouble, for on his return trip his boat was wrecked on the treacherous sandbars at the mouth of the Oyster, leaving him with nothing but the clothes on his back. He had to hike five miles up the road to borrow matches to start his new life.[8]

One of the tales of McIver's legendary strength, recounted by Arthur Mayse, involved the wreck of a French barque on the same Oyster River sandbars. The sad discovery of five bodies washed ashore gave McIver the determination to ensure the men received a Christian burial, though it meant three toilsome return trips to Comox with the bodies of the men slung over his shoulders. "His last trip," recounted Mayse, "was easy because he only had one body to carry."[9]

Another story of McIver's Bunyanesque vigour involved his work on the Oyster River bridge in 1892. This "giant of a man" was paid two men's daily rate because he could pick up one end of a big bridge timber by himself while two or even three fellows struggled with the other end.

To the north of McIver lived another Scot, Joseph Stewart. He established a cattle ranch in about 1885 at what came to be known as Stories Beach. In 1888 Joseph married a widow, Martha Storie, with two sons, William and James. The eldest, William, had been working in Dunsmuir's coal mines since the age of eleven.

The Stewarts' place was a much appreciated layover for Discovery Passage travellers. A writer for a Comox Valley newspaper, *The Weekly News*, described their prosperous ranch: "This is one of the 'out o' the world' places, a ranch on the seashore, with peace and plenty reigning around; the garden well cultivated and very productive; plenty of vegetables, milk, butter, and bacon; plenty of fresh air; trout from the river just at hand, and salmon and cod from the bay."[10]

Joseph Stewart established a ranch at Stories Beach in 1885 and married a Nanaimo widow, Martha, pictured above. His stepson William Storie inherited the Stewart ranch, giving his name to the beach and the meandering creek where their first home was built.
Martha (Storie) Brown Collection, MCR 20102-1

In 1909, a few years after Joseph Stewart passed away, William Storie married Hannah Beech of the Comox Valley and the couple moved into the Stewarts' old log cabin perched on the curving bank of Stories Creek. William's mother Martha lived out her days in the new home that replaced the cabin. This big house was a finely crafted frame dwelling fitted out with milled trim, handmade cupboards and walls insulated with oats. Now a crumbling relic on the edge of the busy Island Highway, it is all that remains of the old Stewart-Storie ranch.

To the north of the Stewart-Storie place was James Knight, a Cariboo gold rush veteran who claimed 160 acres (64 ha) at Shelter Point in 1882, at what is now the junction of Engels Road and the Island Highway. Knight was a hardworking, cash-poor, fifty-seven-year-old bachelor when Eustace Smith, son of Amelia and Horace of Black Creek, hiked up the road, searching for work in 1893. In debt to one or more Comox merchants and badly needing help on the ranch, Knight offered the lad room and board, promising to make him his heir in exchange for his labour. A year later, when the light finally dawned on young Smith that this "rough but kindly and considerate man" had many sprightly years to live, Smith made tracks, following in the footsteps of his timber cruising hero, Jim King.

Shortly after, Knight married a Nanaimo widow, Elizabeth Benson, and adopted another youthful heir as a labourer, Sam McGimpsey. Living continued to be difficult for the Knights, who advertised their place for sale in the *Enterprise* newspaper throughout 1903 and 1904: "I will sell cheap, for cash, my farm of 160 acres, 30 acres cleared and fenced, together with three horses and 45 head of horned cattle, farm implements, etc." But there were no takers, so when James and Elizabeth died within months of each other in 1917, McGimpsey inherited the old couple's beautiful seaside ranch.

An 1890 entry in Nunns' diary describes the battles these ranchers waged against the surrounding wildlife: "Joe Stewart heard one of his pigs squealing in the woods last week and he went out armed with an ax and his stepson with a gun and found a big bear was carrying off his pig. They killed the bear, a very big one. Three days ago Jimmy Knight, a rancher living a mile from Stewart, heard one of his pigs squealing and went out with a rifle and dogs and found a large panther [cougar] and the dogs treed him. Jimmy shot him. He measured seven feet in length. There is $5 bounty for his scalp."

For most settlers, raising stock in a wilderness teeming with large, hungry predators was a serious matter, but George "By-God" Stafford and his storytelling protégé, Bill Law, wove the problem into a humorous tale:

I saw [By-God Stafford] at Campbell River later and I asked him how the pig farm was coming along. He said, "Not very good, by-God, you know, I'm not gaining a bit. There's a bear that comes and steals the little pigs, by-God, you know."

I said, "Why don't you shoot the bear?"

"He's the smartest bear in British Columbia, by-God, you can't shoot him or trap him."

"Well," I said, "I guess the only thing to do is put some lanterns in the piggery."

He said, "I've tried that too, by-God. He never used to come around, he never shows up unless I go to get my provisions, see. I laid for him with a rifle but he don't come around. He knows when I'm home. It's when I go away when he steals the pigs. I tried the lanterns in there and I thought I had him

Hannah Storie and her daughter Martha, c. 1911. Hannah married William Storie of Stories Beach in 1909 and lived out her long life in her sturdy farmhouse, now a sagging relic of pioneer days. *Martha (Storie) Brown Collection, MCR 20101-5*

beat. By-God," he says, "it was all right for two or three weeks. Then one morning I heard a hell of a racket out there and squealing and grunting, you know. I grabbed the old .30-.30 and ran outside...and there was that bear going up the side of the mountain with a pig under one arm and the lantern in the other. He must have heard me pull the hammer back because he blew the light out and I missed him, by-God."[11]

There were settlers, like Cecil Smith, another son of Amelia and Horace Smith, who made their living hunting these predators. "Cougar" Smith was a wiry, slender man with an uncanny knack for tracking game in any circumstance—from pitch darkness to raging winter weather and impenetrable undergrowth. Both a bounty hunter and guide, Smith proudly tallied his kill in 1920 at 1,000 animals, after which he stopped counting.[12] He often took game-hunting clients to the Big Rock area (on the southern approach to Campbell River), an exceptionally beautiful site full of streams and luxuriant growth, which was a natural draw for wildlife. Over the years, Smith killed 150 cougars in this spot alone.

Cecil Smith, left, made his living as a cougar bounty hunter and guide, having developed an uncanny ability as a tracker and woodsman while growing up in Black Creek in the 1890s. Roderick Haig-Brown shadowed "Cougar" Smith for a year in preparation for his book *Panther (Ki-yu)*, published in 1934. *Margaret (Pidcock) Dunn Collection, MCR 11538*

A noteworthy few arrived in the district with the hard-bitten sense to concentrate their efforts on the primary resources of Discovery Passage—fish and timber. Among these seasoned veterans were Reginald and Alice Pidcock, and Moses and Julia Ireland.

The Pidcocks bought property on Quadra Island in 1882 but didn't settle there for another decade. Reginald and Alice were well-educated English immigrants who learned much from their failed attempts at milling and shipping in the Comox Valley in the 1860s and '70s. In the late 1880s Pidcock was appointed Indian Agent for the Kwakiutl district. He used his Quathiaski Cove property as an occasional base while on agency business, then relocated his large family to a grand

The Pidcock family home—"The Big House"—Quathiaski Cove, Quadra Island, c. 1900. Reginald and Alice Pidcock's sons William, Harry, Reginald, George and Herbert developed Quathiaski Cove into an economic hub for the region. Residents of Campbell River, a smaller community until after World War I, had to row across to the Cove for their mail and supplies at Pidcock's store. *David Pidcock Collection, MCR 12722*

new house in the Cove in the early 1890s. Drawing upon a wealth of coastal experience, he worked with his grown sons to develop Quathiaski Cove into a thriving commercial centre, which included a general store, salmon cannery, sawmill and logging operation.

Moses Ireland also settled on this part of the coast in the wisdom of his late middle age. He had gained considerable fame as an expert woodsman during the Cariboo gold rush in the 1860s and as a partner in one of BC's first sawmills, in Burrard Inlet. While notoriety often came his way, fortune continually eluded him. In the early 1880s Ireland was among the first wave of lumbermen to move up the coast from Burrard Inlet. He kept a Victoria address (probably for the winter season) and set up as a hotel keeper, timber cruiser and logger on the Subtle Islands, off Cortes Island. In 1888 Ireland married a Victoria widow, a dressmaker named Julia Ward, whose grown family joined Ireland's businesses. In 1901 the family opened a second hotel and started a cattle ranch at Bold Point on Quadra Island. "He is better known, however," said the *Victoria Daily Colonist* of 1905, "as a forest ranger and timber cruiser, few woodsmen having higher reputations than his in this very exacting craft." Acting on Ireland's advice, men like R.D. Merrill became timber barons. Merrill's descendants still own timberland in the Discovery Passage region, purchased nearly 120 years ago.

Moses Ireland had a storehouse of adventure tales, which sometimes bordered on the fantastic, from his daring rescue of a group lost in a snowstorm during the Cariboo gold rush to his endurance as a Skeena River packer. One of his coastal tales made Ireland the butt of ridicule when he reported to a Vancouver newspaper that he had seen a "bright floating cloud of light travelling on the water." It moved across the water and sparkled "just like an electric light sputters, then glowed white and steady and flashed out." Ireland felt the light was "some sort of notice of the visitation of death, or disaster of some kind." For years after this event any Discovery Islander suspected of spinning a yarn was accused of telling a Moses Ireland.

The legendary quality of Ireland's life and deeds have persisted beyond the grave. A former justice of the peace, Seymour Bagot, wrote in his memoirs that Ireland was the victim of an unsolved murder, and Bold Point residents believe his ghostly presence hovers over his burial plot on what remains of his ranch. But Ireland's death certificate indicates otherwise. After an illness of some weeks he died of heart failure in Vancouver, where he is buried.[13]

The Discovery Islands, particularly Quadra, Read, Thurlow and Cortes, were a magnet for settlement in the early 1880s. With the ocean as their highway the requisites for a homestead were easy access to a safe harbour, fresh water and fertile ground.

Read Island and Campbell River were the first places in the region to be listed in the provincial directory in 1887 and Read Islanders opened the first school in 1894, though it closed shortly thereafter because of insufficient enrollment. The combination of

Moses Ireland, a larger-than-life local figure. The aura of myth surrounding his lifetime of adventure has survived him. Until recent years he was said to have been the victim of an unsolved murder, and his ghost has pestered the current owners of his ranch on Quadra Island. However, his death certificate shows no sign of any such drama: Moses Ireland died of heart failure at a ripe old age and was buried in Vancouver. *BCARS H-02845*

easy logging along the island's steep shoreline and fertile swamps, which could be drained for farming, were its attractions.

An intriguing couple, Edgar and Hattie Wylie, and their family were among the first non-Native people to settle on Read Island, in 1888.[14] Edgar Wylie had just risen in rank from sheriff to police chief in Valley City, Dakota, only a year before he and a group of friends moved to Read Island. At his remote new home in Burdwood Bay, where he was a storekeeper, hotelier, logger and trader, Wylie crossed over to the other side of the law. His lifestyle represented a certain libertarian element in settlement-era society. As the late Bill Hall summed it up, "There wasn't much law around those days."

Edgar Wylie of Read Island (far right), served a rough clientele at his Burdwood Bay Hotel. When his wife Hattie gave up the rough lifestyle and moved to Vancouver, her relatives, the Aldriches, moved in for a time. Left to right, back row: Herb and Cyrus Aldrich, unknown and Edgar Wylie. Front: Jesse, Mary with Earl, and Ruth Aldrich.
Etta (Manson) Byers Collection, MCR 9356

Wylie's transgressions mainly involved bootlegging, shipping crates of "apples" to the neighbouring Indian reserves and making off-hours sales to the loggers of the district. When they finished up a stint of work, men came to Burdwood Bay to await a Vancouver-bound steamship, but some didn't make it to "town" for years. The temptations at Wylie's hotel and saloon easily consumed the profits of a season's work.

Quadra Island visitors (the Joyce family, far right) and Read Islanders at Edgar Wylie's Burdwood Bay Hotel, c. 1906. Wylie's housekeeper, Mary Longe (ninth from the right), inherited his $1,500 estate when Wylie died in 1908. Longe was unable to transfer Wylie's liquor licence to her name, so the infamous Burdwood Bay Hotel was no more. *Genesis 75 Collection, MCR 7812*

The most notorious case to stain the Wylies' reputation was an 1894 murder trial in which the couple had a marginal involvement. It seems a trio of their friends, a lonely logger named Benson and John and Laura Smith, became enmeshed in a love triangle. The newspapers of the day reported that John Smith found his wife in the arms of Benson and clubbed him to death, and the Wylies helped cover up—Hattie cleaned bloodstains from the Smiths' bedroom floor. The trial proved Smith had committed the crime, but he was pronounced not guilty. *The Weekly News* said the jury was unwilling to convict a man "who strikes down the villain who destroys the sanctity of his home."[15] Some time after the trial Laura Smith and Hattie Wylie, unable to continue this wild lifestyle, packed up their children and left their husbands to their tainted Read Island homes.

Wylie lived out his days on Read Island, acclaimed by some as the first non-Native settler and reviled by others for his petty crimes. Upon his death in 1908, Wylie's "housekeeper," Mary Longe, inherited his $1,500 estate, and Wylie's coffin was cemented into the cleft of a rock on his favourite promontory in Burdwood Bay.[16]

Mike and Jane Manson and family, Cortes Island pioneers, 1906. Left to right, back row: Robina, Mike, Wilfred, Ethel; middle row: Margaret (the only child to survive diphtheria, in what came to be known as their first family), Hazel, Jane; front row: Florence, Gwendoline, Flossie. *MCR 9358*

The first commercial activity in the Campbell River district took place on Cortes Island, where there was a brief-lived whaling station from 1869 to 1870. More than a decade passed before settlers arrived, starting with Michael and Jane Manson and family in 1886.[17]

English ranchers were often treated with sneering scorn, but sturdy, no-nonsense Scots like the Mansons commanded respect for their business acumen and dedicated industry—although Michael Manson began his career by eloping with his tyrannical business partner's daughter, Jane Renwick. The couple had endured many trials in their early years, including the deaths of several of their children from diphtheria and the loss of their business to fire. Making a fresh start on Cortes Island, Manson opened a trading post for loggers and Native people at Manson's Landing. In 1888 Mike's brother John joined his business, but in the 1890s recession they gave up their trading post. Mike Manson became a successful MLA for this and other ridings in the province, while John made his living raising sheep on Cortes and Mitlenatch Islands. In 1897 John returned to the Shetlands to marry his childhood sweetheart Margaret. She became a much-loved member of the pioneer community, but she never stopped pining for her Shetland home, so different from the oppressive darkness of the BC forests.

Miners living at the booming little mining settlement of Shoal Bay on Thurlow Island provided a market for Discovery Islands farmers. Numerous mines, backed by international financing, opened in and around Shoal Bay to extract iron, copper and gold in the 1890s. An 1896 Minister of Mines report described Shoal Bay as "the only attempt at a town in the district…a centre of

John Manson, left, with a load of wool ready for market, Sunny Brae farm, Cortes Island. Before leaving the Shetland Islands, the Manson brothers learned both farming and household arts such as cooking, spinning, knitting and sewing, which proved excellent training when they took up homesteads on Cortes Island. *Jon Ackroyd Collection, MCR 7085*

supply for the mining and lumber camps for a few miles around." In 1901 there were 138 people living at Shoal Bay, which boasted two hotels, two stores and a commodious wharf. But the mines petered out and the place slumped into a quiet backwater. A later version of one of the hotels has continued operating on and off through the years.

Euro-Canadian women were in the minority in upcoast settlements until well into the twentieth century, but their presence was essential to the development of community life. Women did not have voting privileges nor the right to own land (unless widowed), and their opportunities for paid employment were minimal.

With the male-to-female ratio at about fifteen to one, family life was the exception not the rule. First Nations women were urged into casual relationships and prostitution, which seldom benefitted them or their children. In a society on the outer fringes of "civilization" it was easy to flout Victorian morality. The terms *housekeeper* and *cook* were often code words for common-law spouse.

Shoal Bay, Thurlow Island, at the peak of its brief history as the largest community in the district, 1901. Its stores, post office and two hotels served numerous mines and logging camps surrounding Shoal Bay, starting in the 1890s. *BCARS D-08207*

No matter what the legal basis of the relationship, a pattern emerged in which women took care of the children and the farms (serious work, if everyone wanted to eat through the winter), while the men laboured away from home when they could, in order to earn cash.

Bill Hall, a pioneer resident, recalled the incongruous expectations placed upon Victorian women, to perform duties not normally viewed as their lot: "Many near impossible things was expected of a woman who married a pioneer. One old timer that I knew put an ad in the paper for a housekeeper and it read: 'Housekeeper wanted by 60 year old bachelor. Must be able to sharpen her own saw.'"

Amelia Smith made the switch from a comfortable English upbringing and continental education to "stump ranching" in Merville, in the hope of finding new and better opportunities for her large family. In between farm chores she walked many miles to teach piano lessons to the children of her fellow settlers. *Pidcock Collection, MCR 10666*

Tales of Mary Bryant, the first non-Native woman to settle on Quadra Island in 1889, have a romanticized tone that may hold grains of truth. With her husband, "Black Jack," working in the logging camps, Mary barricaded the door of her cabin against the "fear-inspiring" Lekwiltok people. "One morning, looking out from the cabin, she saw two squaws examining her washing. [They] wished to exchange their garments for the fine lingerie made in England." In a 1905 speech Mary Bryant laughingly recalled her unfounded fears. She had long since come to value the friendship and support of her First Nations neighbours.

Confined to their homes and gardens, pioneer women like Mary Bryant found that loneliness posed the greatest hardship. As her anonymous biographer wrote:

> The longing for a letter from home led her to visit Quathiaski Cove, where mail was sometimes delivered by passing traders. When she neared a shack that stood upon the shore where the mail was sometimes left, a large black bear stepped out of the brush barring her way. She stood stock still in astonishment, while Bruin snooped up to her, sniffed at her dress, raised himself on his hind legs, and placed his paws upon her shoulders. At this critical moment, a man came out of the shack, picked up a club and knocked Bruin hors de combat. Upon stating her name to the man, and asking for a letter, he informed her that one had come, but that he had returned it [saying] "There ain't no such person on this island."[18]

Cookbooks weren't necessary in the log cabin kitchen, where the standard fare was venison stew. Bill Hall had a favourite story that involved a stew he never tasted. It seems the neighbouring Newcombe family threw caution to the winds when they thought some copper-stained rock on their Gowlland Harbour property signalled fame and fortune. The family celebrated by using a good portion of their winter's savings of $50 for a grand new hat for Mrs. Newcombe, "a fancy one with a big wide brim and a bird, a blue bird, set right on the top of it."

The Newcombes' dreams of wealth were a bust. Years later, after they had moved elsewhere, the ill-fated blue bird of the broad-brimmed hat wound up a plaything for the Hall children. One evening as Angelina Hall stirred the eternal pot of venison stew, she turned her head for a moment, no doubt distracted by the children, and the blue bird dropped unnoticed into the stew pot—a mishap no one was brave enough to announce, as Bill Hall recalled: "And that night at dinnertime, when the stew was dished up, the potatoes was green, and everything was blue and green from the dye out of this bird. She got fishing around in the pot and by the time she got the bird out and saw what it was we were long gone . . . taking out for far away places."

The government's settlement propaganda, which encouraged the Halls and others to take up land, was grossly inflated. But when the 1897 *Year Book for British Columbia* raved about the forest resources of the district, it was a well-established fact: "The country generally is very rugged, and the coast, on both sides of the straits, and the many islands, large and small, which intervene, are heavily timbered. Here are found the principal logging camps of the Province, and a very important supply of the best merchantable timber. Although sparsely populated as yet, perhaps no other area of British Columbia of similar size contains so much and varied natural wealth, represented in timber . . ."

Loggers tackled the forests in partnerships of two and three men working entirely by hand, or in larger settings managed by enterprising lumbermen who secured timber leases upwards of 1,000 acres (400 ha). These large camps were usually aligned to a sawmill operator such as Andrew Haslam of Nanaimo, William Sayward of Victoria or Hastings Mill in Burrard Inlet. The mills provided some equipment and a promise of a tow for the log booms, but the lumbermen made all the local arrangements and supplied the animal power for hauling on land. The intractable bulls of earlier years gave way to horses in the 1890s, but neither of these modes of transport allowed the loggers to haul from more than a few miles inland. Shortly before the advent of steam power (around 1910), men began to complain that the coast was nearly logged out.

The firm of King and Casey operated camps throughout the mid-coast region starting in the 1880s. They managed the expense of caring for sixty oxen by overwintering them on their Comox farm, where they also produced all the hay needed. Each spring, teams of up to fourteen of the massive animals would be rafted on barges to King and Casey's various Discovery Passage camps and dumped overboard to swim to shore, ready to start another season of threats and curses from the bull punchers.

In 1891 Duncan McCallum was running a camp of twenty-five men on Quadra Island. Their ages ranged from nineteen to fifty, with more than half being over thirty.[19] Typical of most foremen, McCallum was an eastern woodsman, as were the majority of his crew. He also employed men from Finland, Sweden, England, Scotland and Austria, and two Chinese cooks. In the blatantly racist climate of the times, the foreman had to manage this cross-cultural mix with care. Chinese workers, in particular, were compelled to live in separate quarters.

Swedes figure larger than life in the history of coastal logging but census records show there were at least as many Asian people as Scandinavians in mid-coast camps in 1901. In one camp there were forty-four Japanese loggers, two of whom were joined by their wives. First Nations people from Cape Mudge and Campbell River also worked in various capacities in the industry, gaining valuable experience, which they later applied to their own logging operations.

Log and slab shanties were thrown up, just good enough to last the one to five years it took to

The first big logging camps around Discovery Passage opened up in the 1880s. Teams of oxen were used to pull the logs to shore, as at Hastings' Camp O on Thurlow Island. *BCARS A-00534*

log a site. The bunkhouses contained two-tiered bunks made from rough slats slung between sapling poles. Men brought their own bedrolls and filched hay from the ox stables for mattresses, which were perfect hideouts for night-crawling bedbugs. An oil-drum stove shed some heat, but only in the centre of the bunkhouse. When it rained hard, and the oxen couldn't work on the slippery skid roads, the men hunkered into their shanties for a day without pay. The camp musician would strike up a tune while Black Jack Bryant dealt the cards and the remainder debated the merits of camp food and their personal prowess, crammed together in the pungent atmosphere of draped and drying underwear, worn boots and oil-stiffened jeans.

They were a rough lot while in camp, distant from the civilizing influence of mixed society and family life, missing all the basic comforts, and sex. Intermittent tangles with women-for-hire, such as "Sore-Neck Annie," brought only momentary satisfaction; then it was back to the brawny swagger of the all-male camps.

A season in camp meant long days of incredibly hard and dangerous work. Safety standards were not a consideration and the accident rate was extremely high. The simple, daisy-filled cemeteries on Cortes Island and Quadra Island contain the unmarked graves of loggers who shipped upcoast from no known address to meet untimely deaths. There were also no protective measures to ensure the continuing viability of forest and fish habitats. A grab-and-dash mentality prevailed in the rush to exploit the rich stands of timber.

These harsh circumstances, the relentless need for stamina and strength, and the giant proportions of the trees they tackled turned these men into a hard-drinking, tough-talking bunch of inadvertent poets. The loggers' lexicon included beautifully evocative descriptors like "misery whip" for the crosscut saw. The two men using it, balanced on springboards notched into the wood above the flaring butts of the firs, dubbed their task "dancing on the Swedish fiddle." Nicknames derived from personal or physical quirks have been passed down through the generations as a fondly remembered loggers' lineage: Bullshit Bill, Skookum Tom, Johnny-on-the-Stump, Johnny-Behind-the-Rail, Step-and-a-Half Phelps, Paperbag Brown and Peg Leg Thompson.

Timber cruisers who bushwhacked the length and breadth of Vancouver Island, searching for the best stands, were the elite of the logger breed. Long-ago cruisers like the King brothers, Hiram McCormack, Moses Ireland, "Big Billy" Dineen and Eustace Smith still command respect for their remarkable abilities as woodsmen.

In the King and Casey partnership, Mike and Jim King were the cruisers while Lewis Casey was the pragmatic camp boss. Together (and individually) they bought, pre-empted and leased thousands of acres along the Campbell, Quinsam and Salmon Rivers for both coal and timber speculation. Their young admirer, Eustace Smith, described the Kings as tall, handsome men who were raised on a Michigan farm in the 1840s. "Jim was quiet and retiring but a great man in the woods," while his brother Mike was a "jovial soul who was more inclined to make friends." Mike King and Lewis Casey married into pioneer families, Mike to Mary Cowie of Fanny Bay and

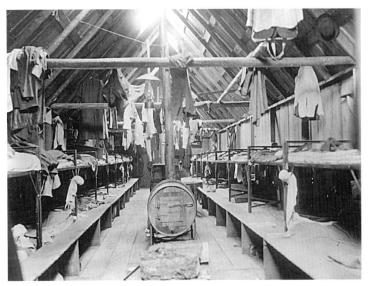

Camp 2, Booker Lagoon, June 18, 1917. The unidentified photographer described this bunkhouse as "typical of the better class of BC logging camps." *Lyford Album, John Dolmage Collection, MCR 10746*

Fallers stood on springboards notched into the tree above the uneven ground to fell massive trees by hand with crosscut saws. They dubbed the job "dancing on the Swedish fiddle," in deference to the legendary strength of Swedish fallers. *MCR 7723*

Mike and Mary (Cowie) King, 1888. Mike King and his partners Jim King and Lewis Casey, of King and Casey, were among the first logging operators in the Discovery Passage region. Mike was fifty years ahead of his time in his vision for the future of Campbell River. He made plans to develop hydroelectric power from Elk Falls to supply an industrial townsite based in Duncan Bay in the 1890s, but his dramatic death and the start of World War I ended his grandiose scheme. *BCARS G-3881*

Lewis to Jennie Creech of Comox. Both men eventually attained enough success to move their families to the urban comforts of Victoria.

Mike King was the most widely known member of the King and Casey partnership. He had a vision of a major town in this region many years before it was to become a reality. Had his scheme come to pass, Campbell River may have simply remained a sport fishers' haven. The town King proposed, Duluth, would have taken advantage of the excellent moorage at Duncan Bay and the long-promised railway terminus, linking Vancouver Island to the mainland via the Discovery Islands and Bute Inlet. By 1893 Duluth, its streets named for his family and associates, was to be a major industrial centre, complete with hydroelectricity generated from Elk Falls. The scheme was promoted far and wide, to the chagrin of Comox Valley folks: "If King and Casey have the faith they profess in Duluth, why don't they offer their lots in this section where the place and its surroundings are known, instead of offering them to the greenhorns who flutter around the Provincial capital..."[20] A few years later an anonymous writer for *The Weekly News* took a tongue-in-cheek poke at Duluth following a camping trip to Duncan Bay in 1895: "Lying quietly on one of the gnarled roots of the weird old trees, in the slumberous afternoon I sleep and dream that I am awakened by the shrill whistle of an incoming train, I look up and lo! the forest is no more; stately mansions crown the once thickly wooded heights, broad streets cross and recross, the electric light, soft yet piercing, throws a faint blue moonlight tinge on sleeping city and silvery sea—and this is Duluth! Am I dreaming or awake?"[21]

Provincial politicians and industrialists toyed with various plans for developing a railway crossing from Duncan Bay to Bute Inlet, using the twin peaks of Ripple Rock as pilings for a bridge. From Quadra Island the trains were to cross the islands by a series of bridges and barges. An intriguing concept offered in 1894 involved the use of "aerial" trains that only worked above water as they were "affected by some magnetic influence" while passing over land. "There can scarcely be any doubt now," said *The Weekly News*, "about the success of the entire scheme." No matter the plans, wild or pragmatic, the railway terminus was continually stalled, a subject of endless scheming and political debate. But Mike King and his partners were willing to wait, holding onto their extensive property at Duncan Bay and carrying their plans forward into the next century.

A new business, on a more manageable scale, presented itself in the 1890s when Sir Richard Musgrave described his 70-pound (32-kg) catch, the "biggest salmon ever killed with rod and line," in the prestigious British sporting magazine *Field and Stream*. Fishermen have never been known for modesty when describing their catch. Musgrave, a British naval officer who married into Vancouver Island's wealthy Dunsmuir family, published several such accounts in British sporting magazines—and the rush was on.

Expert fishermen from Cape Mudge and Campbell River Reserves were paid $3 per day to guide men like Musgrave as they reeled in hundreds of pounds of fish over many weeks of fishing. While Musgrave stayed aboard the family yacht, others suffered the privations of smoke and sand in their rustic camps on Campbell River Spit.

The Thulins, living across the strait at Lund, noted all the action in Campbell River with interest. Here was an opportunity to expand their multifaceted operations as loggers, storekeepers and hoteliers. Campbell River's growing population of thirsty loggers and dapper anglers were awaiting the enterprising Thulins.

Elk Falls, photographed by Henry Twidle c. 1920, was the subject of heated debate and conflicting interests starting in the 1890s. By 1922 conservationists writing in the *Comox Argus* newspaper (serving the Valley and Campbell River) vehemently opposed harnessing the falls. "Dozens of pulp mills can and have been built; but once the beauty of Campbell River Falls is profaned, it is gone—gone for ever." *Dalton Collection, MCR 5135*

Fishers from Britain and the US came to Campbell River for up to six weeks of fishing at a time. They hired the expert services of First Nations fishermen, who paddled the sporting gents against tides and weather for as many as twelve hours per day. *Carl Thulin Collection, MCR 10215*

Sport fishers like Mr. F.J. Barrow of Sussex, England, lived in tent camps at Campbell River Spit, at the mouth of the Campbell River. Barrow captioned his photograph: "The salmon on the right weighed 54 pounds, that on the left some 5 pounds less." *MCR 11490*

CHAPTER 5

Thulinville—The Birth of Campbell River

1900–1914

An Unlucky Logger

I'm a poor unlucky logger, the truth to you I'll state,
I'm skidding for a "Donkey," it seems to be my fate.
High on the Devil's Fraction where he tried to swindle Christ,
But the Redeemer scorned his offer and wasn't thinking twice.
But I might have been a partner with the Hastings in the mill,
Or at least a boss for Gilley, or doing better still.
But I always was fond of women, let them be wives or maid,
They might be fair and pretty, or black as the ace of spades.
And they broke my heart entirely, not a cent forinst my name,
I can work for Dick or Mackie, it is always just the same.
But I was thinking I'll turn rancher, forget my early days,
Take a Homestead out at Stella Lake and try and mend my ways.

Very truly yours,
James Forest Hinchy
Rock Bay, 1906[1]

W hen James Hinchy penned those lines the logging industry was flourishing "upcoast." By 1901 the population of the region stretching from Oyster Bay to Rock Bay warranted the creation of a new census district called Sayward. Of the 361 non-Native people listed, 30 lived on farms and ranches at Kelsey Bay and 13 more at Willow

The Sacht family farm of the 1890s, one of the first non-Native settlements at Kelsey Bay (Sayward), included a farm and store. *BCARS D-02365*

Point and Stories Beach. With Fred Nunns away in the US for an extended period, no other permanent white residents lived at Campbell River in 1901. The remaining 318 were loggers, except for two women—Clara Swanson, the boom man's wife in a Hastings camp, and Albiretta DesBrisay and her son Norman at Camp D.

In 1901 the Hastings Outfit was building a railway logging camp at Stella Lake,[2] which was to become the district's nucleus for years to come. By 1905 Rock Bay ("the Rock") had a hospital, hotel, saloon, boarding house, brothel, store and post office. In the peak years the camp served as a base for 1,500 loggers.

Loggers like Hinchy listed their annual earnings at between $400 and $600. Had he risen to foreman his income would have been between $900 and $1,110 per year. A head cook could earn equal or better the wages of fallers in some camps—but not Charlie Hodack, an Austrian Bohemian cook at Sayward Mill's camp on the Campbell River. Hodack gave his earnings for 1901 as $400. His downfall may have been his love of whiskey; certainly that's what brought him to grief one fine evening at Quadra Island's Heriot Bay wharf.

Bill Hall liked to tell about the night his uncle Charlie Hall's mischievous imagination sprang to life as he watched Hosea Bull, a Heriot Bay hotel keeper, make arrangements for the night watch over a dead logger. Charlie Hodack and a friend were to "keep the rats and mice away from the box" as the body lay in state in the wharf house, awaiting the arrival of the Vancouver-bound *Cassiar*, whose schedule was sometimes unreliable. For a bottle of whiskey each, the men agreed to sit through the night in shifts, spending their off-hours in sociable comfort at the bar. According to Bill Hall, Hodack wasn't in very good shape for such a job: "He'd been drinking for two or three days and was pretty jumpy. While they were changing shifts [my uncle] got a bed sheet and wrapped it around himself and got behind the box. Hodack came on duty and was sitting on a milk case with an old smoky lantern on the floor. He would jump every time he heard a mouse or rat in the shed and would take another drink out of the bottle."

With poor old Hodack well primed, Charlie Hall assumed the voice of the dead logger, moaning forth from behind the coffin, "Ohhh it's cold in here." When Hodack leaped up in fear and amazement, the spectre emerged from the side of the coffin.

"I guess it sure looked like a ghost coming out of the box. Hodack let out a yell and started up the wharf with his long white hair trailing behind him, and [Charlie Hall] behind him . . . Hodack was heading past the hotel and up the road yelling, 'I'll be good! I'll be good!'" Finally some of the fellows caught up with the much shaken Hodack and dragged him back to the bar, where they all had another drink.

Vancouverites seemed inured to the frequent arrivals of corpses from the logging camps until a particularly gruesome delivery of four dead loggers in 1903 caught the attention of a young clergyman. John Antle persuaded the Anglican Church to finance a boat trip upcoast to assess the situation. By the time he reached Quathiaski Cove in the summer of 1904 Antle was forming a plan to create a floating ministry and hospital. What he saw at Rock Bay should have made him think twice. This was not fertile ground for saving souls, but Antle was a man of strong and fixed notions, and these men certainly needed help: "It was Sunday, and a fine day," Antle wrote in his memoirs, "which might suggest church bells and people in holiday attire. But no, the only sound was a sort of subdued roar coming from the saloon, and occasional groans from perhaps fifty or a hundred loggers lying around on the grass, in all stages of intoxication."[3]

The boys weren't in a fit state to heed a preacher—until he mentioned the thin edge of his divine wedge, a medical service, at which point an approving mob flocked around him, filling his hands and pockets with cigars; he chastely refused

Charlie Hodack, an Austrian Bohemian (right), was one of many bachelors who lived by an assortment of means, from logging to guiding sport fishers. His weakness for drink involved him in pranks and capers that have been preserved in many lively tales. *Les and Ivy McDonald Collection, MCR 20148*

the whiskey. The camp bosses were far less enthusiastic when Antle approached them for a contribution, but the coast had just gained another determined visionary. Before a year was out Antle had overcome all obstacles and, together with Dr. Hutton, was cruising from Vananda to Alert Bay in a specially designed mission and hospital ship, the *Columbia*.

By 1905 Antle's umbrella organization, the Columbia Coast Mission, had built a cottage hospital at Rock Bay and started a newsletter, *The Log*, creating a communication link for the camps scattered between Alert Bay and Vananda. In 1906, during one month alone, ninety-one patients

Starting in about 1900, Rock Bay became the logging centre for the Hastings Outfit (BC Mills Timber and Trading Company), with extensive operations throughout the district. By 1905 there was a hotel, store, brothel (sanctioned by the company as a method of keeping men in camp) and the Columbia Coast Mission's hospital at "The Rock." *Marion Adams Collection, MCR 9077*

The hospital at Rock Bay, first opened in 1905 and run by the Columbia Coast Mission, was continually expanded as the demand for hospital service grew throughout the Campbell River and Discovery Islands district. *Mrs. Jacques Collection, MCR 8060*

were treated at the mission hospital, including a young forester who was to become a famous figure in BC industry, H.R. MacMillan.

Prior to 1905 patients were paddled into the strait in search of a passing steamship, or referred to the lay missionary at Cape Mudge, Robert J. Walker. A year of medical training put Walker in the unenviable position of resident emergency doctor and dentist. For the latter task he always kept a hefty pair of pliers at the ready.

In addition to his other accomplishments, Antle took rueful pride in introducing marine gas engines to the region on his reconnaissance trip in 1904. The Cape Mudge lightkeeper, John Davidson, described seeing Antle's sleek little craft moving along at a good rate though the boat's sail lay slack. "I was fair surprised till someone tell't me aboot the contraption called the gasoline engine, and then I kenn'd a' aboot ye."

Gas motors may have suited Antle's cause but "By-God" Stafford did not share his enthusiasm. On a visit to George Verdier's, Bill Law gained a new tale for his repertoire as Stafford's heated one-sided debate with his rebellious three-horse "kicker" drifted across the water to Verdier's shack. In Bill's words:

> He was cursing this thing, you know [and] kicking it too. "I'll give you one more chance, by-God. If you don't go I'll dump you overboard, by-God, yes I will. It doesn't get so rough around here I need you for ballast, by-God, and I ain't gonna step over you every time I want to push on these oars. If I'm gonna row this damn thing I'm gonna row it by myself."
>
> You could hear him out there from the beach, "I'm not gonna be stepping over you." So he worked at it for a little while [longer], "You refuse, aye...well over you go by-God!" And he disconnected that thing and dumped it right there in Seymour Narrows and then he rowed into the bay where George and I were. "I just now dumped that engine, by-God. It wouldn't work! If it don't work it ain't gonna ride when I gotta row, by-God, no."

Finicky as the first engines were, changing technology would soon transform both the fishing and logging industries. The Pidcocks opened a cannery in Quathiaski Cove in 1904 but sold out within two years. The work was slavish. According to a contemporary, the Pidcock boys fished from 3:00 a.m. to 9:00 p.m., using handlines and a dugout canoe, in an attempt to keep up a supply of fish for the cannery. The next owner didn't last long either, also turning the labour-intensive business over within two years. But when W.E. Anderson bought the cannery in 1908 there were new labour-saving devices on the market, like a machine they called the Iron Chink, which decreased the Chinese butchering crew by over 80 percent.

W.E. Anderson had the resources to invest in mechanization. He was among the lucky few who'd made a fortune in the Yukon gold rush. Anderson is said to have bought a mine for $20 that he later sold for $500,000 to a man who in turn became a millionaire.[4] Anderson was a man blessed with the Midas touch. He profited in an assortment of fledgling BC industries, including aviation, Hayes-Anderson logging trucks and the Quathiaski Canning Company. The cannery quickly became his principal concern, garnering the Anderson family a handsome return. W.E., Margaret and their three daughters maintained a large and lively home in the thick of the cannery

The Quathiaski Canning Company was opened in 1904 by the Pidcock Brothers, then sold in 1906 to Atkins and again in 1908 to W.E. Anderson, who developed the cannery into a highly successful operation. In this photograph, taken c. 1921, the cannery building is on pilings at right and the Anderson family home is the large building at centre, just to the left of the company store. *Margaret Yorke Collection, MCR 19521*

W.E. Anderson, who bought the Quathiaski Canning Company in 1908, had exclusive rights to operate seine boats from Oyster Bay to the Adams River. His fleet of vessels were numbered under the name *Quathiaski*, as seen in this photograph by Henry Twidle, c. 1912. *MCR 6011*

Jack Harper, store manager, and the Anderson family outside the Quathiaski Canning Company, c. 1912. The store window is decorated with Christmas goods. Left to right: Jack Harper, Elva Anderson, Margaret Anderson, W.E. Anderson and Mae Anderson (McAllister). *Herbert Joyce Collection, MCR 7274*

complex during the packing season, returning each winter to their stately house in Vancouver's Shaughnessy district.

Lekwiltok men and women were the leading fishers for the Quathiaski Cove Cannery on Quadra Island. Their fishing methods took advantage of expertise developed over thousands of years. Using heavy cotton fishing line, a gaff hook and herring rakes to catch bait, they fished from canoes off the favoured trolling grounds in front of Cape Mudge lighthouse. A visitor saw one Native handliner bring in over 100 fish in one day alone. The cannery offered just two prices, 50 cents for a tyee (from 30 to 70 pounds/13 to 32 kg) and 10 cents for any fish under 30 pounds.[5]

Success only added to the Andersons' natural warmth and generosity. They are generally remembered as exemplary employers and community members. When Robert Willson, a cannery night watchman and carpenter, discovered his youngest daughter had club feet the Andersons paid for a year's treatment in a Vancouver hospital. The Wewaikai fisherman and community leader Harry Assu, after more than eighty years in the fishing industry, still maintained that Anderson was the best man he ever worked for. Anderson also demonstrated uncommon foresight when he had his seine boat crew take time at the end of each fishing season to clean logging debris from the streams within his licence area.

Advances in mechanization also brought tremendous change to the forest industry. Joe Thomson's memories of the introduction of the first smoke belching donkey engine to the district, in about 1905, were recorded by his son-in-law, Wallace Baikie: "They brought the donkey in on

Steam donkeys, as seen here in 1917, extended the distance from which logs could be hauled out of the bush. *Lyford Album, John Dolmage Collection, MCR 18855*

a raft and the engineer had her all steamed up. The whole crew came down with the horse teams to pull it off the raft. Apparently they did not know how to set the rigging for the donkey to pull itself off. Anyway when they were hooking onto the donkey with the horses the pop valve blew off and horses, men and all took to the woods, thinking the rigging was going to blow up."[6]

First Nations people were employed in coastal logging camps from the outset, and shortly before World War I they were opening their own camps. In 1911 the Wewaikai people at Cape Mudge bought a steam donkey to log their reserves, as did the Weiwaikum people of Campbell River a few years later.

As the 1901 census demonstrates, women and children were not encouraged to take up camp life. Lilly Joy Ward, the wife of a Sutil Channel operator and a relation of Moses and Julia Ireland, was among the first women to flaunt opposing biases and move into camp. She kept loneliness at bay by writing a column for *The Log* and helped in the camp kitchen when the outfit was between cooks. Some intriguing correspondence appeared in 1907 issues of *The Log* when Lilly Joy complained of the stove's heat while "doing all kinds of stunts with a hash bowl and chopping knife in our cook house for three weeks…" Rev. Antle praised Lilly's softening influence and pleaded for more women in the camps, but the logger/poet James Hinchy took offence at the tone of Lilly Joy's cookshack complaints, which he felt smacked of the prevailing attitude that loggers were simply beasts of burden: "I was sorry to see that Sister Ward had to work so hard cooking for the loggers...Just roll in a bale of hay, sister, and shake whiskey on it and you won't need to make a fire."

Women who were born and bred on the coast, like Mary (Pidcock) Smith, were spared the huge adjustment required of those arriving from urban centres. Mary's accomplishments were described in *The Log* in 1906: "Mrs. Smith is, in fact, a typical woman of the West, able to turn her hand to anything; can handle a boat and tackle the most lively of Campbell River salmon. She is a first-class shot and the finest buck of the last season fell before her unerring aim. Her skill as a house-keeper everybody in these parts knows and will be ready to congratulate Mr. [Cecil 'Cougar'] Smith on his good fortune in having a life partner so well-fitted to be a 'help meet for him.'"[7]

Conversely, a 1907 *Log* correspondent worried over a new arrival, Eliza Vanstone, making a transition from her English home to a logging camp perched on the edge of the fast-flowing waters of Okisollo Channel: "Mr. Vanstone...visited his home in the Old Country last winter. As a result...he has taken a wife of the fair daughters of England. The change from English cultivated fields [and] hedged lanes to the pathless forests of the 'wild and wooly West' is, doubtless, great, but the comfortable little cottage being erected near the camp...will go far to reconciling her to the change, and in a few months, no doubt, Mrs. Vanstone will have outlived the strangeness of Western life, and will, as others have done, enjoy the wild free life of the British Columbia woods."

Railway logging wasn't quite as hard a sell as the concept of women and children in camp. The Hastings Outfit pioneered the use of trains for hauling in the 1890s when they added an old steam engine nicknamed Curly to their Thurlow and Quadra Island operations. By 1905 railway logging was set to become the dominant hauling method:

When Eliza (Thorne) Vanstone first arrived on the coast as an English bride, her contemporaries worried about her transition to life in the "wild and woolly west." But Eliza adjusted well. She raised five sons on her husband's floating logging camps and later (as seen here in the early 1920s) at their farm in north Campbell River. *Odowichuk Collection, MCR 17875*

> True handlogging is on the decline. The day is fast going by when this strange mixture of lumberman and beachcomber may start out with axe, saw and jackscrew and make big pay while living on the fish he catches and the deer and birds he shoots. Here and there a handlogger's cabin is noticed on the beach, but today there is but one man at it where three years ago there were five.
>
> Amongst the camps, too, time is making changes. Oxen have some years since disap-peared from the woods. But few of the horse teams that succeeded them are now to be found, and the hauling of the great logs of forest giants today is done by steam and cable. Large donkey engines by their whistle, smoke and jets of steam, tell of the camps away back in the woods, where Douglas firs are reeled in one, two and three thousand feet along the skid roads. As a rule one engine, called a yarder, pulls the logs out of the woods...

> [Hauling by rail] adds much...to the cost of the operations, and so railroading takes its place on the big timber claims. The camp is oft-times a division point with locomotive sheds, shops, etc., one terminal being down by the sea, the other up amidst the tall timber. So far railroading propositions are confined to the Hastings and Chemainus operations, but as the good timber is fast receding from the beach, the day is not far distant when the saw log hauling of the coast will be entirely a railroading operation. Rock Bay, Grant Bay, and Sliammon have long resounded to the whistle of the locomotive and the roaring of the log cars.[8]

The writer of this piece concluded with a report of new business activity in the district, "At Campbell River, where last year the Thulin Bros. opened up their new hotel, the Willows, this enterprising Lund firm have now completed a store with Mr. H. Higstrom [sic] in charge."

The Thulin Brothers of Lund were indeed enterprising fellows, who crossed the Strait of Georgia to expand their business activities in 1904, in a place Charlie Thulin once scoffed at as a useless spot in which to settle.[9]

Charles August Thulin was a driven man, possessed of courage, tenacity and an energetic desire to amass a fortune. He left Sweden in 1887 at the age of twenty-four and assumed a new name to fit the American dream. In later years he described his arrival in North America, detailing his wages (which never quite met his expectations) and the high cost of living as he worked his way across the continent from Iowa to Minnesota to Winnipeg and finally to the west coast, where he worked a stint for the Canadian Pacific Railway. "I landed in Port Moody at the beginning of January 1888 with moccasins on my feet and stepped off the car into water up to my knees."[10]

Thulin and several partners undertook a variety of contracts, including clearing lots for the burgeoning frontier town of Vancouver. They boldly plunged into new ventures, sometimes failing, but they were never daunted, which became a lifelong pattern for Charlie Thulin.

Handlogging on the Sunshine Coast proved the most lucrative of Thulin's early endeavours, leading him to a pre-emption on Malaspina Peninsula (on the mainland, south of Cortes Island) in 1889.

Charlie's younger brother Fred joined him in 1889, and the pair set up housekeeping (with the assistance of a cat who licked their dishes clean) in a log shack that had gunny sack window panes and a door made from split cedar, hinged with shoe soles. In a few years they transformed the place into a thriving little village, which they named Lund. Their businesses included two stores, two homesteads, two hotels, a mine, a towboat and a continually expanding logging operation.

Maria (Mary) Johanson immigrated to Winnipeg from Sweden in 1889 and two years later moved to Vancouver, where she met and married Charles Thulin in 1892. With her twinkling blue eyes and easy humour Mary was the counterpoint to Charles, who had a more earnest nature. All four of the couple's children—Anna, Elin, Carl and Lillie—were born while the family were living at Lund.

Campbell River's growing population of sport fishers and loggers presented a business opportunity perfectly suited to the multiple talents of the extended Thulin family. Charlie and Fred, along with a partner, Emerson Hannan, were at first looking for land at Willow Point when they learned of a more suitable property. There are differing versions of how the Thulins decided upon what is now downtown Campbell River as the site for a hotel and store. According to Wallace Baikie, his

Mary and Charles Thulin with their family, c. 1900. Left to right, front: Anna and Elin; back: Carl, Mary (holding Lillie) and Charles Thulin. *Florence Thulin Collection, MCR 15432*

father-in-law Joe Thomson was set to buy the property with Cecil Smith: "Campbell River wasn't anything at that time except a fellow by the name of John Pacey [sic] had 160 acres, where Campbell River now stands. Joe and Cecil Smith had their eye on this place and Pacey agreed to sell it to them for $800. Not having $800 they went up to one of the camps to earn it. When they came back to Campbell River with the money they couldn't find Pacey and went on to Comox and the Elk Hotel. To make a long story short they blew the $800, a typical logger trick."

Shortly after blowing their wad, Smith and Thomson met up with Charlie Thulin and Emerson Hannan: "They were on their way to Campbell River with their little tug to look at a place where Willow Point now stands, with the idea of building a hotel. Joe told them about the Pacey place which they bought... That was the birth of the town of Campbell River."[11]

On an early spring day in 1904 Robert Walker, of the Cape Mudge mission, watched with some surprise as a tug pulling a scow loaded with a horse and wagon and lumber rounded Cape Mudge, crossed Discovery Passage and nosed into the beach at Campbell River. Rowing across the next day he found the Thulins and Hannan ready to start building a hotel on the Peaceys' hayfield, the current site of the Tidemark Theatre.

The Willows, named for the first chosen site, was a thirteen-room, two-storey hotel, which the Thulins and Hannan had ready for business within three months. The small community of non-native settlers in the Discovery Passage region had been enjoying July 1st gatherings at Campbell River Spit since about 1898 so the Thulins and Hannan took advantage of the occasion for opening

The Thulin family started the village of Campbell River in 1904 when they opened the Willows Hotel (at left) and the "Logger's Annex," on the current site of the Tidemark Theatre and the public library, to serve an incongruous mix of loggers and sport fishers. John Beech, a teamster, is seen driving his wagon on the sandy track at the edge of Willow Bay, along what is now Shoppers Row in downtown Campbell River. *Helen Mitchell Collection, MCR 8248*

their new hotel. They rounded up the neighbourhood loggers in their homemade steam tug and treated the boys to such a grand time (to the chagrin of the settlers) that some of the fellows didn't make it back to work for two weeks. The July 1st celebration has, with a few lulls, continued as the key holiday for Campbell River.

At first Charlie commuted between Lund and Campbell River, leaving Emerson Hannan in charge at the new hotel and his brother Fred at the helm in Lund. Hannan was a fellow Swede and logger who'd been employed as a bartender at the Lund hotel. With the Thulin brothers still living at Lund, Hannan was a necessary addition to the partnership because the liquor licensing laws of the day required the licence holder and family to live on the premises. But by 1912 the partnership was on the rocks. Hannan moved on to Prince Rupert, and later to sunny California.

But for now everything was rosy. The hotel and bar quickly became the focal point for the logging camps in the region. Within a year they were ready to expand, wisely moving the bar into a "logger's annex" north of the Willows, putting a suitable distance between loggers and sporting gents. A logger named Frank Dalby had fond memories of the annex: "The men came from all around to drink at the saloon, coming by boat and pulling their boats up on the beach . . . The first saloon was just a bar with a few rooms. There were card games and a drink of whiskey cost 10 cents. Most of the men slept outside in blankets," though a room at the annex only cost 60 cents per night. These thirsty men were good for business and Emerson Hannan and his "brute of a collie" were equal to the task of keeping the boys in line.

The discreet fifty-yard separation between hotel and bar proved insufficient for the high-class sporting set. Sir John Rogers was fond of a nip of whiskey himself but he was less than approving of the loggers' marked enthusiasm for the stuff: "The drawback to the hotel was the logging camp in the neighbourhood," wrote Rogers in his book *Sport in Newfoundland and Vancouver*. "On Saturday night many of the loggers came dropping in to waste the earnings of the week. Drunkenness on these occasions was far too common, and till the small hours of the morning the sound of revelry from the bar was not conducive to a good night's rest."

Mary and Charlie Thulin were on hand to cater to Sir John in 1908, having moved across to Campbell River that year.[12] Mary became an active and positive force in the management of the hotel, while Charlie continued to concentrate on their logging operations. In those days hotel and boarding house management, a logical extension of homemaking, were among the few accepted jobs for women. Though she demurred any grand claims to her part in the family's achievements, Mary Thulin was no doubt the "lady who directed the establishment" in Roger's book.

Aside from his complaints about the Saturday night revellers and some trifling difficulties over getting his boots greased, Rogers was full of praise for the Willows, which was "all that a sportsman could desire." In her ninety-third year Mary remembered how busy the hotel kept them. Their staff included a housekeeper, Chinese cook and waitresses. Their guests, "besides the local ones," were from Scotland, England, New York and "ministers travelling from China." According to Rogers, Mary's handwritten menus and sophisticated choice of dishes included Baked Salmon (Spanish), along with such dainties as Pig's Head a la Printaniere.

One of the frequent customers at the bar mentioned by Sir John Rogers was "Lord B," no doubt the infamous Lord Hughie Horatio Nelson Baron Bacon, a trapper and prospector with a cabin at Buttle Lake. A sign marked the approach to his remote home:

BEWARE

Tread these forest Isles

Softly

Do not disturb the great

forest and storm God

Lord Bacon, The only Lord in America[13]

Rogers described his Lordship as "wizened in appearance and lightly built, but as hard as nails. Persistently drunk for two or three days at a time, he would suddenly sober down, put a pack on his back which few men could carry, and disappear into the woods to his lonely log cabin, only to return in a few days ready for a fresh spree. I always addressed him [as] 'My Lord,' which he took quite seriously, we became quite pals." Whether or not he was a black sheep cast out of the British aristocracy, all agree he was a well-read man who could speak on any subject and quote at length from the classics—which set him apart even in a drunken stupor. As John Perkins Sr. put it when reminiscing about Lord Bacon: "There's a vast difference between a drunken logger and an intoxicated gentleman."

H.H. Bacon, the "only Lord in America," said the secret to his ability as a woodsman was the involved way in which he wrapped the calves of his legs. He is shown here at Gowlland Harbour, 1917. *Mary (Hall) Ritter Collection, MCR 16721*

Jolly Mickey Foy was also on hand, making an impression on Rogers and the other gents at the hotel. According to Sir John Rogers, Foy "had been on the Variety Stage in London and his step-dancing when fairly primed with whisky was something to see and remember."

The International Timber (IT) Company's decision to log in the Campbell River area may have been a factor in the Thulins' decision to locate there. IT began work in about 1906, becoming the first major outfit at the river, with a mainline track running along what is now the ERT Road, to a log dump on the Campbell River. Their inland camp, cresting the hill somewhere between the current Phoenix School and Homewood Road, was described as a model of modernity by *The Log* in 1908: "Everything in the camp is of the best, from the Shay locomotive to the Ericson hot-air pump for the water supply. The dining room is certainly the best we have seen on the Coast. The houses are the Hastings Mills portable variety, nicely painted, and give the camp the appearance of a beautifully situated village. At present there are about fifty men but later there will be as many as 150."

The first decade of the twentieth century was an exciting boom period. The province was filled with youthful exuberance spawned by tremendous growth in all sectors, including logging where there was a frenzy of timber staking. Corpulence, suits and cigars seemed assured for a lifetime—and the Thulins were in on the roll. The opening of the Willows was quickly followed by a small store near the current site of McDonald's Restaurant at Robert's Reach. This was accomplished through yet another partnership, between the Thulins and Elmer Hagstrom, a Swede in their employ at Lund. By 1906 the partners were at work on a bigger and better store, and pressing the government to build a wharf for the little settlement.

Work began on the wharf in the fall of 1906 but the job was bungled,

International Timber Company's model camp at Campbell River, photographed by H.W. Roozeboom, June 5, 1926. *VPL 1459*

Elk River Timber (formerly International Timber) log dump on the Campbell River. *Phyllis Hale Collection, MCR 7098*

The Thulins built their first store near the current site of McDonald's Restaurant at Robert's Reach in 1904–05, and later renovated it to become their family home. The building looked out over the cultivated expanse of their seaside farm. MCR 8339

as John Antle reported in *The Log*: "I was told . . . that two tugs and a crowd of men waited ten days for the foreman to arrive on the scene. The little wait . . . cost $100 per day." Most of the allocated funds were squandered and the wharf was only partially built, but the Thulins and Hagstrom needed it finished: their new store, strategically placed at the head of the wharf, was nearing completion. The partners threw money and time into the project (for which they were later reimbursed), hiring a crew of Lekwiltok men to muscle a winch-driven pile driver. Both the wharf and Campbell River Trading Company Store (where the Georgia Quay building now stands) were open for business by 1907 and Campbell River became a regular port of call—though ships would only stop during fair weather at this new wharf, which was fully exposed to the stormy southeast winds.

Campbell River wharf, 1915, at what is now the Georgia Quay building. It was a community event when the Union steamship made its regular weekly stop to deliver freight, mail and passengers. *Elsie (Joyce) Wargo Collection, MCR 6818*

By 1908 Charlie Thulin had reached middle age and his vigorous drive to achieve still wasn't flagging. He is remembered as being too open-handed to make a complete success of his businesses but what he lacked in fiscal control was compensated for by his sweeping entrepreneurial courage. With a hotel, bar, store, wharf and family home—a small village—all established within four years, he and his brother were ready for their next project, a larger hotel. This one would be positioned close to the new wharf, near the current site of Pioneer Hardware.

Fred Thulin recalled in later years that over 500 people attended the opening of the second Willows on July 1, 1909, continuing the Canada Day tradition. But luck was against the new Willows. Fred Nunns noted tersely in his diary on February 10, 1909: "Midnight the new hotel at beach was burnt down and Thompson, bookkeeper at store, was burnt to death. Cause of fire unknown. Drizzly rain and sleet all day."

The loss gave the partners an opportunity to rebuild on an even grander scale. For the third Willows Hotel a Vancouver construction manager was hired, along with a double crew of fifty men, and they speedily completed the beautiful new hotel for yet another July 1 opening. As with the previous structures, the wood was milled from Thulin's own logs. The eighty-room hotel included separate sleeping and dining quarters for the timber beasts and the anglers. The first

Willows, with its fine lawn, white picket fence and Bing cherry tree in back became an "Annex" to the new hotel, mainly in use for employees and loggers, as was the adjacent saloon.

The sophistication and elegance of the new Willows took more than one urban visitor by surprise: "It was astonishing to find so completely equipped a hostelry so far away from any place of size; brass and iron beds, hot and cold running water in many of the rooms, some rooms with bath and en suite, wide verandas overlooking the water." The "decidedly up-to-date" bar had a tiled floor, handsome mirrors and ornamental iron ceiling while the bar itself was made from a single slab of fir, 60 feet long, 3 feet wide and 14 inches thick (18m x 1m x 10cm). "The Captain had told us there was a good hotel, but we had no reason to believe it would be as good as this."[14]

A Victoria visitor, H. Johnson, marvelled over the sophistication and elegance of the third Willows Hotel, opened July 1, 1910. He added in his journal: "Loggers are restricted to one end of the hotel, and the corridors leading to their rooms are separated from the rest of the hotel by partitions and closed doors, so that the loggers, if inclined to be boisterous, will not interfere with patrons of the hotel of quieter instincts." *MCR 7452*

Mary and Charlie Thulin in their personal lounge, the Green Room, in the third Willows Hotel. *Carl Thulin Collection, MCR 8343*

The dining room of the third Willows Hotel. Nearly fifty years later, during renovations, a verse was uncovered on one of the old dining tables. Carl Thulin recalled that the dining room was fitted out by a "number of old men who did odd jobs around the hotel in return for free board."

> These tables were finished on the first of July.
> By Jack Waters and Graney and that's no lie;
> And old Andy Johnson was our boss,
> He's a good old sort and that is no lie.
> They should have been stained the color of wine
> But the painters were tired working overtime.
> But Oscar the Drunkard at night he came back
> And said "I'll finish the job for you, Jack."

Marion Adams Collection, MCR 5109

The Thulins and their partners retained all the land in what is now downtown Campbell River in a steely grip, but up the river, in Campbellton, land was changing hands. Jack "Klondike" Smith rented Fred Nunns' big log house in 1906, while he assembled materials to build a home on the adjoining 80 acres (32 ha) he purchased from Nunns. Smith is an oft-mentioned player in the community's history, but facts about him and his character are scant. He is said to have got his start when he made a small fortune in the Klondike, although this story is unsubstantiated. While the Smiths were staying in Nunns' home it was destroyed by fire, as were all the Smiths' building materials. Undaunted, Smith amassed more materials and erected his house on the banks of the Campbell, near the current bridges.

Fred Nunns returned to Campbell River a few years after his house was destroyed, ending a four-teen-year period of living in the United States that remains something of a mystery. According to newspapers of the day he went to California for a number of years upon the premature death of his

The main entrance lobby to the third Willows Hotel, built in 1909. This version of the hotel had a separate entrance, dining room, lounge and rooms for the "timber beasts." *MCR 7462*

brother Jack in 1894. Ten years later he was reported to be "dangerously ill" in a Seattle hospital. When Nunns returned to Campbell River in 1909 and took up his diary once again, he was a somewhat broken man with mixed feelings about the changes wrought during his lengthy absence. He wrote, in a letter to his brother in Ireland:

> I am feeling pretty good but never have been the same since my illness some years ago. Of course I am getting on in years, 55 next month. The life suits me fine. I am my own boss, have all the shooting and fishing I want. I make my own butter, bake my own bread, wash my clothes, kill and cure my bacon. The only thing wanting is congenial society. There is an hotel on the beach which I detest as there is such a lot of drunkards there...I have some nice friends on Valdez [Quadra] Island about three miles from here but the waters are rough to cross this time of year. Things look very promising for the future here. The Canadian Pacific railroad is coming this way and will run through our land. The Canada Northern railroad is also coming within ten miles of us. Coal (a 9 and 10 foot scar) has been found just outside our land and they are now boring back of us and no doubt the coal underlies our land and will be a valuable asset in near future.

Other white settlers purchased land in the vicinity of Campbell River. Karl and Morris Petersen, Danish brothers working for the International Timber Company, each bought 10 acres

Fred Nunns' (seated on porch) bachelor shack, Campbellton, east of the current Campbell River Lodge, replaced several earlier residences, including a seven-room house one of his contemporaries described as a "log chateau." *MCR 5997*

(4 ha) from Nunns in 1910, at $150 per acre. In 1912 the McDonald brothers, Charlie and Dave (with his wife Annie and son Les) were the first settlers to take up land on the north side of the river.

The Weiwaikum people's reserve—on marshy land that included the Campbell River Spit, river frontage and a strip along the ocean to the northeast of "Thulinville"—was sandwiched between these straggling developments. The twelve or more families living on the reserve were stymied by the sweeping changes of a new economy and social order that labelled them as inferior. They quietly evolved strategies for coping with unthinking racist attitudes, integrating what they could use of non-Native culture while preserving as much as possible of their own distinct society.

Little changed in the ranch country sprawling between Willow Point and Oyster Bay in the first decade of 1900. Annie Woodhus, her son, Walter and her daughter Bertie were the principal newcomers. Annie, having separated from her husband, bought her property for a combined ranch and roadhouse on the proceeds of her earnings from her Cumberland boarding house.

Christine and Morris Petersen of Campbellton, c. 1900. Morris was one of three brothers from Denmark who took jobs with the International Timber Company and decided to settle in the district. They bought land from Fred Nunns around what is now Petersen Road in 1910. *Mr. & Mrs. W. Cox Collection, MCR 16771*

The McDonalds, seen here in 1912, were the first non-Native family to build a home on the north side of the river. Left to right: Charlie McDonald, Les McDonald (child), Dave McDonald, Annie McDonald. *Les and Ivy McDonald Collection, MCR 20141*

Charlie McDonald and the Perkins children, with the McDonald and Perkins farms of north Campbell River in the background, 1920s. *Les and Ivy McDonald Collection, MCR 20136*

Unidentified Native women, photographed at Campbell River by Henry Twidle. MCR 10268

Woodhus, as the place was simply called, became a popular stopover, halfway between Courtenay and Campbell River.

The road to Courtenay was really no more than a trail, winding through huge trees and sometimes dipping down onto stretches of sandy beach. Mary Thulin remembered attempting to navigate it with a horse and buggy, and having to turn back almost immediately.

Things were developing more quickly on Quadra Island, which had the largest population in the district until the 1920s. There were post offices and government docks at Quathiaski Cove, Bold Point, Granite Bay and Heriot Bay—the latter having the biggest community.

The focal point of Heriot Bay was its hotel, begun by Hosea Bull in about 1896. Hosea's second wife Helen transformed the place from a simple loggers' haven to an oil-and-water mixture of tourists and timber beasts. The Bulls were tireless entrepreneurs who had much in common with the Thulins. They kept a store, post office and sawmill, and presided over the government dock.

The Heriot Bay Hotel, still in business a hundred years later, attracted more than its share of distinctive characters who were not to be kept in check for the sake of summer visitors. Foremost among them was a lean and wiry fighting man nicknamed Skookum Tom Leask. According to the storyteller Bill Hall, Leask was "about the strongest man that I've ever known." One of his famous fights went on for over two hours before being postponed until

Weiwaikum Reserve, Campbell River Spit, 1925, showing "Queen Mary" Kwaksistala's home and family pole. MCR 4568

Heriot Bay on Quadra Island was the largest centre in the district, serving the mines and logging camps that proliferated throughout the Discovery Islands prior to World War I. In addition to its hotel and store, Heriot Bay was one of the first places to get a government wharf, becoming a port of call for the Union Steamship Company freight and passenger service. *Lewis and Mary (Leask) Joyce Collection, MCR 6050*

daylight. Leask, bruised and swollen, lay down on the spot but his beefy opponent, a logging camp operator named David Vanstone, left for more comfortable quarters. That was the latter's undoing; he was unable to drag his punished body back again to resume the match at first light. It's still a matter of pride for the family that this was the only fight Vanstone ever lost.

Wherever there was a bar, Lord Bacon was sure to be amongst the regulars. Bill Hall's uncle Charlie Hall, the prankster, found an opportunity for fun when Lord Bacon arrived one night at the Heriot Bay Hotel packing a .45 six-shooter in readiness for a shoot-out with a man named Hannager. Charlie had the bartender double up on Bacon's drinks and before long he was out cold

Hosea Bull is said to have worked as a baker and a preacher on Lulu Island before buying land at Heriot Bay in about 1896. There he established a logging camp, sawmill, store and hotel. His hotel, now the Heriot Bay Inn, is still in operation. *Helen (Joyce) Andrews Collection, MCR 8523*

The second Heriot Bay Hotel (replacing a partial log structure), was destroyed by fire within months of its opening on December 11, 1911. A new hotel was erected on site, parts of which form the basis of the Heriot Bay Inn, still in use in the 1990s. *Robertson Collection, MCR 19903*

"Skookum" Tom Leask and his Haida wife, Maggie, raised a family on their Hyacinth Bay property. When the couple died prematurely, from separate causes, their children were turned over to a Vancouver orphanage. *Lewis and Mary (Leask) Joyce Collection, MCR 6049*

and firmly tied down in a bed upstairs. When Hannager arrived, packing a long-barrel .44, he was treated in the same manner. Before long he too was out cold and strapped in place alongside Lord Bacon. When the two men came to and discovered their predicament, their shouts at each other quickly turned on their friends as they threatened to burn down the hotel. According to Bill Hall, "They was so set on revenge that they forgot their feud and never did get around to having a shoot-out."

Quathiaski Cove was an interesting jumble of crowded buildings, from the workers' shacks scattered along the shore where the ferry now docks to the various cannery structures and docks jutting into the cove on pilings. On the rise behind the cannery was the combined courthouse, jail, and family home for the constable serving the district. Across from the "jail-

The district jail and courthouse was built in Quathiaski Cove, on the hill above the cannery, in 1912. The charming old jailhouse, with a ghost that was said to press upon sleeping guests in the cold room at the back of the house, was destroyed by fire in 1997. *Ruth Easterbrook Collection, MCR 12824*

house" was the region's first church, St. John's, built in 1917. The majority of these buildings have been destroyed by fires over the years.

Mining was the focus of a lot of attention along the coast of BC, fuelled by a virtual army of prospectors driven by an obsessive desire to strike it rich. The majority met with little or no success. One exception was the Hastings Outfit, who formed a subsidiary company in 1907 to extract gold and other metals from Lucky Jim, a promising ore body that they had discovered in their Granite Bay workings. The mine proved lucrative, though it quickly petered out. Three hundred and thirty-six tons of silver, gold and copper-bearing ore were extracted to make the first shipment delivered to a smelter at Ladysmith. By 1913 Lucky Jim was down to one employee, a caretaker scratching out a living from surface work. Tales of remaining gold and the intrigue of crumbling cabins and machinery obscured by dense bush still tantalize visitors today, just as the hope of riches lured the miners of the past.

The safety and well-being of miners, loggers, fishermen and farmers was greatly enhanced when a telegraph line was extended north from Courtenay to the Thulins' store in 1909. This was a vast improvement on an Okisollo Channel camp operator's futile attempt, reported in the *Colonist* of 1905, to speed messages to Vancouver via carrier pigeons. Just before World War I telegraph lines were cabled across Sutil Channel and Quadra Island and along the rocky shoreline into the logging camps that proliferated on northern Vancouver Island.

Lucky Jim Mine was registered in 1908 at Granite Bay, Quadra Island, by a subsidiary of the BC Mills Timber and Trading Company called the Hastings Outfit. The company shipped a number of profitable loads of gold and other ore before the mine petered out in 1913. The remains of the miners' cabins and a giant iron wheel can be seen at the old mine, hidden in the encroaching forest. *Noble Collection, MCR*

Campbell River, looking south, after the telegraph service was extended north from the village, around 1914. On the right is the old Logger's Annex (converted to a laundry); the first Willows Hotel (serving as a boarding house and annex to the third Willows) can be seen on the extreme left. The Thulins' dairy barn is at centre, in the curve of Willow Bay, which was later filled to create Tyee Plaza. *Carl Thulin Collection, MCR 10265*

Campbell River's first government wharf (at what is now Georgia Quay) was built in 1906. The Thulins' General Store and post office (at right), was at the head of the wharf, across from the telegraph office. *Elsie (Joyce) Wargo Collection, MCR 6816*

Haying on the Thulin farm, 1930s. Mary Thulin is credited with laying out their productive farm, encompassing much of what is now Cedar, Dogwood and Elm Street in downtown Campbell River. *Carl Thulin Collection, MCR 10235*

The Thulins' partner, Elmer Hagstrom, remained in charge at the "Big Store" and post office until his premature death in 1913. The brothers bought out his interest from his widow. Charlie took over the coveted position of postmaster, leaving the functional duties to his daughters. In those pre-banking days most financial transactions were made at the post office. When Einar Andersen finished a season surveying in Strathcona Park in 1915, he and his boss headed to Campbell River, where a warning blast from the Union steamship hastened the latter's departure. In a rush he wrote out Einar's paycheque on a scrap of brown wrapping paper. With this unofficial-looking cheque for $500, representing a full season's work, Andersen was a bit worried as he approached the post office wicket. But Anna Thulin promptly handed him $300, saying, "That's all we have today, but I'll get you the rest tomorrow."

Mary Thulin is credited with the skillful planning and layout of the extensive farm that supported the hotel and village. The Thulins' barn and stables stood just beyond the start of what is now 9th Avenue and was surrounded by acres of fields spreading throughout the flat area back to about Elm Street. They raised cattle, kept a dairy and grew their own hay, vegetables and fruit.

Campbell River's 1910 population was not yet large enough to sustain a school, but someone convinced the authorities the minimum eight pupils were ready to begin. A room in the Willows Annex was made ready and a teacher was requested. Harold Campbell, freshly graduated from a Victoria high school, was deposited at the dock at 1:00 a.m. on August 23, 1910, to become the first teacher. During the three brief months of his stay, before the school was closed for lack of pupils, Campbell (who later became the deputy minister of education) gathered a storehouse of lively memories. Someone let the innocent into the Willows bar, to sip soda and watch the boys in action. "It was an aspect of life that I had never experienced before," recalled Campbell in later years. He was billeted with Fred Nunns, whose morning ritual astonished him. "He got up in the morning, lit the kitchen stove and put on the porridge. Then, still in his pyjamas and slippers, he placed a straw hat on his head and walked down to the river, waded into a deep pool up to his neck, took off his hat and ducked his head underneath the water."[15] Hanging his nightclothes by the stove to dry, Nunns was ready to begin his day.

The two elder Thulin children, Anna and Elin, were at a Victoria boarding school in 1910 but the two youngest, Carl and Lillie, attended the short-lived Annex classroom. Thulin must have made a sweep of the neighbourhood logging camps to urge some of the men to bring their families to the village. By September 1911 there were sixteen children[16] ready to start school in a one-room schoolhouse erected on land donated by the Thulins at 9th Avenue and Cedar Street.

The high rate of accidents in logging camps, together with community needs, made funding a hospital important for Charlie and Mary Thulin. After the Columbia Coast Mission declined their request to build a hospital in Campbell River in 1908, the Thulins took the project on themselves, donating land on what is now St. Ann's Road (the present site of the municipal hall) and raising money from area residents and Vancouver wholesalers. In 1913, shortly before the new hospital opened, Dr. Howard Jamieson and his family moved into the Annex, where he also maintained a temporary operating theatre until opening day on June 4, 1914. The first child born in the hospital was Eve Willson (later Eade), who lived out the majority of her adult life several blocks away on Thulin Street.

Charlie Thulin was a dynamo, the driving force behind an impressive inventory of enterprises, carried out under his various partnerships. He was a rotund and good-natured man, known by all as Poppa Thulin. His serious nature and importance in the community, coupled with a thick Swedish accent and a bit of a stammer, made Charlie the object of more than a few boyish pranks—like the time his massively built pet ram inspired Ed Dalby to paint the animal's scrotum a flashy white and red. Charlie's pet was then released to continue its accustomed rounds amongst the tourists and Thulin rewarded the pranksters with his exclamation, "Now…now…now, yust look at dat; yust look at dat!"

Another incident recounted by Bill Law, a storyteller, involved George Verdier, a noted impersonator who teamed up with Ed Dalby for a bit of fun. Dalby sauntered along to the Thulins' home to discreetly inform Mary Thulin that her husband and a woman were up to no good in a hotel room. Mary promptly made her way to the indicated door, where she could plainly hear Charlie within, trying to "get this girl on the bed; she was protesting, and by-gosh Mrs. Thulin thought he was in there alright." Later on when the jig was up, Charlie stormed into the bar and grabbed George Verdier by the shoulder: "Now…now…now…now Yorge that was no yoke

Campbell River's first school, serving non-Native students, was opened in 1911 on the hill behind what is now the Municipal Hall. *Helen Mitchell Collection, MCR 8335*

The Campbell River Hospital, opened on June 6, 1914, was built through donations raised by the indefatigable Charles and Mary Thulin, and maintained through payroll deductions from loggers at $1 per month. *Carl Thulin Collection, MCR 10219*

you know, the old woman she's madder than hell! That was no yoke."[17]

Predominant in everyone's memory was Charlie Thulin's generosity. He was always ready to help anyone in need, extend credit or donate land and support for the advancement of his favourite cause—Campbell River. He and Mary had a firm vision of the place, which carried on through succeeding generations: "One day Campbell River will be *the* city of the Island."

Mike King continued to cling to his even bigger plans for the district. For nearly three decades this lumberman, timber cruiser and entrepreneur had been holding his land at Duncan Bay, persevering in his dream of a major industrial town powered by electricity generated from Elk Falls. King formed the Campbell River Power Company and just as they were ready to stake the falls (a process similar to staking a mining claim), they received word that a rival interest also planned to stake the falls. King's Victoria attorney, Claude Harrison, dashed along the snowy footpath leading to the falls, photographing his marks just as night began to fall. On his return he spotted the competition, lanterns swinging as they rushed up the slippery trail— too late. The Power Company would invest over $132,000 monitoring the potential of the falls, but King's death and the onset of the First World War would forestall the plan.

George Verdier, "the Mayor of Seymour Narrows," a talented impersonator and storyteller, outside Lewis's store in Quathiaski Cove, where he entertained the Lewis boys with his hilarious tales. *Bob Lewis Collection, MCR*

Mike King's brother Jim died a painful early death from peritonitis at Heriot Bay in 1902. Mike was also destined for a premature end, but his was to be a fittingly grand finale to a remarkable life. Mike was on the west coast of Vancouver Island and due back in Victoria for an important meeting in the spring of 1910. Stormy weather threatened a long delay for the Victoria-bound steamship so, not one to be late for a meeting, Mike decided to walk across Vancouver Island to catch a southbound steamer from Campbell River.

Few men would consider such a solution, but Mike King knew the forests, mountain passes and lake chains of northern Vancouver Island like no other. However, he was sixty-two years of age, pressed for time and ill equipped, and this trip was to prove his last. King tumbled over a 9-metre precipice, injuring an ankle and fracturing several ribs. By the time he reached Lord Bacon's cabin at Buttle Lake, King was in a sorry state: "He was hungry, lame and ill," reported Bacon. "His clothes were torn, his gun was bent and broken...I tried to get him to stay in my cabin for a few days until I could get help to take him out. This he refused..." Mike King struggled on and reached Campbell River from Buttle Lake within one day, which Lord Bacon pronounced "a remarkable feat for any man." He made his meeting, but never recovered from his injuries. He died at his home in Victoria on December 18, 1910. King's gravestone, in Ross Bay Cemetery in Victoria, bears his favourite expression, used instead of the usual foul curses of a logger—"By the Lovely Dove."

Mike King, having amassed a tremendous knowledge of northern Vancouver Island, may have had a hand in encouraging the provincial government to set aside Strathcona Park. Public record suggests the idea came from Premier Richard McBride, a charismatic man who swept into office in the boom-decade at the beginning of the twentieth century. McBride was a fervent advocate of railway development, which he and many others saw as the key to sustained growth. On paper, the idea for a railway terminus at Duncan Bay, with branch lines radiating in various directions on northern Vancouver Island, was imminent. Within this context the idea of creating a wilderness park surrounded by lodges, along the lines of Lake Louise in the Rockies, seemed an excellent investment.

Price Ellison, a government minister, headed up a survey party to assess the potential for the park in 1910. Among the large party of men was Ellison's daughter, Myra, who scaled mountain peaks and traversed icefields in her sensible ankle-length skirt. Some say Myra Lake in the park is named after her, though others say it was named for the Comox Valley pioneer Myra (Thomson) Baikie.

The Price Ellison report was unequivocal— the beauties and potential for the region were as vast as the mountain scenery—and it resulted in the government setting aside 530,319 acres (212,128 ha) of forest, mountains, lakes and rivers in 1911. Strathcona Park is the first and largest park in BC.

Jim Forbes, monitoring the flow on Elk Falls for the Campbell River Power Company, recognized a niche for himself in these grandiose plans when he decided to open a wilderness lodge. Shortly before his marriage to Elizabeth Sutherland in 1911 Forbes purchased land on

The Price Ellison party explored the mountains and lakes surrounding Buttle Lake in 1910 to assess its potential for a park. Some think Myra Falls, Creek and Mountain were named for Myra Ellison, seen here, while others recall that the legendary timber cruiser Mike King named them in 1882 for little Myra Cliffe (later Thomson) of Comox. Taking the six-year-old on his knee, King asked if he could name the beautiful watershed for the child. Following the Price Ellison survey, Strathcona Park was set aside in 1911 and became BC's first and largest park. *Hughes Collection, MCR 10138* the edge of Lower Campbell Lake, a property that was so beautiful the former owner, Cudahy Timber Company, had left it pristine. James and Elizabeth Forbes had the perfect blend of experience, she with the hotel business and he with horses and packing, to actualize their dream for a lodge at Forbes Landing.

Forbes Landing Lodge, c. 1920, was a popular wilderness retreat offering horseback expeditions into Strathcona Park. *Faak Collection, MCR 10445*

The Forbes family used Big Rock, south of Campbell River, as an advertisement and direction marker for their wilderness lodge on Lower Campbell Lake. *MCR 10232*

The couple made a modest start with a little floathouse on the lake in 1912 which they eventually expanded into rustic accommodations on shore. Elizabeth's brothers, Jasper, Bill and Walter Sutherland, served as packers and guides, taking visitors into the splendours of Strathcona Park on horseback. Forbes Landing came to be known as both an idyllic honeymoon retreat and a wilderness hunting and fishing lodge, staffed by an ever-widening circle of the extended Forbes family.

The hopes, plans and schemes for the future for this richly endowed region were boundless, as was the stamina of the people who chose to call the place home. But there were stalls and snags awaiting them. The trouble brewing in Europe, which was already causing a serious market slump well before war was declared in 1914, was about to bring everything to a grinding halt.

CHAPTER 6

Hard Times
1914–1929

In conformity with the slack conditions of business the Social Club will hold a "Hard Times" dance on Saturday evening...Those who have during previous hard times tasted of life in the jungles and can recall the days when real money was non-existent and "scrip" [a promissory note] handed out for strenuous work on the woodpile.

—*Comox Argus*, 1921

Two days after war was declared between Britain and Germany in August 1914, the first Canadian Pacific Railway train, decked out in bunting and flags, pulled into the new Courtenay Station. "It was a great day," wrote one of the spectators, "whistles blowing, crowds cheering and carriage horses pranced with either fear or delight." The Thulin family were no doubt on hand to participate in the celebrations. After years of speculation and surveying, CPR crews were beginning to lay track to Duncan Bay. Courtenay would act as a connector for it, with a second line, the Canadian Northern, coming from Port Alberni. Land prices throughout the district were skyrocketing. "When communication by rail across Seymour Narrows is established," wrote Rev. Thomas Crosby, "there is no doubt that a remarkable development will occur in this part of the Province."

The Thulins were beautifully positioned to take advantage of a land boom. By 1914 the family owned all the private businesses and land in what is now downtown Campbell River, along with hundreds of acres west and south of the townsite. Those wishing to settle in the district had to beg a purchase from the irascible Mr. Nunns of Campbellton, to the north of town, or buy raw land on the north side of the river, which did not have a bridge yet. With their businesses established, the Thulins were prepared to wait for the arrival of the railway—but it would prove a long wait. The demands of the war overseas shelved this and many other development schemes across the country.

Union Steamship vessel at the dock at Campbell River, c. 1915. The freight and passenger service from Vancouver included routine stops at Campbell River, but only when the weather was fair, as the dock was exposed to the blast of southeast winds. *Carl Thulin Collection, MCR 10214*

The Thulin family logged their extensive property surrounding the townsite of Campbell River, dumping the logs via a chute that crossed what is now the Island Highway at 6th Avenue. *Carl Thulin Collection, MCR 8699*

There were other disquieting side effects of the Great War. The intense and rapid mechanization required for war production caused escalating inflation and a recession in Europe, which eventually made its way to BC. The settlers weathered the recession as they had previous "hard times," retaining their exuberant optimism while doggedly forcing a living from stump ranches and farms that provisioned the lumber camps. For children like Eve (Willson) Eade of Quadra Island this hand-to-mouth lifestyle left an ingrained memory:

> In summer there was hay to be got in. A neighbour would cut the main fields but we raked it all by hand into windrows and then haycocks, then taken in the barn by wagon. After the oat field was cut and in, Dad would make us go over the field and pick up every piece of oat stalk that was missed.
>
> We had a huge garden to weed and hoe and water. We picked the apples, pears, etc. and they were kept under the ferns we cut in the winter so they wouldn't freeze. Dad dug the potatoes and we sorted them to different sizes, little ones to be cooked for the pigs, ours to eat and the best to sell.
>
> We had three wells for water on our farm, one close to the back door, one down by the barn and one out in the pasture to water the animals. In summer the house well ran dry and we carried the water by pails from the creek…Being the smallest and lightest of the family, Dad chose me to clean out the wells; this was done every summer and it was a chore I dreaded. In those days you didn't say "no" to your parents, in fact, you didn't dare think "no," so the preparations would start. Dad would tie a galvanized pail onto a heavy rope and this was my chore, to get into the pail and be lowered down the 30 feet or so to the bottom. He would tie a shovel to the rope also and I would have to clear out all the guck and he would pull it up a pail at a time. There were snakes—lots of snakes to be shovelled into the pail and they would squirm out on the way out and fall back down on me— how I dreaded the cleaning out of the wells! When it was done to my Dad's satisfaction, I stood in the pail, hung onto the rope and was pulled up into the beautiful sunshine until next summer.[1]

The Weiwaikum people were living in straitened circumstances well before the recession caused by the war. By 1914 their population had reached a low of sixty-one people attempting to meld their existing skills and lifestyle into the priorities and restrictions of the non-Native population expanding around them. They seemed destined to fail. The general assumption was that the First Nations people were on the brink of extinction.

The main economic support for the Weiwaikum people at the outset of the war was fishing and cannery work, for which they earned about $200 a season, augmented by trapping on their northern reserves and picking hops in Washington state. Chief Lul-kaweelis (Charlie Smith) described the circumstances of the Weiwaikum people to a Royal Commission touring the province in 1914:

> Since the white men have come and are still coming more and more they are making our places here smaller all the time and that is what pains our hearts. This land of ours here has been measured three times now and each time it has been

An unidentified group on the Weiwaikum Reserve, Campbell River, c. 1912. MCR 8356

made smaller, and I ask that this reserve be returned to us at its original size.

We also want to use the traps that our forefathers used to use on these rivers because it is a very much easier way of catching the salmon... We ask permission that we may be allowed to fish on the river with nets even if it is only a short one. Nearly every winter we come next to starving because we are not allowed to take the fish out of the river which is our principal food... We also ask that we may be allowed to shoot what game we want for food; that is another thing we are not allowed to do by the white men.

The drinking house over here is too close to our reserve. That is another thing which gives trouble in this place. Why is that not put a stop to? It is a very bad thing. It is just like murdering people... Indians and white men as well.

Commissioner McDowall was sorry to hear the hotel was a problem, but "the best thing the Indians can do is to keep away from it." His simplistic advice was of no help, but a temperance movement then in full swing was pushing for a law designed to address this very real concern. When the Prohibition law, banning all liquor sales "except for medicinal purposes," was passed in 1917, it (and a rapid succession of calamities) put the Thulin family's indomitable spirit to the test.

On the eve of Prohibition, in the fall of 1917, a horde of loggers converged on the Willows Hotel for their last legal spree. From a vantage point on the hill behind the hotel, the women of the village watched as about "300 ravenous timber wolves from the different camps of the north" wreaked havoc. Within two hours the hotel's beautiful tiled floor was awash with broken bottles, glasses, window panes and furniture. When the fun developed into a full-scale brawl, which seethed past the clutter into the open air, Carl Thulin quickly boarded over the broken doors and windows to bar the men's return. "It was a good thing for the hotel keeper," reported the *Argus* newspaper, "that the constable [from Courtenay] was on the job, otherwise there would have been no limit to their actions." Sweeping up the mess, the Thulin family considered the serious economic setback they faced: the liquor trade amongst the "wild men of the woods" was an important mainstay.

The bar in the third Willows Hotel, shown here c. 1914, was made from a single slab of fir 60 feet long, 3 feet wide and 14 inches thick (18 m x 1 m x 35 cm). The regulars perched on a bench along one wall, where they spun endless yarns of their prowess in the woods. *Helen Mitchell Collection, MCR 7143*

And to make matters worse, a rival dry goods business was opened in 1917 by Walter Crawford, near the International Timber Company tracks northwest of "Thulinville." Raised on a Comox Valley farm, Crawford came to Campbell River in 1910 to work for the Thulins in logging and freighting, later becoming the town's first wharfinger. Within a few years Crawford was joined by a man named Brannigan, who opened a flophouse, which some think was the forerunner of the Quinsam Hotel, in the upstart new community of Campbellton.[2]

Once the problems started rolling in there seemed to be no stopping them. On December 9, 1917, the little group of buildings at the head of Campbell River wharf were muffled in drifted snow. The Thulins' "Big Store," with its coal oil lanterns, barrels of wares and shelves of dry goods, was decked out for Christmas shopping. The cordwood was stacked high on the front porch and

The Crawford family's store, opened in 1917. Left to right: Verona (Forbes) McNeil, Campbell Crawford, William M. McNeil, Grace Tyson (Devitt) and Oscar Olsen. The Crawfords' store was the start of Campbellton, a rival community to Campbell River, located in what is now the Quinsam Hotel parking lot. *Baldwin Collection, MCR 307(a)*

the stovepipe was glowing hot—too hot. The store went up in flames and was nearly a complete loss, which Charles valued at $40,000. The Thulins quickly got the business up and running again in temporary quarters in their newly completed business block nearby, but it was three years before the store was replaced.

The following year was no easier for the Thulins and their neighbours, in spite of the long-awaited end of the Great War in the fall of 1918. With the returning soldiers came a virulent strain of flu, called Spanish influenza, which had been raging throughout Europe. By the time the epidemic ran its course in the western hemisphere, the casualties far outstripped the number of lives lost on the battlefields.

North Island folks took precautions against the spread of the disease, banning

The Thulins' general store, which burned down in December 1917, was relocated to a new business block (seen here behind the store) for several years until the family could erect a new structure. *Helen Mitchell Collection, MCR 8064*

Jim McNeil and A. Kollquist on the steps of Thulins' General Store, c. 1915. *Carl Thulin Collection, MCR 8346*

The large new general store opened by the Thulin family in 1920, at the head of the government wharf (current site of Georgia Quay), included apartments on the upper floor. *Baldwin Collection, MCR 1889*

public gatherings and closing schools and churches, but the flu spread rapidly through the logging camps and farms. The death of hard-working Arlette Willson of Quadra Island left a young family of seven to their father's care. Campbell River's first doctor, Howard Jamieson, died during the war years, and according to Hannah Storie the new doctor, W.R. Shaw, was a poor replacement. It was six weeks before he visited Hannah, who was pregnant and dangerously ill with the flu: "He left pills and left saying he didn't know if he could save me. Somebody told my husband when I took sick to hang onions in the roof of the house—and I was the only patient for miles around that survived."

First Nations people had little resistance to the flu. At one point every able-bodied adult on the Cape Mudge Reserve was sick, making it necessary to hire someone to cut wood and haul water.[3] The Salmon River Reserve had only a few remaining permanent residents when the flu epidemic struck. Most of the survivors relocated to Cape Mudge and Comox, leaving the poles and houses of a once great village to fall into decay.[4]

Between the flu and heavy winter gales there was good reason for people to stay close to home as Christmas approached in 1918. One of the worst storms wiped out the Campbell River wharf, the town's lifeline to the outside world. Fred Thulin recalled in later years that people chided him and Charlie for building a wharf directly exposed to the blasting southeast storms. The wharf stubbornly survived for eleven years, until the gale of 1918 proved the naysayers right, smashing out the mid-section and leaving the wharfinger's prized new car stranded at the end of the dock. With typical pioneer ingenuity they rigged up an innovative skyline cage to transfer freight to shore, while Walter Crawford anxiously counted the weeks until the wharf was repaired and his car safely on shore again.

Trouble seemed to haunt the Thulins and the little village of Campbell River toward the end of World War I. As Christmas approached in 1918, just one year after the Thulins' store had been destroyed by fire, the lifeline to the community—the wharf—was smashed apart in a winter gale. A skyline cage was rigged as a temporary device for moving freight and passengers to shore until the wharf could be repaired.
Helen Mitchell Collection, MCR 8349

These islanders retained their frontier resilience and youthful belief in the promise of a bright future in spite of the hardships of the war years. Toward the end of the war, in 1918, the Thulins opened a dance hall, the Lilelana Pavilion. The name was an amalgam of the names of the three Thulin girls, Lillie, Elin and Anna, who presided over the Prohibition-era soda fountain. Old-timers still speak fondly of the Lilelana's fine acoustics and the comfort of its adjoining lounge.

The Thulins built the Lilelana Pavilion (seen here to the right of the Willows Hotel, at what is now the corner of St. Ann's Road and Shoppers Row) in 1918 during the Prohibition years, when it was illegal to manufacture or sell liquor. The pavilion, presided over by Charles and Mary Thulin's daughters, Lillie, Elin and Anna, was named for them. *Yeatman Collection, MCR 4203*

Music was usually supplied by local amateurs like Dutchie Neuberg or Moody's Band from Courtenay, whose talents earned them special rank in the community. (Actually, "special rank" was accorded to any musician—good, bad or indifferent.) The drummer for the Moody Band, Alvin Parkin, recalled the illegal booze stashed behind the band, and the fights that were a regular feature of dances. "The fights would start about anything, just for the love of fighting. Many times there'd be twenty tangled up in it, and women included. Nothing to see a woman knock a man out cold. Names excluded."

An International Timber Company locomotive engineer, Spoolie Kusha, had the job of delivering the eager dancers from the IT camp (which by this time was 14 miles [22 km] south of town) in the company train. Rounding everyone up again at night's end was not so easy. Standing at the doorway Kusha would sound the curfew with an impatient cry, "Time to go! Time to go!" as he herded the lingering dancers out the door.

Young folks thought nothing of taking lengthy trips in open boats to attend all-night dances at

Spoolie Kusha, a popular locomotive engineer, loaded party-goers on the International Timber Company's train and brought them into town for regular dances at the Lilelana Pavilion. *Gertrude Kusha Collection, MCR 14968*

the various halls in the far-flung Discovery Islands communities. A hall was opened on St. Patrick's day in 1917 on Quadra Island (which was still called Valdes Island, though the name had been officially changed to Quadra in 1903). Frank Gagne, a congenial community leader, brought the dancing crowd across to Gowlland Harbour in the *Blue Goose* and deposited his well-dressed charges on a boomstick dock, leaving them to inch their way to shore. Lillie Thulin still enjoyed a laugh in her senior years, remembering the time a mischievous impulse caused her to push one of her tottering escorts into the "chuck." But, it was all worth it; the Valdez Island Social Hall had the best dance floor north of Vancouver.

When the Thulins' bookkeeper died from influenza, George Francis was brought in as his replacement. His wife Marion was struck by the gaiety of the little community's social scene: "On the weekend, the loggers would come into town and the stores downtown would sometimes be open as late as 11:30 on Saturday nights. On Sunday nights there was a singsong in the Willows Hotel, but the town's main source of entertainment was cards. Bridge was the favourite game. At Christmas time, Mr. Thulin would invite everyone to the Willows Hotel for Christmas dinner."

Labour shortages during the war broadened the spectrum of work available to women and, after decades of lobbying, white women were finally allowed voting privileges in 1917. (Native people, male and female, and people of colour, did not get the right to vote until many decades later.)

Before the Great War, Yuko Shinmoto moved to Campbell River from Cumberland to look after the children of Mr. and Mrs. Cobb of the International Timber Company. In Campbell River she met and married an IT logger, Abie Shinmoto. Later Yuko became a partner in the Sugo family's Uneeda Laundry, opened in 1920 in the old Logger's Annex. Looking back, Yuko marvelled over how labour-intensive the business was in those pre-mechanization days. Every piece was washed by hand and strung outside on a line to dry in fair weather or draped about in the attic of the former saloon when it rained.

Charles and Mary Thulin's four children took an active part in the family businesses, including the harvesting of a bumper potato crop, c. 1918, in the field behind the Willows Hotel (current site of the bingo hall parking lot). Left to right: Lillie and Elin Thulin, Margaret (McNeil) Thulin, two unidentified men and, seated in front, a Japanese gardener known to the family as Elmer. *Carl Thulin Collection, MCR 7505*

Employers like R.L. Cobb at first resisted hiring women for non-traditional jobs, but the labour shortage of World War I forced them to call upon Ma Murray's Hiring Agency in Vancouver to choose six "mature" (settled, middle-aged) women. The six selected, who were not all technically "mature," were among the first women to work in logging camps on this part of the coast. The youngest of the lot, Gertrude Payne (later Kusha), jumped at the chance to earn $50 a month plus board, though her mother quaked at the thought of Gertrude working among such rough men. Mrs. Payne hopped aboard a Union boat for an impromptu inspection of Gertrude's new circumstances and was happy to find the men's behaviour above reproach. The "timber beasts," bereft of the sight of women and children, held each other to an Arthurian code of conduct. For Gertrude this was a vast improvement over what she had experienced working the night shift in downtown Vancouver. "We were treated with all respect. Give me a logger any day over any man in the street."

The women were prepared to wear men's aprons in the dining room but they weren't about to be called flunkies—logger lingo for dining room help. When the women received their first paycheques, labelling them flunkies, they marched to the camp manager's house to announce: "We're waitresses!" Whatever the title, the job involved gruelling eleven-hour days, seven days a week. The International Timber Company brass were impressed with their new help, and one woman was rapidly promoted to assistant cook. Gertrude, tired by the exhausting schedule, gave up her job but was back within six months as the wife of the IT locomotive engineer, Spoolie Kusha. The newlyweds moved into a canvas-and-board shack in the IT's new "married quarters," where she was once again one of three women living in a 200-man camp.

There was a surprising degree of support for one of BC's early feminists, Emmeline Pankhurst, when she addressed a Campbell River audience on behalf of the Council for Social Hygiene in 1921. Pankhurst, billed as the "well known champion of women's rights," was given the free use of the Lilelana Pavilion, where the audience donated the largest amount of money collected at any place on Vancouver Island.

Mae Anderson (McAllister), another woman of independent spirit, was among the first people—male or female—to drive a motor car along the narrow trails of Quadra Island. One day, rounding a bend, Mae and her noisy beast of a car surprised a man walking. He leapt into the bush with alacrity, preferring the safer avenue of the dense forest.

Mae Anderson (later McAllister), daughter of W.E. Anderson, owner-operator of the Quathiaski Canning Company, was one of the first people—male or female—to drive a car on Quadra Island. *Ed McAllister Collection, MCR 20126*

Carl Thulin sits proudly at the wheel of his father's new car, with his family arranged around him, c. 1919. *Courier-Upper Islander Collection, MCR 10210*

The first cars in Campbell River, brought in by Charlie Thulin and R.L. Cobb of the International Timber Company, signalled an important change in transportation. Instead of a six-hour boat trip to Courtenay, Cobb and Thulin could now bounce their way along the dirt track in half that time. By 1920 Thulin had a "squadron" of seven cars for hire, with his son Carl as chauffeur.

In the early 1920s Frank Lalonde set up a coach service, using a big touring car to run passengers and freight between Courtenay and Campbell River. Stanley Ritchie took over the business in 1924, advertising a fare of $3 per person, $5 return (more than a day's wage) and 25 cents for parcel delivery.

A new man in the district, Constable Jack Williams of the Provincial Police, had an abrupt entry into the art of motoring. When he arrived at his posting in 1920 there was no house, office or jail at his disposal (the district jail was on Quadra Island), but there was a boat and a new Model T Ford.

Jack received a full half-hour of driving instruction in Courtenay before setting off for Campbell River on a trip worthy of a Charlie Chaplin film. Unable to stop the car, Constable Williams

The Island Highway between Campbell River and Courtenay, c. 1915, was little more than a cattle trail that wound around stumps and dipped down along stretches of sandy beach. To drive the beaches, motorists had to stop their cars and partially deflate their tires. *J.H. Dalton Collection, MCR 6950*

wiped out a whole section of farm fencing as he careened up the infamous road that snaked around tall timber and down onto stretches of beach. On another occasion the infernal Model T's brakes failed as Jack manoeuvred a steep hill one dark night. He flung himself clear, leaving the car and his dog to crash through the brush and cross a deserted street, where it slammed into a tree. When he returned the next day to confront the wreckage, Jack found his faithful dog peacefully asleep in the back seat of the car.

Through the early 1920s the Thulins hung on to thousands of acres of property extending from the townsite southward, though the promised rail link to Duncan Bay was now a dim prospect. As a consequence life remained static in the village of Campbell River, but in the new community of Campbellton, and across the river on the north shore, things were progressing at a slow but steady pace.

The Pidcocks were among the families who settled in Campbellton in the 1920s. Reginald Pidcock Jr. ("Uncle Reg" to all who knew and loved this gruff-edged bachelor) and Herbert and Dolly (Smith) Pidcock bought adjoining riverfront properties from their old friend, Fred Nunns, in 1921. The Pidcock Brothers dissolved their partnership at Quathiaski Cove that year, leaving Uncle Reg, Herbert and Dolly to enjoy semi-retirement as fishing and hunting guides. All three, raised on the coast yet steeped in their English heritage, shared an exuberant love of the outdoors.

John Perkins Sr. took a job with his countryman David Vanstone before sending for his wife Effie and their son, who booked passage on the *Titanic*. When they found they could not get accommodation in steerage they were forced to take another liner, which passed the wreck of the *Titanic* too late to help. The Perkins family purchased property in North Campbell River one day before World War I was declared. In 1921 David and Eliza (Thorne) Vanstone, with their seven sons, bought the McDonald brothers' property next door to the Perkinses—and made a gradual switch from logging to farming and property development.

Eliza and David Vanstone raised their family of seven boys in a series of logging camps, with occasional spells at a Vancouver home, until Vanstone bought farm property in north Campbell River from the McDonald family in 1921. *Eileen Odowichuk Collection, MCR 17863*

In the spring of 1922 the International Timber Company bought approximately 100 acres (40 ha) from the Weiwaikum people, land they had already been leasing for about two decades for their log dump and booming ground. The property stretched along the river from just behind the Quinsam Hotel to the tip of Campbell River Spit. Some Campbell River Band members feel that this deal, encouraged by the Department of Indian Affairs (DIA), was purposely signed at a time when the literate members of the band were away working. Those who put their X to the lengthy legal document had to rely on DIA and logging company officials to interpret the agreement they were signing. The sale price of $150 per acre, plus a steam donkey and four thousand feet of lumber, may have been commensurate with prices of the day, but it took prime real estate out of the hands of the Weiwaikum and left them with a relatively small allotment of marshy land.

Department of Indian Affairs officials were also behind an intense push to enforce a law forbidding potlatches, a key social and economic structure for the Kwakw<u>a</u>ka'wakw people. Some Native groups throughout the area continued to hold potlatches, openly or secretly. When Lekwiltok families participated in a large-scale potlatch held in 1922 in a northern village, charges were laid against the chiefs. A deal was struck to commute some of the jail sentences, and in exchange the families involved were required to surrender their ceremonial masks and dancing

The remains of the Quatelle family's traditional big house at Campbell River Spit, Weiwaikum Reserve, c. 1923. *Clinton Wood Collection, MCR 6013*

The home of Mary Kwaksistala, Campbell River Spit, Weiwaikum Reserve, was the site of one of the last potlatches to take place on the reserve, following the enforcement of the ban on potlatching in 1922. *May (Quocksister) Henderson Collection, MCR 5173*

regalia to the federal government. Many Lekwiltok people decided to step out of the potlatch system at this point, while others continued with more simplified potlatches held in secret.

June Painter, who moved to the Campbell River Spit (on former reserve land she and her husband leased from the International Timber Company), recalled the excitement of the music and crowds arriving for another giant potlatch held at the Spit in 1922. June was invited to attend but in the press of setting up her new home she decided to wait for another occasion, a decision she regretted to the end of her days. The enforcement of the potlatch ban made this the last one at the Campbell River Reserve for many decades. It was only some years after the ban was lifted that people began potlatching again.

From canvas and board shacks erected amid the sand and flowers at the Spit, Ned Painter established a boat building business to supply specialized rowboats for sport fishing. Ned built up to fifty boats a year, which were rented at $3 per day, plus $8 for a guide, who worked the tides for a fourteen- to sixteen-hour day. When disgruntled Willows Hotel patrons, fed up with the noise of the loggers, urged the Painters to erect tent-shack accommodation at the Spit, the family began a new phase of their business. Out of these humble beginnings the Painters developed a tourist resort that far outstripped their initial plans.

Ned and June Painter lived in a rustic cabin at Campbell River Spit, seen here c. 1926, where Ned built his specialized sport fishing boats for sale and hire starting in 1922. *Meredith Collection, MCR 4073*

One of the Painters' many interesting customers in the early years was Mrs. Butler, the wife of a principal of the International Timber Company. June Painter described Mrs. Butler as a "terribly keen fisherwoman" who was attended by a cook and chauffeur for six weeks of serious sport fishing (she always brought her retinue for her annual trips). "It was a real performance when she came; it was just like catering to a queen."

Campbell River Spit, c. 1928, showing the International Timber Company's booming ground. *Einar and Hazel Andersen Collection, MCR 15468*

Ned Painter's finely crafted boats are still regarded as the perfect design for salmon fishing in Discovery Passage. The Painters started out by offering boats and guides for hire and soon branched out into providing rustic accommodation at Campbell River Spit. *Pidcock Collection, MCR 11080*

June Painter was the dynamo behind the expansion of the family's resort, which started with cabins on the Campbell River Spit and was expanded when they built a lodge on their north Campbell River property. *June Painter Collection, MCR 11891*

A long-time Campbellton resident, Jack "Klondike" Smith (who bought land from Nunns in 1906), cashed in on the fact that there was no land for sale between the village and Willow Point. He subdivided his 80-acre (32 ha) farm in 1922, at the current site of the bridges crossing the Campbell River. Smith was among the first in the district to create town-sized lots, which he offered for sale at between $150 and $225 apiece.

In a flush of enthusiasm Smith donated a 50x100-foot (15 x 30 m) lot and a $500 loan at 7 percent interest to the Parent Teacher Association. Smith intended the land to be used for a new school, but the PTA and a recently formed Community Club used his donation and bought an adjoining lot to erect a community hall. The site has long since been replaced by a swath of pavement at the Campbellton Mohawk gas station, but happy memories are still cherished by those who enjoyed parties, dances, school socials and the special thrill of seeing their first motion picture shows at the old community hall.

Acquiring a new school remained an important goal through the early 1920s. Forty students were packed into the old one-room school behind the Willows while a compromise was worked out on the siting of a new school accessible to both the village and the growing community of Campbellton. Land was purchased from the Thulins on the boundary between the two communities, at what is

Mrs. Butler (pictured here with her guide, Herbert Pidcock), fished by the exacting rules of Campbell River's Tyee Club. The club requires fishers to use light tackle and a rowboat to land fish weighing over 30 pounds (13.5 kg) to receive pins. *Pidcock Collection, MCR 11064*

The land for the community hall in Campbellton (present site of the Mohawk gas station) was centrally located but it was subject to flooding from the river. In 1935 rowboats were used to ferry people across flood waters covering the government road. *Roderick Haig-Brown Collection, MCR 4501*

now Elm Street and Island Highway, and the Weiwaikum people were persuaded to donate a strip of land to enlarge the school property, with the understanding that their children could attend the new school. It was opened in 1924 with two teachers and 58 pupils, but when Fanny Roberts of the Campbell River Reserve (whose husband Bill had served in the Great War) arrived on opening day to enroll her children she was told they must continue to attend residential school, as her family were not

The ladies' auxiliary of the community hall raised the money to build and maintain the hall, the focal point of community life from 1922 on. The founding group, some of whom may appear in this photo, were Mrs. J. Brunton, Mrs. C.H. FitzGerald, Mrs. C. Petersen, Mrs. M. Petersen, Mrs. M. Palmer, Mrs. McDonald, Mrs. R. Pidcock and Mrs. T. Morrison. *Les and Ivy McDonald Collection, MCR 20145* taxpayers.[5] It would take another eleven years before the Weiwaikum people could construct their own school on the reserve.

With all the new development and bright promise surrounding his Campbellton subdivision, "Klondike" Smith should have been a happy man, but that was not the case. On a business trip to Vancouver in 1925 Smith went missing from his bloodstained stateroom. Investigators found half his clothing, an open knife and $30 beneath his pillow, which proved the only clues to a death his contemporaries attributed to suicide.

Another long-time Campbellton resident died uncommonly in the early 1920s. Fred Nunns suffered for years with toothache, which he usually treated with home remedies such as blistering doses of carbolic acid. On a business trip to Courtenay in 1923 Nunns decided to have six of his troublesome teeth removed and shortly afterwards collapsed in the home of a doctor. His death was attributed to a suspected overdose of novocaine. The *Argus* called him "the father of Campbell River" and sadly noted that "with the death of Mr. Nunns goes another link with the past of ox-wagons and trails."

Tom Hudson bought the site of a former logging camp on the river's north side in 1925, joining the ranks of British immigrants settling on the outskirts of Campbell River. Hudson had the advantage of agriculture college training and a bit of family money to get him started. He became fast friends with the Painters, Pidcocks, Smiths and FitzGeralds, who eased the newcomer through the adjustment to isolation, loneliness and the eternal rain of a coastal winter. Tom's first letters home were brimming with optimism, but as the winter wore on Vanstone's offer to buy his property looked tempting: "The chief disadvantages of this place I find are that the winters are too wet, with not much sunshine, also that Campbell River is too far away from anywhere and there is nothing to do except work on the farm."[6]

Like so many before and after him, Hudson came to find that the peace, beauty and opportunity of life on the coast were more than adequate compensation for the months of grey weather. By the time Hudson met Mavis Adye (on holiday at Painters as a companion to a Victoria family), he was passionately attached to his river-mouth property. Tom and Mavis developed their place into a fine farm, now in the hands of the Hudson family's second generation and one of the few remaining in production.

The little townsite of Campbellton expanded under the pressure of this influx of residents and the ever-increasing logging industry surrounding it. A small cafe, the Dewdrop Inn (whose huge overhead sign wisely proclaimed it a Cafe & Cash Store) opened in the early 1920s. It was advertised in the *Argus* newspaper as "a cheery, hospitable restaurant, cafe and store where the logger, the tourist and everyone can get excellent meals, well cooked, at very reasonable prices and at all hours." And Mr. William McNeil offered "modern tonsorial service" for the "logger or anyone else" in his barber shop in the ramshackle cluster of businesses on the west side of the IT tracks. A Courtenay baker, J. Mort, opened the Pioneer Bakery across from the Quinsam Hotel in 1922, selling loaves by the dozen to area logging camps. In 1928 he erected a fine new building, which remains standing at the corner of the Island Highway and Petersen Road.

An intriguing character named Jim English bought the Quinsam Hotel, then under construction, in 1923–24. The Bishop, as English was known, bought the place with the proceeds of his successful Oyster River businesses—a store and the Fisherman's Lodge. The prohibition on alcohol sales was dropped in 1920 but the tough restrictions placed upon where and when alcohol could be sold and consumed required some crafty side-stepping by those determined to succeed at this trade. Jim English was a charismatic character with an uncanny ability to remain on the right side of the law, while serving his customers no matter the time of day or night. By 1926 he was able to expand the Quinsam to include a restaurant and barber shop. As Joe Meredith of north Campbell River recalled, "he used to be at all the bootlegging trials but they never pinched him; he had a lot of followers I guess." English is thought to have gained his enigmatic nickname, The Bishop, when he was called upon to say a few kind words over the grave of a friendless logger who happened to die at his hotel.

The exact date the Quinsam Hotel was built is not known, but it is thought a man named Brannigan opened a flophouse in Campbellton before beginning to construct what is now the Quinsam Hotel in 1923–24—when Jim English, The Bishop, bought the place. *Baldwin Collection, MCR 7686*

Though English managed to remain above the law when it came to bootlegging, he was not above the pranks of his clientele. In a taped interview Darrell Smith related an old-timer's tale of two fallers grieving the death of their workmate, a bucker who died on the job early one morning. That night as the fallers sat glumly over their beer at the Quinsam it suddenly occurred to them that their belated friend ought to join them for one last round. They inveigled a taxi driver to help them pinch the corpse from the rustic shack that served as a morgue and propped their pal up at a corner table in the bar. The Bishop was hesitant to serve the "drunk" in the corner but finally agreed to the first round. When called upon for a second round, English flatly refused to serve their drunken friend; after all, The Bishop had his reputation to preserve. The next day when a crew in the bar asked English if he'd heard the news about the death of the man he so clearly remembered barring from the hotel the night before, he was incredulous. "When did he die?" he demanded. "Well," they said, "he got killed yesterday morning." "Like hell he did," responded English, "he was sittin' right here last night!" When the superstitious barkeeper finally realized he'd served a corpse he was shaky for days.

The World War I recession, which dragged on beyond the war and into the early 1920s, is remembered by area residents as being more difficult than the Great Depression of the 1930s. Certainly that was the case for a number of Discovery Passage businesses that went into receivership just as the recession was reaching its end in 1923–24. An overextended credit system, carried throughout the lean years to a highly mobile workforce, was their undoing.

The custom of the day, especially in a small centre with no banks, was for businesses to operate on an involved credit system which was sometimes extended over very long periods. Some say Charlie Thulin was generous to a fault and a few imply he simply couldn't say no. By 1923 the Thulins were owed thousands of dollars and they, in turn, had exceeded their credit limit with their Vancouver wholesalers. It wasn't just the loggers who were racking up debts at both the Campbell River Trading Company Store and

Jim English (seated), owner/operator of the Quinsam Hotel. He was a charming and forceful community leader who is said to have made a stake by bootlegging from his tavern on the Oyster River during the Prohibition era. *Waldref Collection, MCR 9441*

the hotel. The Campbell River Hospital, also in serious trouble, had outstanding accounts at the store of over $3,000.[7]

The mounting debts for the Thulins were fuelled by an expensive buyout, a few years earlier, of their partner Emerson Hannan, at a rumoured sum of $21,000.[8] The Prohibition years brought a decrease in profits at the hotel, as did the growing competition in Campbellton. When Prohibition ended and the loggers once again ruled supreme at the Willows bar, the Thulins' sport fishing clients sought accommodation elsewhere—beginning a gradual decline in their specialized tourist trade.

The Lund operation is said to have kept Campbell River afloat through some of the hard times, until the Thulin brothers' Vancouver wholesalers decided to call in their debts in 1923, seizing control of both the Lund and Campbell River businesses. The Credit Men's Association assigned Melville Haigh to audit the Thulins' books[9] and to manage their affairs in Campbell River until their assets could be disposed of to pay off the debts.

North Vancouver Island residents made the best of the lean years of the early 1920s by living off the land. Seen here in 1924, left to right (standing): Tom Taylor, Leonard Waddington (teacher), Les McDonald (boy); (seated): Lorne Higgins, Dave McDonald. *Les and Ivy McDonald Collection, MCR 13229*

One of Haigh's first initiatives was a vain attempt to rebuild the hotel's flagging sport fishing business. He bought a new fleet of rental boats from Ned Painter, and in 1924 joined forces with an international group, headed by Dr. Wiborn of California, to form the Tyee Club. The club, with its exacting rules, went on to become an enduring part of the Campbell River sport fishing mystique, but the hotel continued its decline.

The "Big Store" was sold to Frank Cross and David Vanstone in 1926, and they turned it over to their eldest sons to manage. The hotel, annex and Lilelana Pavilion were sold in 1927 to the Isaac family for $27,500. When all the debts were cleared the Thulins were left with their home, farm and a portion of their once extensive property holdings.

The Thulins were not alone in their troubles. The Credit Men's Association also foreclosed on the hospital in 1924 for debts to Vancouver wholesalers. As a result the hospital was closed, leaving loggers and residents once again to rely upon distant hospital service at Rock Bay or Comox for about two years. In 1926, 200 people gathered at what the *Comox Argus* described as the largest public meeting in the history of the district. Three prominent logging companies stepped forward to settle the bulk of the hospital's $4,000 debt, and it was reopened as the Lourdes Hospital, under the efficient management of the Sisters of St. Ann.

The Bull family of Quadra Island experienced both personal and financial losses at the end of the World War I recession. Following a lingering decline, Helen Bull passed away in December 1924 and within months the hotel and store, once the nucleus of the largest population in the

The Campbell River Hospital was another victim of the World War I recession, but the debts were paid off by area logging companies in 1926 and the hospital was put under the management of the Sisters of St. Ann. Left to right: Mary Rose Yvonne, Mary Kathleen, Mary Mark and Mary John Leonard.
Sisters of St. Ann Collection, MCR 8179

district, went into receivership. Bull disappeared into poverty in Vancouver, where he was last seen selling blankets on a street corner.[10]

As roads and motor vehicles took precedence over boats, becoming the dominant mode of transport, Quadra Island gradually gave way to Campbell River as the main economic hub for the district. In 1924 the local headquarters for the BC Provincial Police was moved from Quathiaski Cove to Campbell River. Stewart Wheldon Dawson used his own boat and a car to serve a vast territory from Oyster Bay to Port Neville.

Vehicles and roads had speed and flexibility in their favour, especially important in a place where the wrong combination of wind and tide were life-threatening. In spite of the advantage of a lighthouse booming out warnings, Discovery Passage continued exacting a toll on mariners.

A notable wreck of the 1920s occurred in the Strait of Georgia while Discovery Passage folks danced the night away at a Christmas party at the Lilelana Pavilion. As the SS *Northwestern* forced its way through driving snow on its approach to the Passage on December 13, 1927, Velma Kipp (later Cuthbertson), a Quadra Island schoolteacher, glanced out the dance hall window and wondered how she'd be able to get home. Passengers aboard the SS *Northwestern* looked out into the same snowstorm with much more intense concern. Their fears were well founded. At 5:00 the next morning, with the seas still running high, the sleeping townsfolk at Campbell River were called to the aid of the 187 people aboard the *Northwestern*, piled up on the shoals east of Cape Mudge.

The wreck of the SS *Northwestern* off Cape Mudge in December 1927 was a harrowing event for the passengers, but all were rescued, brought to town and treated to a dance at the Lilelana Pavilion while they awaited a ship to take them back to their home port in Seattle. *Herbert Joyce Collection, MCR 7915*

The ship was on a yuletide mission, taking freight and passengers from Seattle to Alaska for the holiday season. She was loaded deep with Christmas stock: china, canned goods, boxes of gumboots, eggs, turkeys, chickens, cows, sacks of flour and sugar, fruit and bales of hay. Corporal Dawson, in his small police boat, joined forces with a halibut boat to attempt a joint rescue but it was eight hours before they were able to get alongside the *Northwestern*. The Willows Hotel was bustling with preparation. Hot coffee awaited the cold and distraught passengers, along with basic accommodation for all, and messages were tapped out to family and friends from the telegraph office. Fortunately the dance band was still in town, so that night the townsfolk treated their stricken guests to a dance at the lovely Lilelana Pavilion.

When word spread that the 1,000 pounds (450 kg) of insured freight remaining aboard the *Northwestern* was destined for salvage, the stump ranchers and fishermen of Quadra Island decided it was fair game. Before customs officials arrived to take stock, some of the freight had been paddled ashore as Christmas bounty. A few folks got their loot by more legitimate means when soiled goods were tossed overboard by the salvage crew, but others persisted in boarding the ship in spite of warning gunshots blazing over their heads, and an announcement that every house on the island would be searched. For years after the wreck of the *Northwestern*, crates of ill-fitting gumboots, canned lard and coffee (which, fifty years later, one old-timer still maintained was the best he'd ever tasted) were pulled from hiding behind walls and beneath floorboards. It was a memorable Christmas for many a cash-poor islander the year the SS *Northwestern* was gored on the shoals at Cape Mudge.

High winds and foul weather plagued the people of north Campbell River, who were forced to paddle across the river to buy and sell supplies and get their children to school. The capricious river, difficult to navigate in winter storms and spring floods, often stranded children in town overnight with no way to send word of their whereabouts. Residents took every opportunity to pressure the government to build a bridge across the Campbell, but in the end it was the needs of the big lumber camps at Menzies Bay that swung the government into action. No matter the means, Campbell Riverites were jubilant when a bridge was erected in 1928. Arnold McDonald, with an ear-to-ear grin, proudly drove the maiden journey across the new bridge with a delivery of groceries from Crawford's Store, and the Perkinses served homemade potato wine at an impromptu bridge party.

For the Painter family the bridge brought an immediate advantage. Some years prior they had purchased a few acres on the north side of the river from their friend, Tom Hudson. The new bridge made it possible to expand their business on their own land, where they built guest cabins.

By the late 1920s both Campbellton and Campbell River were in the hands of an interesting new mix of residents and entrepreneurs, with David Vanstone in the forefront. Family lore has it that Vanstone left England as a youth and wound up in Victoria in the early 1890s in a curious combination of trades, teaching ballroom dancing by day and driving a "honey wagon" (emptying outhouses) by night. Sometime in the Gay '90s Vanstone came north to work in the logging camps as a teamster; within a few years he and a partner were running their own camps.

Vanstone was a robust man in his fifties when he officially retired from logging to become a financier and property developer. Joe Meredith recalled that Vanstone got his start as an investor when a friendly debt of $1,000 was repaid in brewery stock, which brought a handsome return with a Prohibition-era product called near-beer.

Starting with the purchase of the Thulins' store, Vanstone astutely scooped up property at every opportunity. He built family-style tourist bungalows on the waterfront north of the river in the late 1920s and constructed several business blocks in downtown Campbell River in the 1930s. In 1935 David Vanstone was publicly proclaimed Charlie Thulin's successor, a man "doing his bit" to build up the town of Campbell River.

As the Thulin family businesses were sold through the 1920s, a new mix of entrepreneurs put their stamp on the village. David Vanstone built the Vanstone Block, second building from the right, in about 1928. In the late 1990s the much-refurbished structure was still in use, in the 900 block of Shoppers Row.
Ryan Collection, CRM 7123

Fred Thulin's son Oscar opened a garage and marine ways (boat haulout) in 1921 near the current site of Georgia Quay. He followed the family tradition by involving various members of his extended family in the business. Oscar's wife Agnes was the company bookkeeper, and his brother Clarence joined the firm in 1924 as a mechanic, at $50 per month. Some years later Agnes's brother, Einar Andersen, bought into the business. This second generation Thulin business avoided the family losses of 1923–24, only to fall prey a decade later to overextended credit during the Great Depression. The marine ways portion of the business, now called Ocean Pacific, is still operating.

Oscar and Agnes Thulin, along with Agnes's brother Einar Andersen, operated Campbell River's first car garage and marine ways from the early 1920s to the 1930s. In the late 1990s the marine ways portion of the business was still in operation in the original location on Pier Street, under the name Ocean Pacific. *Einar and Hazel Andersen Collection, MCR 13014*

Others in the second generation of the Thulin family also remained in the thick of the Campbell River business scene. After a few years of struggle Carl and Margaret (McNeil) Thulin opened the Bee Hive Cafe and Confectionery in 1929. Then in 1937 they built a business block for both the café and a new store, Pioneer Hardware. According to family legend Margaret began the Bee Hive confectionery with "a half a box of candy." Within short order Margaret built the business into a "bustling hive of activity," with a mouth-watering selection of penny candy in big glass jars, a poolroom, newsstand, and café. Both the Bee Hive and Pioneer Hardware remain vital downtown businesses, the latter continuing as a Thulin family enterprise.

By the late 1920s the economy was moving again. New businesses were opening and area logging camps were operating at full capacity. Then, seemingly out of nowhere, came the 1929 stock market crash, which precipitated the Great Depression and flattened the economy once again.

Margaret (McNeil) Thulin and Jim Whyte at the 50th parallel marker, Island Highway. *Carl Thulin Collection, MCR 10241*

The effects were at first minimal on the resource-rich coast. The regulars at the Bee Hive blandly swapped snippets of titillating news over the brims of their coffee mugs, while New York tycoons leapt from windows as their investments vanished overnight. North Island folk, resourceful and adaptable, were relatively well-placed to weather more hard times, but they would also, eventually, share in the deprivations of the Great Depression.

CHAPTER 7

Depression and War
1929–1945

Mae West at "River"

Comedienne Leaves Valuable Gift at Elk Falls

Campbell River, July 25 [1934]—Mae West and Sue Carroll, internationally known screen stars, of Hollywood, in a tour of the Island, visited Elk Falls and while there enjoyed afternoon tea with Mrs. Frank Masters [who operated a little tea house at the falls] last Monday. They were greatly struck with the beauties of the district, particularly with the Falls. It is not unusual for visitors to carry away souvenirs, but rather odd to leave them. Mrs. Masters was given a beautiful camera as a memento of the comedienne's visit.

—*Comox Argus*, July 26, 1934

The *Comox Argus* newspaper completely ignored the stock market crash of 1929, choosing instead to run a two page spread on the massive logging camps at Menzies Bay. One of the companies—Bloedel, Stewart & Welch—had between 550 and 600 men at work in their camp, which the newspaper described as the "headquarters for the largest logging operation in the British Empire." Their standard-gauge railway lines, growing by 65 miles (104 km) of track per year, radiated in all directions, totalling about eighty spurs. The camp dining room was constructed in the form of a large *T*, with each of the three arms able to accommodate 120 men at once, for a total of 360 men at a sitting.

The executives of another large logging operation, the International Timber Company, sold out just in advance of the Great Depression. The new owners of what was now called the Elk River Timber Company (ERT) faced declining markets and the rise of unionism.

R.L. Cobb, the manager of the IT Company (which he had served for twenty-nine years), stayed on to become the manager of the ERT. Both ERT and IT before it were largely owned by

US companies operating in the Pacific Northwest, where the earliest experiments in reforestation began. Cobb's awareness of the need for reforestation probably sparked his interest in getting a project going in BC. In 1922 Cobb had offered the Forest Service 12,000 acres (4,800 ha), several miles to the southwest of Campbell River, but the offer was declined, perhaps because government officials suspected it was only a tax dodge. In 1929 Cobb made the offer again, this time as an executive of the newly formed Elk River Timber Company. The terms remained the same, though Cobb had narrowed the donation to a choice of 1,000 acres (400 ha) from within the originally offered 12,000 acres, to be maintained in perpetuity as a reforestation demonstration project.

The Bloedel, Stewart & Welch camp at Menzies Bay was touted by the *Comox Argus* newspaper as the largest camp in the British Empire. The T-shaped dining room, in the centre of this 1935 photograph by W.M. Forrest, could accommodate 360 men at one sitting. *BCARS F-02349*

The Campbell River experimental forest, which later came to be known as the Beaver Lodge Lands, was legally transferred to the province in 1931. A covenant on the deed required that the land be used for "experimenting in reforestation and scientific forestry management." That spring, 15,000 two-year-old trees were planted in what the *Argus* believed to be the first large scale reforestation of logged land in British Columbia. Once the planting was complete the experiment was left to the whims of nature and time.

As the world market plummeted with the weakening global economy, wages in the logging industry were slashed to pre-war levels, from an average of $4.50 a day down to $2 (minus 90 cents for board and blankets), and crews were cut to a minimum. A 1932 service club representative for the village of Campbell River reported on the general conditions of the time: "We have three of the largest logging operations in the Province within 10 miles of us. From the above you will realize that we are in the heart of the Logging Industry, the Camps employing up to 2000 men when operating in full swing. At the present time on account of the general conditions throughout Canada, the Logging Industry is hard hit, and not more than 500 men are employed."[1]

The big-time operators successfully blocked early attempts at union organization by blacklisting those suspected of union activity. Companies shared their blacklists, effectively blocking union members from getting any work within the industry. Men who saw the need for change, not just in wages but in safety standards, were forced to circulate union literature and bring in motivational speakers under cover.

In 1934 the call for a strike vote was circulated throughout the crews working for Bloedel, Stewart & Welch. Einar Andersen, having given up his partnership in the Campbell River Garage in favour of working in the woods, attended a strike meeting with ambivalent feelings. Many shared his feelings, but within minutes of hearing a gifted union orator named Gunrad, they were ready to take action.

An important difference between this and previous attempts at strikes was the effective organizing of the campaign. In the past, striking men lit out to "town" (Vancouver) on a spree, thereby unwittingly hastening their need to go back to work. But this time a shantytown was set up on a tourist campground in north Campbell River, where sobriety was a requirement. The strikers were also required to maintain a respectable presence in the community, enforced by loggers wearing arm bands, who patrolled the hotel barrooms to ensure strikers were staying out of trouble.

The loggers' strike of 1934 was one of the first to succeed, due in part to efficient organization. The strikers set up a shantytown in north Campbell River to keep the loggers from going to Vancouver, where their meagre resources would quickly be depleted and they would be forced to return to work.
Bergren Collection, IWA

The mild winter conditions of 1934 eased life in the shantytown, where strike pay consisted of a $1.50-a-week "milk allowance." Walter Antifave and Johnny Garat used their fancy touring car, complete with curtained windows, to make regular trips to local farms to collect donations of vegetables and milk while organizers hustled groceries from the Fraser Valley. Stanley Isaac of the Willows Hotel provided lumber for the tent camp and Gertrude Isaac kept the men supplied with pies. Alex McLean, the new owner of the Campbellton store, extended credit to the strikers for the duration, and citizen committees held dances to raise money in their aid.

As the strike of 1934 gained momentum, spreading beyond Campbell River to camps in Comox and at Port Alberni, upwards of 4,000 men walked off the job, making this the first major strike on the coast.

After three and a half months the strikers won a partial victory. Public pressure forced the provincial government to establish a 40-cent-per-hour minimum wage for the entire industry, resulting in a 15 percent increase for Bloedel, Stewart & Welch workers. Union membership rose by 3,000 during the strike and the union gained new impetus as organizers continued to push for improved working conditions and union recognition.

By the 1930s it was becoming more acceptable for men to bring their wives and children to live with them in logging camps. In 1937 Helen Mitchell abandoned urban comforts to join her husband at the Campbell River Timber Company camp. She later wrote about her early years in camp, the bravado and lingo of her husband's world and, in particular, the rusticity of her first home:

> The bus stopped at the Willows Hotel at that time... Medrick [Levesque] was driver of the seven-passenger limousine that I and several loggers crowded into a short time later for the 12-mile trip to the beach camp at Menzies Bay. Not realizing that I still had a long way to go, I declined the invitation to eat in the Willows dining room, and sat in the limousine while the loggers ate a hurried meal, afraid I'd miss the taxi and lose my way. Consequently, I arrived at the beach camp starving. There, I learned I still had 22 miles to go by speeder on the company's railroad, to the woods camp.
>
> Night was falling and I counted 22 deer in the dusk... It was about 9:30 when we arrived, and pitch black. The loggers were dropped off at the water tank where a path led, I later learned, up to the bunkhouses. The speederman took me a little farther along to where the commissary and storage and sawfiling shacks were located at a "Y." My husband was waiting there for me with a flashlight and I followed him for about a quarter of a mile up the railway track, tripped over spikes and ties in the darkness, till we reached the one-roomed shake shack I was to call "home" for the next three years.
>
> The CRT was one of the largest logging camps on the coast when I lived there. There were about 45 families, and 79 children, about three single girls and almost 500 men working in the woods.
>
> I couldn't wash the floor because the lumber was very rough and covered with splinters. I didn't need a dustpan. The cracks were more than an inch wide before we got them covered so they were handy for sweeping the dirt into. The creek was my first water supply. I had to take my buckets, scramble down the hillside and kneel on a levelled-off log to scoop the water out of the creek... I had no sink, just a counter space I built for myself from tie-mill planks, with shelves underneath for food and dishes.
>
> We had to send out for most of our food, of course. I sometimes sent to Woodward's in Vancouver for an order, enough to last a month. I always enjoyed "freight days," and spent hours unpacking and exclaiming over the various items I had ordered. Most of the time, however, we camp wives ordered weekly from the "Big Store," Cross and Vanstone in Campbell River, or from Alex McLean in Campbellton [formerly Crawford's]. On Friday mornings the speeder came up from the beach, towing a trailer-load of groceries and meats from the Campbell River stores.[2]

For several decades the smaller operators, known as gyppos, found a continuing niche in the industry by moving floating camps into areas that were otherwise inaccessible. Their outfits could be as simple as a single tarpaper shack or as elaborate as a floating village, such as the one described by Francis Dickie, an upcoast magazine writer, in an unpublished manuscript titled "Let's Go Places":

> Upon a gathering of enormous rafts of cedar logs a cluster of houses lay. Though made up of sections, the whole was held together by boom chains and cable, presenting to the viewer an air of compactness, a community stability, that certain something one senses only in established places.
>
> Ridiculous as this impression seemed regarding a so obviously transient arrangement, the feeling grew stronger upon me as I stepped upon the planking of the City. I started along the main street of this astonishing floating aggregation of one-storey buildings. All were of frame, from one to five rooms in size. Several were of tar-paper covering, others of cedar shakes, other of neat boards. In little yards at the front and back of these, flowers and vegetables flourished in earth held in old dug-out canoes, long boxes, barrels and tins. From the nearby shore pipelines, tapping mountain springs, had been carried to supply the householders with running water.

Floating logging camps, as simple as one scruffy shack or as complex as a floating village, were a favoured means for logging less accessible sites. These camps were the domain of independent loggers, usually run by extended families. Float camp operations like this one, at Simoom Sound, were among the first to welcome women and children.
Edna May John Collection, MCR 14140

One industry that experienced substantial growth during the Depression was gold mining—a result of high public demand for hard currency. The Donaldson family tenaciously clung to their farm, one of the last, in the failed farming community at Cape Scott until rumours of long-ago Spanish gold discoveries in the Zeballos area netted them a rich claim. From the first stake in 1931–32 the rush was on, and by mid-decade there were more than twenty mines in production, giving rise to the boom town of Zeballos. The Privateer mine, the largest operating out of Zeballos, reputedly shipped $6,500,000 worth of gold and silver between 1938 and 1948, when the gold petered out and the mines closed.

The majority of north Vancouver Island residents managed to continue earning a living during the Depression, albeit a meagre one, augmented by a plentiful supply of fish and game. As Gladys (Dawson) Thulin recalls, "as long as there were deer running around in the bush we didn't have to go hungry." Men came to her father, Corporal Dawson, for permission to hunt out of season and he'd send them away with a few bullets to aid the cause. Ione (Crawford) McDonald, whose father lost his Campbellton store in the Great Depression, still has an aversion to venison stew. A favourite saying of the day was: "I ate so many clams my stomach began coming and going with the tides."

The mild climate and the ability to live off the land made the coast a mecca for hundreds of out-of-work men from across the country. The *Argus* reported that those seeking relief must be British subjects "in need of the necessities of life, or destitute and without means of subsistence" in order to register with the several funding agencies that provided basic relief in exchange for work on public projects. A 1938 analysis of a large relief camp at Elk Falls estimated that 75 percent of the inhabitants were from out of province; only five men, in an earlier study, were found to be Discovery Passage residents.

Some of the relief crews were housed in unoccupied logging camps. Men received their board plus $7.50 per month for labouring on road construction between Oyster Bay and Campbell River, and tree planting on logged-over lands, using stock from a new tree nursery at Quinsam Prairie. At Elk Falls, which finally gained official park status in 1940 (after two decades of strenuous lobbying), a large tent camp was set up for a crew building roads, trails and bridges to enhance this treasured beauty spot.

During the World War I recession single men had established driftwood shantytowns near the fishing grounds—Cape Mudge, Francisco Point, April Point (then known as Poverty Point) and Menzies Bay. Men who proudly disdained going on relief joined these bachelors, to earn a very basic living, fishing by hand for the cannery, using a ragtag assembly of rough boats.

Campbell River's Depression-era population was 250 people.[3] The main thoroughfare through the village was a dirt track, dusty in summer and sloppy with rain and wind-driven sea water and driftwood in winter. On the southern boundary of the village was the "big hill," cresting near what is now 1st Avenue. Following the government road toward the village, on the bluffs at what is now Sequoia Tree Park, were the log buildings of the forestry station, built in 1929. To the north, across from the current Fishing Pier, was Corporal Dawson's family home and the police station, and farther along was the main business precinct, the Campbell River Garage, Mrs. McCarthy's Ladies Wear, the Bee Hive block, the Cross and Vanstone store (formerly the Thulins' general store), the government wharf and the Willows Hotel. Behind the hotel was the Lourdes Hospital. On the shore of Willow Bay (now Shoppers Row) was the Lilelana Pavilion, the new Vanstone

Apartments and Ritchie's car garage. At the bend in the road, just past the Thulin family home (near the current McDonald's Restaurant), was the first radio-telephone station, opened in 1929. Behind the main drag, on the flats that now comprise much of the business core, was a sloppy swamp called Cod Fish Flats, and the Thulins' expanse of farm fields.

Before crossing a bridge at Nunns Creek and the marshy expanse of the Campbell River Reserve on the right, the road passed the school and a new church, opened near the school in 1931. The land for the church is sometimes said to have been donated by Mr. and Mrs. Charles Thulin, augmented by the purchase of fifty additional feet from an unnamed source.[4] The community raised $3,000 and the Anglican Church chipped in a loan of $1,000 for the construction of St. Peter's Church. In accordance with Charles Thulin's request, the church was to serve the needs of both Anglican and United Church congregations, until the latter could build their own place of worship.

In 1931 Campbell River's first official church was opened near what is now Elm Street, on the edge of Campbellton, near the town's second school (at right). *Carl Thulin Collection, MCR 10218*

The circumstances of the Lekwiltok people were improving by the 1930s. At the height of the Depression the Weiwaikum Band opened a day school for their children. On opening day, in November 1935, Chief Johnny Quocksister served as interpreter for the children who were not yet fluent in English. That same year Bill and Fanny Roberts cleared land beyond the telephone office for a "fully modern" house.

A new family moved to the Campbell River Reserve during the Depression. James (Jim), Sam and Katie were the grown children of Kenneth Henderson, a *Grappler* shipwreck survivor, and Lucy Johnson, a Nakwoktok woman from a northerly Kwakw<u>a</u>ka'wakw village. In his family memoirs

Jim describes a childhood plagued and blessed by the challenges of being equally fluent in the languages and cultural expectations of both his parents. Jim married "a pretty little girl from Campbell River" in 1925, stayed on and was joined in 1929 by his siblings Sam and Katie, both of whom also married into Lekwiltok families. Sam married May Quocksister in 1935[5] and the couple went on to have sixteen children, including two sets of twins.

The government road beyond the Weiwaikum Reserve was lined with clusters of spreading maples, countrifying the rough and ready appearance of Campbellton: an ERT warehouse, the Quinsam Hotel, Pioneer Bakery, a meat market, cafe, barber shop and a bit farther along, the community hall.

By the 1930s Charlie Thulin was no longer of an age to rise above adversity. His life had been a classic rise and fall, from his beginnings as an ambitious Swedish farm lad[6] who became a highly successful businessman, to his return to the life of a simple farmer. Charlie attempted to develop and sell some of his land holdings, but nothing was moving in the sluggish Depression economy. The only land he relinquished was given over to employees in lieu of overdue wages. But Charlie retained his dignified status in the community to the end. As a respected elder of the town, he presided over social events and represented Campbell River's interests when needed. In his last year of life Charlie took an active role in the push for hydro development. He and Cecil FitzGerald acted as representatives of the Campbell River Board of Trade at a Victoria convention, pressing the BC Electric Company to dam the Elk Falls.

After a brief illness, "Poppa" Thulin passed away in April 1932 at the little hospital he had worked so hard to establish and maintain. Hundreds of people from all over the coast flocked to town to "pay their last respects to the old pioneer," showering the family with 112 floral tributes. Charles was remembered for his role in establishing both Lund and Campbell River and for his "cheery smile and buoyant spirit." His was the first funeral at St. Peter's Church, and he was one of the first to be buried in the new cemetery in north Campbell River, on land donated by David Vanstone.

The Thulins retained their extensive farm, backing what is now downtown Campbell River, through the Great Depression. *Baldwin Collection, MCR 1886*

The death of Charles Thulin left Mary and her two unmarried daughters, Elin and Lillie, to cobble together a Depression-era income. They converted their home, the much renovated and expanded first store of 1904–05, into a residential hotel they called Thulin Court. Elin applied to fill her late father's position as post master, and though she had carried out all the duties for years as "assistant post master," the coveted political plum was awarded to a man from out of town. Her sister Lillie, a determined woman with an innate business sense, took the lead in family business affairs, stepping into the role of property manager. When the Depression eased in the latter part of the 1930s, Lillie began what was to prove a highly successful career in real estate.

In 1932, the year Charles Thulin passed away, a newcomer arrived who was to become a vital champion of the woods, lakes and rivers of the Discovery Coast. Roderick Haig-Brown's original plan had been to work in Washington state as a temporary transition between a traditional English public school education and his launch into a career in the foreign service. When a temporary logging job took him to the Nimpkish River in 1927, Haig-Brown was a young man with no particular focus. A year on the river brought him to both his natural home and his life's work—expressing his passion for the woods and rivers of British Columbia as a writer, sportsman and conservationist. In about 1930, Haig-Brown left the Nimpkish and fulfilled a family obligation by returning to England, but after yearning for and writing about BC he was back in 1932 and ready to tackle a book on BC's elusive predator, the cougar. Following in the tracks of the renowned cougar hunter Cecil Smith, Haig-Brown gathered material for a story told through the eyes of a cougar.

For a man contemplating marriage to a Seattle debutante, Campbell River offered a modicum of civilized convenience on the edge of his beloved coastal wilderness. Roderick Haig-Brown and Ann (Elmore) took up residence in a cottage on "Uncle Reg" Pidcock's property on the Campbell in 1934[7] and later bought the adjoining Herbert and Dolly Pidcock property. From his study overlooking the river Haig-Brown wrote twenty-seven books and countless articles woven from his complex understanding of the natural world. The Pidcock/Haig-Brown home is now a heritage site in use as a bed and breakfast and public education centre.

Roderick Haig-Brown, Campbell River's best-known resident, c. 1930. He came to BC to work for a logging company on the Nimpkish River in the late 1920s, and revelled in the fabulous hunting and fishing to be had on the coast—a sportsman's paradise that deepened his respect for the natural world. Haig-Brown went on to express these convictions in many books and articles, and in determined campaigns to preserve wildlife habitats threatened by pollution and development. *Edgar Landsdown Collection, MCR 9403*

Throughout the Depression there remained a solid core of well-heeled sporting enthusiasts eager to fish the famous tyee pools at the mouth of the Campbell River. Working as a fishing guide was an important secondary income for many Campbell Riverites.

The guides who worked for the Painters over the years amassed a treasure trove of lively memories of the fast and famous, from the Marx Brothers to Zane Grey. The most exciting party to visit in the 1930s was the entourage of the King and Queen of Siam (now Thailand). They were brought to town by Herbert Pidcock, Chairman of the Board of Trade, which had been formed in 1930 to promote tourism. Everyone in town was dragged into the media-hyped extravaganza of catered meals and guided fishing trips for the royal party. The elite of the Discovery Passage guides, keen to promote their livelihood, donated their time. For the two days the party stayed in the district both Herbert Pidcock and Cecil FitzGerald guided the King, with various others including Chief Johnny Quocksister, Dan Assu and John Perkins Sr., guiding other members of the royal party. The Queen's early catch remained the largest taken, though the King extended their visit in an attempt to meet or exceed her luck.

Darrell Smith (nephew to Herbert and

In 1936 Ann and Roderick Haig-Brown purchased Marguerite (Dolly) and Herbert Pidcock's home and acreage on the banks of the Campbell River. The Haig-Brown house is now a heritage site owned by the province and operated as a bed and breakfast and education centre. *Ann Haig-Brown Collection, MCR 12735*

Dolly Pidcock) laughingly recounted stories of his client, a sixteen-year-old prince who lost interest in fishing toward the end of a full day in the boat. "He asked if he could try rowing and I said, 'absolutely,' so I got back in the swivel chair and took the rod, and the prince he rowed the boat and I sat back there and fished. So I can honestly say I was taken fishing by a prince!"

As the Depression finally began to ease in the late 1930s the district experienced one of the most disastrous events imaginable for an economy dominated by the forest industry.

The summer of 1938 was exceptionally hot and, in hindsight, critics said the government should have called for a full shutdown of all logging camps. But mindful of the fact that such a move would put hundreds of men out of work, the authorities allowed the large camps to keep working. On July 5, when sparks from a passing train at the Bloedel, Stewart & Welch camp

Herbert Pidcock guiding the King of Siam (now Thailand), 1931. The royal party thoroughly enjoyed their fishing trip to Campbell River, in spite of the fact that no one in the extensive family group landed a tyee (a fish over 30 pounds/13.5 kg). The Queen of Siam caught the largest fish taken during the holiday, which was hosted by the Campbell River Board of Trade. *Pidcock Collection, MCR 11100*

between Gosling and Boot Lakes ignited in a cold deck (a stack of logs ready to load), a small fire quickly became an out-of-control blaze.

As the fire gained momentum, men reported seeing snags burning like great roman candles and balls of flame "crowning"—leaping through the air at an estimated 90 miles an hour (144 km/h) to reach fresh timber. Boot and Gosling Lakes were nearly drained and Loveland Lake dropped four feet as water was pumped into the flames.

The police rounded up all the young men in the district and sent them to fight the fire alongside the loggers, who were organized into crews, digging firebreaks in an effort to try and direct the blaze. As the fire escalated, 100 unemployed men were brought in from Vancouver to assist, while hundreds of other unemployed men there mounted a huge protest and occupied three downtown buildings. Makeshift quarters were arranged for them at a tent camp by the Campbell River bridge.

Margaret Thulin made 250 lunches at the Bee Hive Cafe, along with huge vats of coffee prepared in wash boilers. As the blaze continued to spread, two Navy ships were anchored offshore at Duncan Bay, ready for a call to evacuate Campbell River. Townsfolk buried their prized possessions in their backyards, but the fire skirted the town, narrowly missing Elk Falls Park (thanks to hastily prepared windbreaks and trenches), and swept out of control toward Courtenay.

Residents and loggers had a vested interest in attempting to stop the fire, but the unemployed men from Vancouver were unused to the gruelling work of building trenches and barricades. Forbes Landing Lodge, in the path of the blaze, was one of the firefighting headquarters until the lodge itself came under threat. The family turned their attention to saving the lodge, and when

Smoke and ash from the Great Sayward Fire, sometimes known as the Bloedel Fire (as seen at the Campbell River estuary), drifted as far as Seattle, Washington, as the fire spread from behind Campbell River to Forbidden Plateau in the summer of 1938. The town of Campbell River was spared, but 74,495 acres (30,000 ha) of prime timberland was left a smoking ruin. The fire started when sparks from a train ignited a pile of logs. *BC Archives NA-06497 OR MCR 16835*

the place seemed secure all but young Gordon Forbes retreated to Vancouver. Had they been at hand when the fire once again turned toward the lodge, it would have made little difference, for when the hoses and pumps were hooked up there was no response. Saboteurs, thought to be some of the malcontents from Vancouver, had cut the hoses and filled the water pumps with sugar. The beautiful resort was a complete loss.

John Hough, head lineman and troubleshooter for N.W. Telephone Company, was caught in the second fire at Forbes Landing, along with his fourteen-year-old son. They made a narrow escape when the Elk River Timber Company sent in a crummy covered with wet gunny sacks. Exhausted by their experience, they walked from Campbellton to the telephone company

Unemployed men were brought in from Vancouver, where a huge protest was taking place, to fight the Great Sayward Fire. They were given their meals and beds on the ground. *BCARS NA 06458*

The bleak landscape after the fire. *BCARS NA 06497*

Forbes Landing Lodge, a long-standing family business on Lower Campbell Lake, was destroyed during the Great Sayward Fire of 1938. When the pumps and hoses were mustered to keep the blaze away from the lodge, firefighters discovered that saboteurs had filled the pumps with sugar and slashed the hoses. The protestors who had been brought in from Vancouver were generally believed to be the culprits. *Elizabeth Forbes Collection, MCR 7711*

office in Campbell River to call for transportation back to Courtenay, where they found the only line in use by a young reporter. The smoke and ash of the fire largely bypassed the town, but when Pierre Berton telephoned in his report, he added dramatic emphasis with frequent coughs and a muffling cover over the telephone mouthpiece.[8]

The fire spread southward and the sky was blackened as far away as Seattle, where people reported sweeping ash from their cars. Finally, after six weeks, the weather changed and the Great Sayward Fire petered out, climbing toward Forbidden Plateau. Eustace Smith and a team of timber cruisers were called in to assess what remained of the timber in a burned-over wasteland of 74,495 acres (30,000 ha).

As a result of the fire, a massive tree-planting project was initiated in parts of the burnt and logged-over lands, and Bloedel, Stewart & Welch were confronted with lawsuits and tremendous corporate losses.

The first large-scale tree-planting operation in the area was undertaken after the Great Sayward Fire.
BCARS H-03103

The devastating effects of the Great Sayward Fire paled by comparison with the atrocities taking place in Europe, where Germany was once again on the march. Within a year of the fire, Canada joined its British allies in the fight to stop the rise of fascism. A relatively small number of north Vancouver Island men were allowed to enlist for the war. Jobs such as logging, fishing and ranching were classed as essential services. Whatever a man's moral and political convictions, if he was working in these fields, he was required to stay at home and sustain production.

Signal corps members leaving Campbell River to train for World War II service. *Amber (Bayer) Jontz Collection, MCR 18267*

Though war brought worry and restraint, it also initiated a period of sustained growth and full employment for both men and women, a welcome relief after the long stretch of the Depression years. For the majority there was a rewarding sense of purpose attached to the sacrifices required by the war effort.

Seven of the area's vital young men died overseas. Each sad telegram announcing a death reignited the grief shared throughout the district.

Another grim reality of the time, marked in this case by a resonating silence, was the political decision to evacuate all Japanese Canadian residents from the coast. The announcement was made in 1942 as a reaction to the bombing of Pearl Harbor and the general escalation of Japan's ambitious war campaign. Canadian military and police officials opposed the idea of evacuation but political pressure prevailed. Long-standing racial tension, propelled by a very real fear for the vulnerable BC coast, ruled the hearts and emotions of Canadians. Later, in hindsight, many found themselves in silent opposition to the scale of the measures taken. The right and wrong of the decision to remove Japanese Canadians and strip them of their property for a nominal return was blurred by the awful reality of war.

For others the war was an opportunity to advance a long-standing push for racial homogeneity. Shortly before internment was announced, the local member of parliament, A.W. Neill, made his stand on the "Japanese Question" abundantly clear. Playing upon the prevailing sentiment that Japanese Canadians were potential traitors, Neill stated, "Fifty years from now, unless something is done to stop it, all west of the Rockies will be yellow."

Neill's views, at least on a plan for removing the Japanese from the coast, were generally supported by fishermen. Japanese Canadian fishermen, working in this highly competitive industry, pooled information and fished together in exclusive clusters at favoured fishing spots. In the dog-eat-dog environment of commercial fishing even the Japanese Canadians' beautifully built boats, constructed by master craftsmen like Kiyomatsu Atagi, were held against them as an unfairly gained upper hand.

As the fear of a Japanese attack on the hard-to-defend BC coast escalated during World War II, all Canadians of Japanese descent were interned away from the coast, many of them in makeshift camps. Their fishing boats and other possessions were seized and sold. *R. Lewis Collection, MCR 17257*

When the long-anticipated evacuation notice was delivered to the Atagi home on Quadra Island, Kane Atagi stood quietly at the doorway watching the receding back of a stranger, the Victoria police officer who had brought the notice. Kane and her husband Kiyomatsu had twelve hours in which to pack their personal belongings—whatever would fit—in two suitcases and a clutch bag apiece. Kane's hard-won accomplishments as a Canadian citizen disappeared as she watched the police officer continue his grim round.

It had been twenty-seven years since this delicate-seeming woman had begun her Canadian life attached to the Quathiaski Cannery and her husband's job as a boat builder. Coming from a privileged background, Kane faced the multiple challenges of learning domestic chores while adapting to an unfamiliar language and environment. Her efforts to learn English using her children's school texts gave Kane what her children called a "dictionary" accent, but nonetheless she had become conversant in English.

Kane and Kiyomatsu Atagi clung to the police officer's prediction that they would only be detained for a few months, but they knew their fate was uncertain. They sold off some of their possessions to friends and closed up their comfortable home and boat-building workshop. According to their daughter, Ayako (Atagi) Higashi, while they were in enforced exile in the Kootenays, the government sold their property.

> The [BC Security] Commission rented my father's boathouse to someone, but they always needed more than the rent to make necessary repairs to the machinery and the buildings, which were in tip-top condition when Dad left. The Commission had access to our bank account and just took what it wanted when they wished. One day the Commission asked for our deed to the house and property. My father respectfully replied that he did not want to sell...However, the Commission told us that it was selling the property and would draw up a new deed, and that he could just throw away our deed—it was no longer relevant.[9]

The issue of whether or not to allow the Japanese Canadians to return to the coast was hotly debated for four years beyond war's end. Their welfare was championed by a vocal minority, including Rod Haig-Brown:

> The feeling against the Japanese is at present so blind, so widespread and so cruelly expressed out here that it may not be in their best interests to return at the present time, even in small numbers...This is a matter for shame since it shows that we have not learned the first principle of democracy, which is tolerance of minorities...I asked the Member to approach any discriminatory action he felt forced to take at Ottawa with a sense of failure and humility and with a resolve that at all costs his action should not set any precedent for further persecution of minorities. I asked him to remember the extent of human suffering already caused.[10]

Japanese Canadians were finally granted permission to return to the coast in 1949, but very few came back to this district. Most, like the Atagis, were not prepared to once again reshape their lives.

Meanwhile, in 1942, Rod Haig-Brown was appointed country magistrate for a 10,000-square-mile (26,000 sq km) radius surrounding Campbell River, having been pressed by a local constable to put his name forward.

> I came into the job in what seemed to me an extraordinarily casual way, simply because there was no one else around who wanted to take it on...At thirty I felt far too young—magistrates should be old and wise and grey.
>
> "It's mostly by the book," the Corporal said. "And what isn't written down is just common sense. You owe it to the country anyway—you've got the education and the time."
>
> I heard my first case on the day I took the oath. I sat at a desk, feeling small and confused, flanked by two magnificent policemen in the imposing uniform of the Provincial force.[11]

From this casual and intimidating beginning, Haig-Brown went on to become a highly respected judge known for his fairness and compassion.

During the war, Haig-Brown was also made a commanding officer of 200 "rangers" in the Pacific Coast Militia Rangers (PCMR), formed as a home guard in response to the fear of a Japanese attack. Other local units preparing to defend the coast were the Air Raid Patrol and the fishermen's contingent, dubbed the Gumboot Navy. About 10,000 volunteers for the PCMR were issued uniforms and rifles and trained in guerrilla warfare tactics. Martin Fossum, bull bucker at Bloedel, Stewart & Welch's Camp 5, recalls: "Active training was held after working hours and during weekends. Sometimes it proved quite rough and rugged—crawling flat on our bellies through swamps and underbrush with heavy equipment on our backs. We became quite efficient with Sten guns, Bren guns (a machine gun) and 30-30 rifles."[12]

Wages were locked in at a relatively low rate during the war but so were the prices of basic commodities. Labour unions like the International Woodworkers of America (IWA), which had become the major union for the logging industry, agreed to observe a standoff on strikes until war's end. Strong markets for wood, full employment and the union's support for World War II conscription led to big increases in union membership and public empathy in spite of the wartime freeze.

A maverick in the logging industry, Alfred Simpson, was the first employer in BC to sign a bargaining agreement with the IWA.[13] Simpson professed limited knowledge of logging when he took over a marginal operation at Iron River during the war years, but he turned the company into a success. To create a booming ground on the exposed curve of sandy beach at Oyster Bay he dragged in a fleet of ruined ships to create a breakwater, which the locals dubbed Simpson's Folly. Eventually the breakwater included fifteen hulks: sailing ships of the last century like the *St. Paul* (once a swanky American gambling vessel), several defunct Union Steamship Company boats, a whaler, coastal traders and decommissioned naval ships.

Iron River Logging Company at Oyster Bay erected a breakwater made from the hulls of old ships, including a World War I destroyer, the *President Burns*, and a four-masted sailing ship, the *St. Paul*, which arrived at Oyster Bay complete with spars, yardarms and a "wonderfully carved" figurehead of a woman with flowing hair. *Baldwin Collection, MCR 13294*

Shortly after Simpson signed the bargaining agreement in 1944 he sold out to H.R. MacMillan. Whether or not he liked it, H.R. had to negotiate with the IWA, whose push for better wages and working conditions resulted in a strike at war's end. MacMillan's wartime views on the union movement, published in a biography written by Ken Drushka, were surprisingly astute: "I have a feeling that we are quickly heading into a new era also in labour relations and cost of production. We are too far out of line with some American practices, rates of pay, and overtime; therefore it would appear that because of active and well-informed leadership of the workers...we will have to be brought up to [American] levels." The thirty-eight-day strike resulted in significant gains, a forty-hour week, a pay hike and a huge boost in union membership which, as a result of the strike, became the largest union in the province.

Menzies Bay continued to be the nucleus of the largest logging operations on the coast. Various small-scale companies rose and fell in the decades prior to World War II, consumed by rising conglomerate corporations. In 1939, H.R. MacMillan bought the bankrupt Campbell River Timber Company, operating a 200-man camp out of Menzies Bay.[14] Bloedel, Stewart & Welch (which later became MacMillan Bloedel) established Camp 5 in 1943. It provided housing for 550 men and 63 families at Brewster Lake. By the end of the war the operation had 70 miles (112 km) of mainline and spur tracks in use.

H.R. MacMillan also owned a controlling interest in the BC Packers Company, which bought the Quathiaski Canning Company in 1937. The cannery had been a steady success for its previous owner, W.E. Anderson. When his failing health forced him to sell, Anderson invited his top fishermen to decide among themselves which company he should sell to. According to Harry Assu of Cape Mudge the decision was difficult, but eventually the majority decided upon BC Packers as their preferred new employer.

Four years later, at the height of the packing season, the cannery burst into flames. Ruby (Hovell) Wilson recalls being jarred from sleep by repeated warning blasts from the cannery whistle on August 29, 1941. She was at term in her first pregnancy, so Ruby sat tight in her cannery shack while the young women around her ran to the cannery to untie the boats from the dock, reserving Ruby's father's boat for rounding them up. But when Mr. Hovell's little Easthope motor failed to respond, Ruby was called to the scene to help. Unfortunately local residents had not responded to the cannery whistle, thinking it was simply a call to work. The small crew fighting the fire had given up on the cannery, which was completely engulfed in flames, and were concentrating on saving the net loft: "Years ago my dad had taught my niece and me to run his seven-horse Easthope [and] that came in handy when the cannery burnt. I finally got it going and watched them [rescue] two boats. I was on my way back to my little shack [when] I slipped because it was so watery there and that's the last thing I remember. The next thing I knew I had a baby; she came early. She was three days old before I saw her...before I became really conscious; they had me sedated. The girls saved all the gas boats, picked them all up and tied them to the little island there."[15]

The cannery was a complete loss. The former owner, W.E. Anderson, who died just prior to the fire, would have suffered enormous regret but H.R. MacMillan likely saw it as a passing annoyance. His company was consolidating their operations into a few central locations so the Quathiaski Cannery was not replaced.

For women, the loss of the cannery was a major blow to their economic independence. Most women worked on a production basis, trimming fish to fit cans on "the line." Some of them, like

Ruby Wilson, started out with the cannery as children, earning 15 cents per hour delivering baskets of empty cans to be filled by their mothers and aunts. For those who were fast with their hands, the job brought decent returns. Many men continued on as commercial fishermen after the fire, transferring fish to the big packer boats sent up to the Cove on a regular basis, but for women there were no equivalent jobs in the community.

W.E. Anderson's failing health made it necessary for him to sell the Quathiaski Canning Company in 1937. He invited his highline fishermen to choose between several potential buyers, and after some discussion they settled upon BC Packers. This photograph of the cannery was taken in 1935. *Margaret Yorke Collection, MCR 19520*

Ranching and farming, though a minor aspect of the coastal economy by the 1940s, were classed as essential services during the war. Alf Vanstone, son of one of the district's early logging operators and entrepreneurs, tried to enlist when his brother Dave was killed overseas. But, as his wife Ramona recalls, he was promptly sent back to the family farm to "grow more beef cattle" after one day in the army recruiting centre.

A few large seaside farms and ranches between Oyster Bay and Willow Point maintained production throughout the

When Quathiaski Cannery was destroyed by fire in 1941, women like Eve (Willson) Eade lost a source of local employment—working "on the line," trimming fish to fit the cans. *Eve (Willson) Eade Collection, MCR 17410* war. What is now the UBC Experimental Farm was a pansy seed farm (supplying a US market) owned by Darrell and Guy Smith, the third generation of the Amelia and Horace Smith family of Black Creek. The area's oldest ranch, started by the Knights at what is now the Island Highway and Engels Road, was in the hands of the McGimpseys. The Storie family sold milk and produce from their long-established ranch at Stories Beach as did the Swanskys, to the north, at Erickson Road.

George and Margaret Adams gave up prairie farming to establish a store and gas station at Willow Point in 1939. By the war years their store and a community hall built in 1940 was becoming the hub for a new business centre. Bill Erickson donated the land for the hall, which remains in use. The late Dorothy Edmonds, who lived at the Simms' dairy ranch at what is now Hilchey Road, remembered an attempt to "pave" the road at Willow Point by slicking it down with clay mined from a site below "the big hill" leading up to what is now 1st Avenue.

Clay surfacing was a crude acknowledgement of the importance of transportation improvements required for war-era production. Two such projects, the subject of years of intensive lobbying, were finally achieved in the early 1940s. A road connection linking Sayward and the logging camps north of Campbell River to the rest of Vancouver Island was accomplished with relative ease, but the removal of old Ripple Rock, a lurking menace in the main shipping lane for the coast, wasn't an easy fix.

Local fishermen, for the most part, had learned by white-knuckle experience how and when to navigate Seymour Narrows, skirting around the jagged twin peaks of Ripple Rock by holding to the Maud Island shore at slack tide. But awaiting the change of tide and sidling around Ripple Rock was not cost-effective for the international traffic entirely dependent upon the Inside Passage during the war years. When the Americans registered a strenuous complaint, tenders were put out in 1941 to "decapitate" Ripple Rock.

The British Columbia Bridge and Dredging Company of Vancouver won the contract and plans were formulated in 1943 for a surface attack. A scow was built to accommodate the drilling crew, whose mission was to bore multiple holes for explosives. Concrete anchors weighing 250 tons (225 tonnes) each were sunk on either shore and heavy steel cables were strung across the Narrows to hold the barge in place. The *Argus* reported that the cables immediately proved insufficient for the task. "Vibrating uncontrollably in the riptide [they] snapped like threads!'" Try as they might, little progress was made. By summer's end the project was dropped. Numerous alternate plans were suggested, from torpedoes to dropping an atomic bomb on the rock. One wild proposal suggested tunnelling in from beneath the rock to set explosives in place, an idea that was immediately rejected.

Work began in 1945 on a second attempt which offered only a minor variation on the 1943 approach. This time 10-ton (9-tonne) cables were fixed to "spar trees" on either shore to secure the cables in the air above the tidal action. But this arrangement proved as futile as the first, and just as engineers were once again considering alternative plans yet another tragic accident was added to the toll at Ripple Rock.

When the shift ended on March 11, the men working near Maud Island attempted to leave the job site at full flood tide in a boat that was later deemed to be entirely inadequate. In a flash the 28-foot fishing boat, of shallow beam and overloaded, was sucked into a giant whirlpool. Two men somehow managed to pluck hold of the boat's guy wires and hang on as the vessel

Several attempts were made in the early 1940s to bore holes into the surface of the treacherous Ripple Rock, so that explosives could be inserted. But the racing tides of Seymour Narrows defeated these projects, and the 1945 attempt resulted in a tragic loss of life. BCARS G-03794

plunged into the vortex. One of the survivors, M.E. Nilson of Vancouver, described his lucky escape to an *Argus* reporter:

> "It happened in a second," Nilson said. "All of a sudden the boat was over and the men were in the water. The tide was at the flood then, exceptionally strong." Nilson and Mohlan, clinging tenaciously to a guy wire, were whipped about in the water as the fury of the whirlpool tossed the boat over and over. The crew working at the Nymphe Cove end of the project, discovered the tragedy as they nosed out from the cove in their boat for Menzies Bay. William Beech, in charge of the rescue boat...disembarked his passengers and then with two other men, sped to the scene...
>
> Nilson told Constable MacAlpine how he and Mohlan escaped. He was sitting in the cabin of the gasboat when he suddenly felt the craft heel over and the cabin filled with water. He leaped out and when he broke the surface he was alongside the partially overturned hull of the gasboat. He grabbed a guy wire and held on, noting that Mohlan was hanging on to the other end of the boat.

Stan Beech recalls that by the time his brother William had unloaded his passengers, the fishing boat had righted itself and was drifting towards Race Point, where it was possible to retrieve Mohlan and Nilson from the wreck. The bodies of the other nine men were never recovered.

The useless work of blasting away at the surface of the rock continued after the accident, but at summer's end the project was dropped, not to be taken up again for nearly a decade.

Building a road as far as Sayward in 1944 was a more manageable task, simply requiring linkages between an existing network of logging railway grades, as well as forty-seven trestles to create one contiguous route. There were about 100 permanent residents living in the Kelsey Bay area in the 1940s, along with numerous transient loggers and their families. All told, approximately 250 men were working for Salmon River Logging, under Dewey Anderson, who arranged a celebration for the opening of the road. A cavalcade of motorists from Victoria and points north attended a feast at Anderson's boom camp, prepared by Stanley Major, former chef at the Harrison Hot Springs Hotel. The assembled guests still recall the dishes served: "tasty appetizers, turkeys, tongues, cold meats, cakes, jelly rolls and other creations," which Anderson described in his welcoming speech as "just a few leftovers from the regular camp meal." There were lamb roasts "got up" into the shape of ducks or swans and jelly rolls made to look like logs—"bark, knots, everything." Campbell River could no longer claim the distinction of being at the end of the road.

For most of the residents of Discovery Passage the war years were a busy time when people lived for the moment. As part of war measures, residents were required to carry documentation ready for random security checks, and food and beverage rationing dictated inventive new ways of cooking. Butter, sugar, coffee, meat, tea, gasoline and alcohol were all rationed, and consumption was controlled by coupons. Logging camps, where platters of beef were considered vital, were the only exemption to meat allocations. But limits were placed upon the men's thirst for spirits, as the Campbell River writer Helen Mitchell later recalled:

> Beer and liquor were strictly rationed so when the [Union steamship] hove into sight the bartenders at the Willows Hotel promptly closed their taps, to save their rations for the local customers, and the thirsty passengers who sprinted up the gangplank in search of a cool one were forced to control their impatience and wait till their journey's end. The Quinsam Hotel, being a little off the beaten track, didn't close as often and if the ship was going to be in port an hour or more, the more enterprising of the passengers taxied out to Campbellton for a quick one. The only trouble was that, unless the wind was just right, the toot, indicating the vessel was leaving in 15 to 30 minutes, couldn't be heard out there, and many a logger found the ship long gone by the time he made his way back to the dock.[16]

There were no quotas on the excitement that followed the armistice announcement of May 8, 1945. Constable MacAlpine spread the news far and wide—running past Elk River in his power boat, he hollered out to John Perkins, Jr. and his co-workers, "The war is over in Europe!" The next day was a full holiday for everyone, and amid the celebration a rumour spread, sourced to R.J. ("Bob") Filberg of Comox Logging Company, that there was "something big" in the works for Campbell River.

CHAPTER 8

The Smell of Money
1945–1969

"It might be said that the story of this bustling town [of Campbell River] revolves around giants. Giant trees! Giant fish! Giant river and falls! Giant industries! Yes, and even giants among men!"

—C.P. Lyons, 1958

Just as World War II was coming to a close, Premier John Hart made an announcement that touched off an explosion of development in Campbell River. The government's campaign to utilize the technological advances of the war years included a "rural electrification program" to ensure "every farm kitchen would have an electric washer, toaster, ironer, and all the other appliances of a modern city home." The beautiful rush of water at Elk Falls, long the subject of testing and scheming, would be dammed by the newly formed BC Power Commission. At first the dam was described as a domestic power source, but within months of the premier's announcement the scale of the project expanded to a series of dams, making it the main power source for much of Vancouver Island. The ability to tame and control this magnificent environment, which had stamped a determined individuality into the lives of its people, was now within the grasp of provincial leaders and corporations.

Mike King, timberman and entrepreneur of the 1890s, would have enjoyed seeing the realization of his long-ago vision for industrial development at Duncan Bay, powered by hydro generated from Elk Falls. The sneering tone of editorials in the Courtenay newspaper of King's era gave way in the mid-1940s to patronizing approval: "Campbell River has definitely shed her swaddling clothes and can honestly look to the future with confidence."

R.J. Filberg of the Comox Logging Company had much in common with old Mike King. Filberg is thought to have been behind the government's final selection of the Campbell River (over their originally preferred site on the Nanaimo River) as a major power source for Vancouver Island.

Aerial view of Campbell River and Discovery Passage, looking north to Seymour Narrows, 1947—a time when the district faced enormous change and growth. A massive hydroelectricity project was installed in phases in the Campbell River watershed. *Jim Haigh Collection, MCR 16790*

According to an electrical contractor, Len Rossiter, "Filberg had probably already gone to them [the BC Power Commission] and told them that there was something in the wind on a mill to go in at Duncan Bay." Though Filberg did not make any public announcements on the subject for several years, rumours of a mill continued to circulate as he obligingly allowed the BC Power Commission to use his company's Duncan Bay property as a terminus for off-loading heavy equipment for the hydro project.

Filberg's life story is yet another rags-to-riches tale. By the 1940s he was a powerful force in BC business circles, his "boot strap" achievements having been gained through skill and a winning personality. At the age of seventeen, the Seattle lad took a job as a surveyor's assistant at Campbell River and Union Bay. Within a few years he was hired by the Comox Logging Company, a subsidiary of the Vancouver-based Canadian Western Lumber Company, where he began a long career that would elevate him to the company's top echelons.

A key strength for Filberg was his ability to garner the respect and appreciation of those around him, including the boss's daughter, Flossie McCormack, whom he married in 1916. Soon after his marriage Filberg was promoted from the engineering crew to logging superintendent at Comox, and by the late 1930s he was director for the parent company, Canadian Western.[1]

The rumours about Duncan Bay were officially confirmed in 1947. The project involved both the Canadian Western Lumber Company and the Comox Logging Company, working in collaboration with Crown Zellerbach to develop a "wood processing mill." The partners neatly divided their spheres of interest. Filberg was to manage the logging operations, and Crown Zellerbach would look after the milling end of the business, as an adjunct to their Ocean Falls plant.

Crown Zellerbach, a giant US paper manufacturing firm, was not a newcomer to the Campbell River scene. As Crown Willamette the company held the water rights on the Campbell system through most of the 1920s. Their plan, stalled by the Depression, had been to develop a commercial hydro plant and open a paper mill.

With a government supply of electrical power now assured, the next item of business for the Elk Falls Mill partnership was securing a local timber source. According to the logging historian

Ken Drushka, Filberg lobbied hard to acquire one of the province's first Forest Management Licences (FML) to supply the mill. This controversial new licensing system, which favoured large companies, gave Comox Logging long-term control over 200,000 acres (80,000 ha) of timber, mainly on the islands in Johnstone Strait. They were required to manage the forest under the new "perpetual yield" system, which restricted them from active logging until the 1970s. Meanwhile they were free to take the dead and fallen "junk wood" to be processed at the mill. The small operators and gyppo loggers protested vigorously, but the government closed the deal in order to secure the new mill. As the gyppos predicted, the move destroyed a way of life and the economy of the islands, which had long supported an independent population based on logging.

Things were shifting on every level following the war, above and below ground. On the quiet Sunday morning of June 23, 1946, an earthquake took North Island residents by surprise, sending them leaping from their beds, tractors and Sunday school classes to flee the effects of a quake measuring 7.2 on the Richter scale.

It was fortunate the earthquake occurred on a sleepy Sunday morning, leaving empty school desks and grocery store aisles to bear the brunt of the havoc. A Campbell River Sunday school was a blessed exception. Milton MacAlpine, a police officer, reported: "the minister continued the prayer until the last child had left and reached a safe distance from the building, then the chimney toppled down in the doorway through which the children had passed."

The district was littered with fallen chimneys following the quake. Householders watched in awe from the safety of their yards as their chimneys arched back and forth like giant dancers before crashing to the ground. Gaping chasms appeared in roads, dykes and farm fields, but the wreckage resulted in only one death. The thirty-second quake left the north islanders a lifetime of vivid memories and humorous tales, including one by Tom Hall: "One of the stories going around was about an old man we called Heart Attack Harry who was riding his bike back down the highway to his home in Willow Point. He'd had a few heart attacks and when he began to have trouble keeping his balance and steering he got off the bicycle and lay down on the ground. A passerby asked him, 'Are you having a heart attack?' He replied, 'Well, if I'm having one, my bicycle is having one too.'"

Ray Compton, whose home was in the centre of town, had just started his day when "everything started to shake, rattle and roll. Larry, our son, started yelling, 'God's blessing from Heaven.' I grabbed the goldfish bowl and ran outside. Everyone was outside; some had no clothes on. My car, a Dodge taxi, was rolling back and forth. Our neighbour, Jack Prout, was trying to stop the car by holding it away from his shack."

Don Corker recalls hearing about an elderly couple in the Willow Point area, "who had just installed an electric fence to keep roaming cattle out of their garden. On that Sunday morning the irate gardener discovered the cattle trying to get through the fence and turned the switch on. Suddenly the house and everything in it started to shake. 'Quick!' yelled his wife, 'turn that thing off before you shake the house down!'"

Dave Malloy watched a river of liquor run out from under the door of the liquor store in Courtenay, and Herbert Joyce leapt off his moving tractor as his Quadra Island farm field rolled beneath him like the swells of a heavy sea. One fellow, after a drunken night of carousing, wakened during the quake to marvel at what he thought was a particularly violent hangover, popped two aspirins and went back to bed.

The earthquake of June 23, 1946, toppled chimneys and ripped gaping chasms into roads, dykes and farm fields such as the Marshall property on Read Island. *Hayes Collection, MCR 5676*

The 1946 quake, which measured 7.2 on the Richter scale, caused the end of Rebecca Spit (now a provincial park on Quadra Island) to slump down into the sea. *D. Clandenning Collection, MCR 12965*

Next year, in December 1947, Premier John Hart sent power zinging through the lines of the giant hydroelectric development above Elk Falls as he flipped the switch inaugurating "the electric age for Vancouver Island."

Roderick Haig-Brown watched the event with concern, later reflecting that the government's master plan for successive levels of dams on the Campbell system took him off guard.[2] The capacity of the first dam was increased in 1949, leaving behind a mess of dead standing timber and floating debris on Lower Campbell Lake. In 1951 the BC Power Commission began work on the Ladore Dam, and a year later there was talk of a third dam to be built in the headwaters of the Campbell River system on Buttle Lake, much of which is in Strathcona Park. It was this announcement that sparked a reaction from Roderick Haig-Brown and others from across the country who valued the pristine wilderness of BC's first major park.

Constructing one of a series of hydroelectricity dams on the Campbell River watershed in the late 1940s through the early 1950s. *Phyllis Allen Collection, MCR 20106-157*

Mrs. McDonald, an eighty-one-year-old descendant of John Buttle, the man who had first charted the beautiful lake in 1865, made an impassioned plea. "My father, as long as he lived," she claimed, "vowed that lake was the most beautiful sight he ever saw." She went on to say, having last made the trek into the remote lake in her late seventies: "I would defend that place, for the sake of future generations, with my life if I could. It's all wrong to dam Buttle for a few filthy dollars and take away the heritage of the children of tomorrow... This isn't an agricultural country, and when our timber and minerals have been exhausted, we will have nothing but a wasteland."[3]

Roderick Haig-Brown threw himself heart and soul into the fight to save Buttle Lake, where the water level would be raised by about 50 feet (15 m). "I am afraid for the wonderland of Strathcona Park because its fate lies with a Cabinet of dreary old men who have lost their capacity for wonder, if indeed they ever had any," said Haig-Brown.[4] After more than four years of

The government's plan to build a dam on Buttle Lake in the early 1950s incensed people who valued the pristine beauty of the lake and Strathcona Park. They mounted one of the province's first environmental campaigns, the Battle of the Buttle, which ended in a partial victory for conservationists.
Hughes Collection, MCR 10135

protest, mainly championed by organizations like the Affiliated Fish and Game Clubs of Vancouver Island, conservationists won a narrow victory. The government agreed to locate the third dam on Upper Campbell Lake instead of Buttle Lake, with about 20 feet (6 m) of flooding projected for the latter as reserve storage. Haig-Brown was outraged that flooding, simply to create a reserve, was still in the plans: "Strathcona, the most accessible, most highly protected park in the Province had been destroyed as easily as this. A sleepy cabinet is being allowed by an apathetic public to sell out the finest park in British Columbia for a few miserable kilowatts...The storage that will damage the park is merely the tag end of a considerable project. It is 'necessary' only as an additional subsidy to pulp and paper companies...[This] will destroy every natural beach and landing spot along the lake shore. It will destroy most of the trout spawning areas by flooding every creek mouth. It will flood out the magnificent timber flats of Wolf, Marble, Myra, Phillips and other streams..."[5]

The flooding of Buttle Lake was not to be stopped. Concessions were made, the shoreline was cleared and new beaches were created. When the dams were complete, what had once been a chain of three pristine lakes, connected by miles of river, was now one massive lake covering 800 acres (320 ha). The three rivers (Elk, Salmon and Quinsam), enriching thousands of acres of timber and supporting major salmon runs, were diverted into the hydro system.

Roderick Haig-Brown's colleague and friend, Arthur Mayse, felt the "ravaging of his river" broke Haig-Brown's heart and his fighting spirit. But Rod's son Alan says his father's perspective on the "Battle of the Buttle" has been a continuing source of inspiration to him as he, in turn, continues to champion environmental causes: "When the word came that the dam would be built

Burning timber on Lower Campbell Lake, August 1947, during the construction of the John Hart Dam.
Arthur Price Collection, MCR 6634

I said, 'You lost, eh?' He very carefully and thoughtfully answered to the effect, 'No, we didn't lose. We got them to move the dam down to Upper Campbell, which was already logged, and flood it back into Buttle raising it only 18 feet. While this is a great loss of that virgin forested lakeshore, we have shown that the public can influence the developers. People will take heart from this and go on to fight against ignorant developments."

The Battle of the Buttle was one of the first major conservation campaigns in the province. The relatively small band who fought the hydro project learned many valuable lessons, which were to be applied throughout the coming years. The driving motivation of people like Haig-Brown and his protégé Ruth Masters was a passion nurtured by years of active enjoyment of the lakes, mountains and forests. As hikers, hunters, trappers, fishers and mountaineers they developed a complex knowledge that made their arguments, calling for a balance of economic and wilderness values, hard to ignore.

Electric power for the masses was just one of a number of modernization goals actively pursued following the war. Transportation improvements also changed the economic future for Campbell River. In 1945 community leaders stepped up their campaign for a new breakwater and wharf, sending a flamboyant pile-driver operator named Frank Gagne to Ottawa, where he persuaded the government to fund the project. With Campbell River poised at last to offer secure moorage, the fisheries office was moved from Quathiaski Cove in 1947, though it was yet another three years before the project became a reality. The opening ceremony in January 1950 attracted a sizable crowd, huddled together against the cold. With a foot of snow highlighting the outline of the new docking facilities, people cheered the arrival of a flotilla of fishing boats. Overhead the clouds parted occasionally to allow prophetic glimpses of two BC Airlines planes buzzing the event. Air

Roderick Haig-Brown, pictured here c. 1950, took an important leadership role in the Battle of the Buttle environmental campaign, which resulted in the government deciding to flood the lake as a backup water supply rather than build a major dam there. *Weishlow Collection, MCR 19719*

transport was poised to become a major rival to freight and passenger services like the Union Steamship Company and Canadian Pacific, which had been keenly awaiting better docking facilities at Campbell River.

Bob Langdon was undoubtedly at the controls of one of those BC Airlines seaplanes. Langdon, a young, slightly built man with barely two years' previous experience, arrived at Campbell River as a fill-in pilot in 1946. Within months he was in charge of the small float plane operation based on the beach in front of the Willows Hotel.

Langdon was destined to become a local hero. His scrapbooks from those early years demonstrate a devil-may-care humour, bravado and full-hearted commitment to the needs of his customers. His clippings tell of endless daring rescues in gale-force winds and zero visibility, transporting injured loggers, farmers and pregnant women from the outlying islands and inlets to the Lourdes Hospital. Mrs. Robertson of Cortes Island wrote a tribute to Langdon: "Bob may not look like a guardian angel—but in times of need, many of us felt that's what he was." Langdon and his crew made an average of four flights a week for stretcher cases, "90 percent of them from logging camps where time can mean the difference between life and death."

Townsfolk who seldom needed Langdon's seaplane service may not have recognized how crucial a part his company played in solidifying Campbell River's position as an economic hub for the north island. BC Airlines quickly expanded as Langdon scooped business from the fading Union Steamship Company. He took rueful pride in his airline's triumphant rise to dominance: "When I came up I used to follow the Union steamships around and see if there were any passengers that got off at a Union Steamship stop that would want to fly to a logging camp maybe a couple of miles away. The captain used to laugh at this funny-looking Seabee that used to follow him around but he's unemployed now; we've got all the passengers now."[6]

Langdon's clients flooded him with letters of appreciation upon his retirement three decades later. Most remembered his heroics with heartfelt appreciation, but Rita Ogren took a tongue-in-cheek poke at his willingness to fly in any weather: "Yes Bob we had a few flights with you in your flying machine. One time we flew back to Ramsay Arm from Campbell River in a snow storm. None of the other pilots would take us and I had visions of another day in the big city of Campbell River to spend a little more of the old man's money but no dice, along came Bob and away we went. We made it of course and back to housework and five kids. Sometimes Bob you were just too good of a pilot."[7]

After years of lobbying, Campbell River residents finally got a new wharf (at centre) and breakwater (right) in January 1950. The new facilities were destined to become a less important component of the community's shipping and transportation activities, as trucks and seaplanes supplanted water vessels. *Carl Thulin Collection, MCR 10217*

After BC Airlines opened a small seaplane base on the beach in front of the Willows Hotel in the late 1940s. The seaplane quickly became one of the most important means of moving loggers, their families and their equipment around the scattered camps on the Discovery Islands and mainland inlets. *Carl Thulin Collection, MCR 6682*

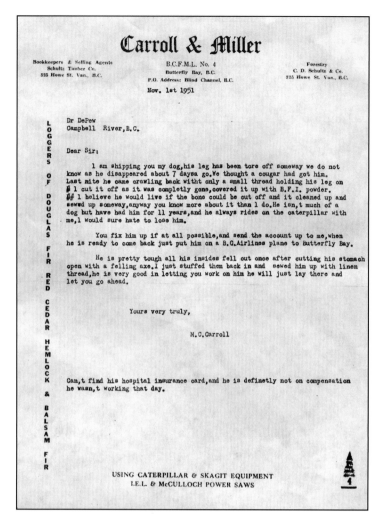

Carroll & Miller

Bookkeepers & Selling Agents
Schultz Timber Co.
325 Howe St. Van., B.C.

B.C.F.M.L. No. 4
Butterfly Bay, B.C.
P.O. Address: Blind Channel, B.C.

Forestry
C. D. Schultz & Co.
325 Howe St. Van., B.C.

Nov. 1st 1951

LOGGERS OF DOUGLAS FIR RED CEDAR HEMLOCK & BALSAM FIR

Dr DePew
Campbell River,B.C.

Dear Sir:

1 am shipping you my dog,his leg has been tore off someway we do not know as he disappeared about 7 daysa go.We thought a cougar had got him. Last nite he came crawling back witht only a small thread holding his leg on # 1 cut it off as it was completly gone,covered it up with B.F.I. powder. ## 1 believe he would live if the bone could be cut off and it cleaned up and sewed up someway,anyway you know more about it than 1 do.He isn,t much of a dog but have had him for 11 years,and he always rides on the caterpillar with me,1 would sure hate to lose him.

You fix him up if at all possible,and send the account up to me,when he is ready to come back just put him on a B.C.Airlines plane to Butterfly Bay.

He is pretty tough all his insides fell out once after cutting his stomach open with a felling axe.I just stuffed them back in and sewed him up with linen thread,he is very good in letting you work on him he will just lay there and let you go ahead.

Yours very truly,

M.C.Carroll

Can,t find his hospital insurance card,and he is definetly not on compensation he wasn,t working that day.

USING CATERPILLAR & SKAGIT EQUIPMENT
I.E.L. & McCULLOCH POWER SAWS

In foul weather the Seabees were parked on an empty lot in the centre of town, joined there by a gaggle of odd vintage cars and boats. Villagers took exception to this eyesore, along with the danger of Seabee planes crossing the main drag. As a result his base was relocated to Tyee Spit.

Campbell River's earliest newspaper, the *Courier*, was on the scene to cover all the action, starting with a scrappy-looking mimeographed newsletter in 1945. Helen Mitchell, the author of Campbell River's first history, *Diamond in the Rough*, was one of the *Courier's* initial reporters, working at the rate of 10 cents per column inch:

> Gathering the news in those days was a more leisurely and more co-operative effort than it is today. When I first started working for the *Courier* there were two other news hens here reporting for the Courtenay papers—Mrs. Jean McNeil and Mrs. Lee Hoby.

Every Monday we three gathered at Jean McNeil's house on Thulin Street and compared notes on what had transpired in the town since the previous week. On the way down to Jean's I'd stop off at the old Lourdes Hospital and get a list of the patients, the new babies, and any logging or road accidents. Similarly, on her way up to Jean's, Lee Hoby stopped off at the police station on the highway and found out about accidents, thefts, or anything else on the police blotter that was newsworthy. Jean was the only one of us who had a phone and we would make use of it to check up on other items.[8]

Campbell River's leading citizens tried to keep abreast of the fast-paced growth transforming their town. The Board of Trade pressed for village incorporation in a plebiscite on April 30, 1947. The population within the proposed village boundaries was 2,200, with 255 registered voters. Of the unspoiled ballots, 181 were in favour and 67 were vehemently opposed, the latter fearing another level of government would mean the loss of the old casual ways of doing business—and more taxation. When the first election was called on December 11, 1947, Carl O. Thulin, a calm and fair-minded man, was elected as the chairman of the Campbell River Village Council. The first commissioners included Carl's cousin Oscar F. Thulin and John (Jack) Baikie. They needed

Bob Langdon of BC Airlines (checkered shirt, left) meets Roderick Haig-Brown (at centre, leaning on rail) and other townsfolk concerned about the environmental impact of moving the BC Airlines base from in front of the Willows Hotel to the Campbell River estuary. *Joan Whitmore Collection, MCR 13070*

all of Carl's smooth diplomacy to steer them through the first years of debate over new bylaws, which rocked the town—like one that ruled against keeping cows and chickens in the village.

The *Courier* reported that in 1947 School District 72 (formed in 1945 to serve Oyster Bay to Sayward and the Discovery Islands) took an option on 13 acres (5.2 ha) on "hospital hill" for "a new twelve division school complete with auditorium, gymnasium, cafeteria and all the buildings now considered necessary in a modern school." There was a hue and cry about placing the school so far out of town, in the bush, but a vote was taken in its favour through a plebiscite, and a new multi-grade school was opened in April 1950, on the current site of Phoenix School. Alan Haig-Brown recalls that a Seabee plane flew over the town, dropping leaflets urging citizens to vote yes: "My friends and I were delighted and ran all over Campbellton collecting the pamphlets. I was only in grade three and couldn't read much but we all wanted the new school. My first year in the new school I was in grade four and had a seat by the window

Helen Mitchell, who arrived in Campbell River in the 1930s to join her husband at a logging camp, collected a wealth of material on the town and wrote its first history, *Diamond in the Rough*, published in 1975. *Courier-Upper Islander Collection, MCR 18175*

Campbell River's first village council at their fire hall meeting room, 1947. Left to right: Robbie Robinson, village clerk; Commissioner Oscar F. Thulin; Chairman Carl Thulin; Commissioner John Baikie. *Courtesy Municipality of Campbell River*

in a classroom along the front of the school," a seat from which Haig-Brown dreamed about his future, "watching the fish boats and tugs line up for the narrows and wondering what was on the other side of the mountains."[9]

Ramona Vanstone remembers the luxury of the town's first movie theatre. Young couples from both the Vanstone and Perkins families pulled on their boots and winter coats to trek through a snowstorm to attend the opening of the Van Isle Theatre (now the Tidemark Theatre) on January 2, 1947. Removed from the chill of winter, the sold-out audience sank into plush seats to be transported into the lives and loves of Hollywood. The event was such a thrill that most sat through both the matinee and the evening screenings.

The Dubeau family home was converted to the first municipal office, seen here in 1959. *Baldwin Collection, MCR 18255*

It was not just the announcement of the pulp mill that inspired all the civic development around town in the late 1940s. Following initial exploration in 1949, the Argonaut Company, a subsidiary of the Utah Construction Company, opened an iron mine at Upper Quinsam Lake. According to the *Argus*, Japan was their target market. "It is reported that the United States, planning to rearm Japan, has been pressing U.S. groups in the western states to ship ore to Japan. They, being reluctant to use their U.S. resources for this purpose, have turned to British Columbia."[10] The company's preferred site for loading ore onto cargo ships was on the Weiwaikum Reserve. Band leaders were not initially in favour of the idea but after months of discussion they accepted a proposal for a twenty-five-year lease and a connection to the municipal water system in which water would be piped in from one of the penstocks above the John Hart dam.

The Argonaut Company opened an iron mine at Upper Quinsam Lake in the early 1950s and built a dock for shipping ore on the Weiwaikum Reserve at Campbell River Spit. Though the mine has long been closed, the Quinsam Coal Company was still using the Argonaut Wharf in the late 1990s. *Wieshlow Collection, MCR 19756*

Baikie Brothers, independent logging operators raised on Denman Island, bought milling equipment used during hydro construction and set up a mill in Campbell River slough in 1950. There had been other sawmills in various locations around the slough over the years, including one run by old "Sawdust Bill" and Joe Zanatta, which was destroyed by fire in the late 1940s.

Logging continued to be the largest industry in the province in the 1950s, when surging technological advances following the war brought power saws and logging trucks into common use. Pre-war loggers would never have predicted the advent of trucks over steam, which had been viewed as the absolute pinnacle of mechanization in the woods. But by the mid-1950s, many camps had converted to trucks, which allowed them to access steeper grades. Arthur Mayse, who worked in the woods as a youth, described the social impact of these changes:

When truck roads supplanted railway lines in the British Columbia coast logging woods, a change took place in the logger's way of life.

He was no longer shackled to his work-place for 24 hours a day. With a road to the outside world, he was free to live away from his job, coming and going in his own car or in one of the knockabout woods buses called crummies.

The logger acquired a different, and smoother, profile.

From a single "Tame Ape" whose only approach to a home was a camp bunkhouse, he became a family man with wife and child, house and mortgage. He ceased to be a bird-of-passage between the monastic confines of the woods and the fleshpots of Vancouver. Unionized and well-paid, his working conditions vastly improved, he became a pillar of his community.[11]

The fleet of S & S (Schnare and Schnare) Trucking, Oyster Bay, 1945. By the 1950s, trucks had replaced railways as the primary means of moving logs. *Ted Boggs Collection, MCR 13308*

The opening of the Elk Falls Mill in 1952 was the most important event in the town's history. Jobs at the mill assured decent wages in a stable, unionized, year-round industry with growth potential. At the peak of the construction phase, starting in 1950, there were 1,000 people at work on the $21-million project. When the mill officially opened in June 1952 there were over 200 employees on the payroll, "making newsprint for the free world." The editor of the *Courier* announced that stability and plenty had come to stay.

Within a year of opening in January 1953, Crown Zellerbach bought the Canadian Western Lumber Company and its subsidiary, Comox Logging Company, for $35 million, retaining R.J. Filberg as vice-president for their BC operations.

Art Backlund, Bob White (salesman) and Martin Fossum, bull bucker, standing by one the first D-30 Burnett power saws to be tried out at a logging camp. This photograph was taken at Bloedel Camp 5 in the 1950s. *Bloedel-Camp 5 Collection, MCR 14503*

Bloedel, Stewart & Welch's (later MacMillan Bloedel) Camp 5, Menzies Bay, 1950. Camp 5 was one of the last of the major village-style camps to operate in the district. Former residents, who formed a tight-knit community, have enjoyed several large-scale reunions at the now abandoned Camp 5 site. *Godfrey Baldwin photo, Baldwin Collection, MCR 1622*

The Elk Falls Mill site, Duncan Bay, prior to construction in 1950, photographed by Godfrey Baldwin.
Baldwin Collection, MCR 1210

Aerial view of Elk Falls Mill, Duncan Bay, 1950s, photographed by Godfrey Baldwin. *Baldwin Collection, MCR 3218*

Mill management, following Filberg's success with the Comox Logging Company, encouraged their employees to make their homes in Campbell River (rather than building extensive on-site housing) to assure themselves of a stable work force. Twenty-six stylish new homes were scattered about behind the town.

By 1953 Campbell River's population of 2,626 showed a remarkably high proportion of young people, with 408 being children under the age of six. There were 776 dwellings, the majority of which were simple homes of four or fewer rooms.[12]

The mid-century growth did not affect the essential nature of the town, or its rustic appearance. It remained a friendly little place where pranks volleyed back and forth between downtown merchants were public news and the simple style of most of the houses stamped the place as a working-class town. A *Vancouver Sun* reporter wrote a frank appraisal of this gawky transition phase, in a community she said was "boiling" with activity from a "welter of half-formed plans": "The overflowing bounty of nature seems almost to have given the town an inferiority complex. The Island Highway passes through the shopping district and the houses straggle along it backed by a steep bank. Nondescript, many of them sagging and in need of paint, they are not prepossessing. A few new, trim buildings only serve to point up the drabness of the whole."[13]

The Bee Hive Cafe (at left) and the old general store (right), late 1940s. The businesses had run through various hands over the years, from the Thulins to Cross and Vanstone. When this photograph was taken, Lavers of Courtenay owned the store. *Baldwin Collection, MCR 1839*

Fran MacDougall was similarly unimpressed on her first sight of Campbell River. Arriving aboard a Union Steamship vessel in 1946, to take a nursing position at the Lourdes Hospital, Fran's first question as she looked down the dock into the rough-edged town was "When's the next boat out of here?" The answer was one week, which proved long enough to capture Fran as a life-long resident.[14]

Dr. Dick Murphy didn't even realize the place was a town on his first pass through. Raised on the Irish seacoast, Murphy spent his first few years in Canada on the prairies, a period that affirmed an overriding need to live by the sea. He packed up his "trunk full of medical tools" in the summer of 1948 and made a reconnaissance trip up Vancouver Island. Dick recalls that near Courtenay someone told him he couldn't get lost on the way to Campbell River, and waved him onward: "It's at the end of the blacktop." But miss the little town he did. Following a trying drive up "a really ratty road" he found himself crossing the wooden Campbell River bridge, where the road switched to a dirt track in quiet farmlands—the signal that he had somehow entirely missed Campbell River.

Later, while he was on a fruitless search for work in the Victoria area, a former first aid attendant on the John Hart Dam advised Murphy to return to Campbell River. This prophet didn't mince his words. "Look, the only hope for you is in Campbell River, it's the only place on the island that's moving. There's hope in Campbell River." So back came Dr. Murphy, ready to view the place afresh.

Jim English of the Quinsam Hotel helped the doctor settle on where to locate an office. "I met old Jim English one day [in Campbellton], walking down the middle of the road, which he always did, and he put out his hand and stopped me and said, 'Hey young fella, if you want to practise medicine in this town you practise it at this end of town!' Under The Bishop's direction the doctor found a house in the centre of Campbellton which he bought fully furnished for $3,300.

Campbellton, corner of Petersen Road and the Island Highway, c. 1950. The Pioneer Bakery (later a hair salon) is at right, across from the old Crystal Grill café. *MCR 16707*

Painters Lodge, c. 1950, showing the Tudor-style lodge and cabins, photographed by Godfrey Baldwin. *Baldwin Collection, MCR 3223*

In 1950 Dr. Murphy was sworn in as a village commissioner and opened a second office downtown, on what is now Shoppers Row, north of St. Ann's Road, retaining the Campbellton house as his residence and evening office. His shifts spanned daytime and evening hours, to serve the needs of loggers and their families. House calls were routine. When a huge bulk of a man like John Perkins Sr., one of north Campbell River's first settlers, could not raise his head from the pillow, Dr. Murphy packed his black bag and was off. "John was in bed and I examined his chest; he had a bit of a bronchitis. We chit chatted for a while and I wrote him a prescription. As I was leaving he said, 'Doctor, I think you better take a look at the missus too.' So I said, 'Sure John.' I thought she was out in the kitchen…but this little lady pops up her head, she was right in the bed, behind big John."

Dr. Murphy found respite from the rigours of his practice by greeting the early morning tide on the tyee fishing

Bob Hope (right) is one of many famous guests who have stayed at Painters Lodge over the years. *Baldwin collection, MCR*

grounds. He was a great fan of the sport and an admirer of Ned Painter's finely crafted boats. Things were changing for the Painters the year Dick Murphy came to town. The famous resort on their north Campbell River property included a handsome Tudor-style lodge with a dining hall, lounge and accommodation for about twenty people, along with the twelve original beach cottages.

Painters Lodge was an extended family operation owned by June Painter's two half-brothers, Peter and Herbert Barclay, and her husband Ned. June was an integral part of the operation. "I was running around all the time, involved in everything from soup to nuts. We had a staff, but I cooked, cleaned, everything that was necessary…except beds, I never did make beds." In 1948 the family decided to sell because, as June noted in her memoirs, her husband and brothers were not agreeing. "I was very upset about selling at the time, but I wasn't particularly consulted. Women weren't in those days."

David Vanstone lived to see Campbell River achieve the bright promise he and others had so long predicted, but not beyond. Vanstone passed away at home on the morning of January 14, 1948, after a brief illness. Since the Depression, Vanstone had taken an increasingly silent but crucial role in the business affairs of the town, as a financial backer behind a long list of businesses, from a gas station and hardware store to tourist resorts.

His bright-eyed daughter-in-law Ramona Vanstone—who was used to her quiet girlhood home on Cortes Island—was impressed by the regular procession of businessmen calling upon David Vanstone to pay court, discuss plans and make loan payments. When the last installment of a loan was retired David would give the nod to his wife Eliza, who would fetch crystal glasses and a brandy decanter for a celebratory settling up of accounts. In more than a few instances it was necessary for Vanstone to write off a loan, as with the death of a businessman leaving behind a family. "He would tear up their debt notes. He would not consider asking a widow to pay." Vanstone's position, generosity and influence made his name a byword in the district.

Ramona Vanstone describes her father-in-law as a large man with "unbelievably blue" eyes, a hearty chuckle and a winning personality, though his gruff exterior sometimes belied his kind ways. He was a wonderfully smooth and accomplished dancer, which was particularly striking for a man of his size, and even as an elderly gent he took pleasure in dancing an old-time waltz.

When Vanstone passed away, his estate was divided amongst his extensive family. Ramona Vanstone recalls that some of the family used their inheritance "to fulfill their interpretation of the good life," buying new cars and taking trips abroad, while others made it their sustaining income. One of David's sons enjoyed

David Vanstone (right), one of Campbell River's most influential businessmen, with his wife Eliza (centre) and her cousin Mary Watson, c. 1936. They were photographed outside the Vanstone family home on the waterfront, at the mouth of the Campbell River. *Ramona Vanstone Collection, MCR 18432*

flashing around large cheques for sums upwards of $14,000 as if they were a regular occurrence, though in fact they were the result of gradual payouts from the liquidation of the family assets.

High-octane alcohol continued to be an accepted ingredient in life on the coast. A taste for rum and whiskey crossed all social, ethnic and economic lines, from the "wee" drop of Scotch served at bridge parties to the loggers' determined boom-and-bust cycles. In 1954 alcohol sales for the district, recorded at the government-controlled liquor store, were a whopping $487,145.

Dr. Murphy remembers the difficulties arising from alcohol abuse, which he characterized as a "massive" problem for the district. It was especially pronounced among the old bachelors living in shacks around town, who suffered from delirium tremens, a violent after-effect of heavy alcohol use:

> We couldn't expect the nursing staff to look after these people and it wasn't safe to leave them at home. Our rate of suicide at that time was pretty high too, with older people. We used to get the family or the friends to go to the hospital with the patient and they would look after the physical aspects of the patient thrashing around…I remember one day the Camp 5 Ambulance brought a patient down with a broken leg and the first aid man came with him. While I was talking to the first aid man and looking after the patient, we heard a tremendous explosion of glass breaking. One of the nurses ran out and said, "Somebody has jumped through the window." The first aid man and I doubled around the back of the building and here's a guy with a little hospital shirt on heading across to Alder Street. We took off after him but couldn't have caught him except that they were putting in the water main up Alder and he fell into the ditch and we grabbed him. He went right through the window, glass and everything—with the DTs.[15]

In the doctor's opinion this male-dominated, hard-drinking community was not a suitable place for women, who were pressed into marriage at too young an age: "The men had their jobs and they had their beer parlours and the rest of it. The women had young families and they used to get married very, very young. In fact, I think it was kind of a status thing with young girls that the younger they got married, the higher they were in the pecking order. They used to get married at fourteen and fifteen. They'd have three or four children by the time they were twenty-two or twenty-three. And they carried a load. It was not nice for women at all."[16]

There was plenty of business for prostitutes in the district, some of whom offered a distinctive brand of rural service. Mr. and Mrs. Homewood set the tone during the Depression when they moved from Vancouver, with $3 between them, to establish a family farm on Homewood Road. Mrs. Homewood, a lanky, thin-faced women in her forties, augmented the family income through prostitution, protected from rough handling by her faithful husband. Following this homey pattern in the 1940s were two sisters who lived with their logger husbands on neighbouring farms. Under the protection of their men, they added to their family incomes by selling fresh milk and sex.

It was not just loggers who provided an income for prostitutes. The crew on a ship loading ore at the Argonaut Wharf were subjected to a random raid that sent local prostitutes scurrying down the gangplank in a southeast gale. As one of the more infamous women emerged, the wind whipped open her fur coat, exposing her charms to the assembled crowd.

Women's options for work in a range of fields expanded tremendously during the war, only to constrict again at its conclusion. "Nice girls" became nurses, teachers or secretaries. Young people who couldn't afford advanced education took jobs as shop clerks or domestic servants at a very meagre income. A few found creative means to skirt these limitations. Mrs. Brunton supported her family by bootlegging from her home (at first a tent), conveniently located behind the Quinsam Hotel. Lillie Thulin's business didn't have to be discussed in hushed tones, but her male peers sometimes viewed Lillie askance as she became one of the first female real estate agents in the north Vancouver Island region. At first Lillie worked from her home, until the business grew and she opened a downtown office in 1957.

Lillie's first subdivisions were built on family property. She developed both Thulin Street and "Swede Hill" in the 1940s, naming the streets that bisect the hill in alphabetical progression from Alder Street to Beech, Cedar, Dogwood, Elm, Fir and so on. Thulin Street, extending as far as 5th Avenue, was built with picks, shovels and horses. Taking an exacting personal interest in the work, Lillie would carry the dynamite for her road-building crews and later, when bulldozers came into use, she'd don a pair of sensible overalls and join Ernie Polglase in the cab of his bulldozer, directing his work "in no uncertain terms." When times were lean Lillie relied on her father's practice of offering contractors in-kind payment, a 50x120-foot (540 sq m) lot valued at $35 (or three for $100) in exchange for their work.

More tolerant views of First Nations people and minority groups began to emerge slowly following the war. Voting rights were finally extended to Chinese and Indo-Canadians in 1947, and to Japanese Canadians and First Nations people in 1949.

There were noteworthy changes for First Nations people at mid-century. The earnings of some Native fishermen brought them respect and a voice within their industry. The law banning potlatching was dropped in 1951, encouraging a renewal of traditional art and culture, and the school district was the first in the province to end the segregation of Native children. At first it was just scholastic achievers who attended the new high school, while the younger children continued at the little elementary school on the Reserve until 1959.[17]

First Nations people formed an advocacy organization, the Native Brotherhood, in the 1950s. Young men like Frank Assu and George Quocksister, who served on the executive in the district chapter, were outspoken representatives of a strong new generation. In 1950 Assu was impatient for some long overdue changes: "At the present time we are not Canadian citizens," he said in an address to a Chamber of Commerce meeting at the Willows Hotel. "We have no member in the legislature. Indians cannot borrow money from a bank. We have no voice in Indian

Frank Assu, at the wheel of his boat, photographed by May Baldwin c. 1950. Assu was a strong advocate of First Nations people, following in the footsteps of his father, Chief Billy Assu. He was one of the few to speak out against the internment of Japanese Canadians during World War II.
Rose McKay Collection, MCR 15027

Affairs. We cannot collect old age pensions—but we do pay personal income tax. What we want is equality. We are living in a democratic country, let us make it that way."[18]

Frank Assu learned his skills from men like his father, Chief Billy Assu of Cape Mudge, whose exemplary leadership brought him universal respect. The Wewaikai people were admired for their ability to turn adversity into success, achieving a high standard of living within a relatively short span. Chief Billy Assu's name is still revered as the powerful and determined force behind these achievements. He was awarded a Coronation Medal by King George VI in 1937, and later decorated by Queen Elizabeth for his "meritorious service."

Alan Haig-Brown retains a childhood memory of being introduced to Billy Assu on a Campbell River street. It was clear to the boy, in this fleeting encounter, that Billy Assu was a man his father honoured and respected. Roderick Haig-Brown later wrote a moving tribute to the man:

> He was, by any standards, a truly great man. Had the chances of birth and education been different, it is easy to imagine him a leader in world affairs, a delegate to the United Nations or perhaps its secretary-general. That he was called to play his part on a smaller stage should not detract from our pride in his memory.
>
> His strength and native wisdom led a formidable people into peaceful and successful integration and if the scale is small, the achievement is great. He retained his dignity and his powerful personality to the very end of his long life. Few leaders can have faced greater changes or found sounder ways among them.[19]

The Campbell River Rotary Club, the business bastion of the community, invited First Nations families to participate in the July 1st parade starting in the 1950s. There were some, on both sides, who viewed this intermingling of cultures as a mixed blessing.

The public display of masks, button blankets, and aspects of the dramatic traditions of the First Nations opened the eyes of the world to the brilliance of their culture. The Kwakwa̱ka̱'wakw artist Mungo Martin, working from a traditional style big house at the BC Provincial Museum in Victoria, captured an international following and acted as a mentor to a whole new generation of artists. In Campbell River, Sam Henderson and his large family became noteworthy carvers. They also joined Elizabeth Quocksister, training young people in traditional music, dance and crafts.

Social changes were taking place on every level. A new

Sam Henderson, a Kwakwa̱ka̱'wakw man who married into the Quocksister family of the Weiwaikum Band of Campbell River, became a renowned carver. Numerous members of Henderson's large family trained under him and now have an international following. This photograph was taken in 1971. *Courier-Upper Islander Collection, MCR 18054*

class of people were attracted to Campbell River—educated professionals, who filled skilled union jobs at Elk Falls Mill. Their requirements for health, education and recreation services placed new demands on the town, as did their expectation of a welcome (which was not immediately forthcoming) at the eternal bridge parties of the town's ruling elite.

Joining the struggle to expand hospital services proved an easier stepping stone into community life, integrating the old guard and the new. Ed Cooley, with his engineering degree from the University of Oregon, was one of the professionals Crown Zellerbach transferred to Campbell River. Cooley made a place for himself in the social life of the town through active involvement in service clubs, and he joined a study group formed in 1952 to assess health services in the community. The outcome wasn't a surprise: there was an overwhelming need for a new hospital with modern equipment, but the Sisters of St. Ann were in no position to finance a project on the scale required.

The need for a sophisticated new hospital for the growing municipality resulted in a difficult severing of ties with the Catholic order, the Sisters of St. Ann, who were not in a position to fund the new hospital. *Courier-Upper Islander Collection, MCR*

The Sisters, in their chaste habits, presented a somewhat incongruous aspect to the rough-edged boom town, but they had served the place well. The change to a secular hospital was a difficult transition for everyone, resulting in a range of views and emotions. Some wanted the hospital to remain in the hands of the Sisters of St. Ann, others felt the town had long outgrown a church-run hospital managed by a non-nursing order, and badly required a new facility with the latest equipment.

After five years of planning the new Campbell River and District General Hospital was opened on September 7, 1957. The hospital was built on a unique double-corridor plan, with the wards on the periphery and the work areas in the centre. Like the pulp mill, the hospital was a state-of-the-art facility that became an example to others. Many community members contributed funds for the hospital. The Wewaikai Band donated the fixtures for a room, as did Mary, Anna, Lillie, Elin and Carl Thulin, who furnished a room in memory of the hospital's first benefactor, Charles Thulin.

Another project that proved a rallying force for Campbell River's transforming population came about after the old community hall in Campbellton collapsed. The hall was squashed under two feet of wet snow the night before the annual New Year's Eve dance of 1949–50. The Woods sisters, whose family owned an auto court and gas station at Shelter Point, were all set for the big event when word flashed around the district that the hall was a ruin. Under the sad heap of flattened timbers lay a stack of fine memories, like jitterbugging and dancing the Lambeth walk to Mrs. King's orchestra, or perching on hall chairs and watching Clarke Gable and Jean Harlow fall in love on a lopsided screen.

The old community hall in Campbellton collapsed under the weight of a particularly heavy snowfall in 1949, just hours before the start of a New Year's Eve dance. *Baldwin Collection, MCR 1467*

The Royal Canadian Legion had already begun making plans for a new social and sports hall on their 11th Avenue property. With the need compounded by the loss of the old hall they were joined by the Kinsmen and Rotary Clubs, who led what many still consider a stellar example of spirited community effort. Weekend work bees were arranged through much of 1954, each one co-ordinated by changing shifts of businesses, service clubs and tradespeople. The hall was pressed into use before it was even complete, for a fiftieth anniversary dance on July 1, 1954, celebrating the start of business in Campbell River in 1904.

The July 1st parade of 1954 was celebrated as the fiftieth anniversary of Campbell River, which started with the opening of the Willows Hotel on July 1, 1904. *Amber (Bayer) Jontz Collection, MCR 18277*

Some cod fishermen noted a correlation between the opening of the mill and the decline of their fishery—the mill pumped its effluent out into the middle of Discovery Passage—but the majority rarely gave more than passing thought to the potential effects of pollution. When management announced a move into pulp production, no opposition was reported in the local press. Most were satisfied with Harold Zellerbach's claim that sulphate (as opposed to sulphite) would not have a harmful effect on salmon. Moreover, he assured the public that the rapid development of science would soon find a solution to the problem of air pollution from the mill's giant stacks. But for the time being, the erect plumes of acrid-smelling smoke must be endured; it was the smell of money.

Quadra Islanders made an urgent plea for car ferry service in 1956, as Union Steamship service dwindled. Where freight and passenger ships had once made twice-weekly calls at four island docks, they were now making just one weekly stop at Quathiaski Cove. The loss of the Union

Steamship service effectively stranded people who had relied upon goods coming in by mail order from Vancouver. Estelle Rose of the Quadra Island Ratepayers' Association challenged Campbell Riverites to support the islanders' bid for a ferry. Not only would a ferry enhance business at "The River," charged Rose, but the town was at fault for the decline of Vancouver shipping services: "Why has the Union SS made this drastic cut? Well, it appears to be Campbell River's fault. Why? Because Campbell River has grown, progress has come and now that trucking services pick up freight in Vancouver one day and deliver it to Campbell River the next, it doesn't pay the people of Campbell River to use the Union SS freight service."[20]

Rose also chastised the village for the inadequate size and location of its breakwater and wharf, which had not been built to accommodate a ferry. "Campbell River is no longer just a resort town. You have built up your village to where Quadra and the surrounding islands look to you for their main source of supply."

Helen Mitchell described a less tangible loss: a romantic aspect to coastal life ended as air service and trucking came to dominate the coastal trade: "It always thrilled me to hear [the *Adelaide's*] whistle on a lovely summer's evening, look out, and see her gliding into the old wharf. Sometimes the ship's public address system was going and the purser's voice, giving advice to the passengers, could be clearly heard up on the hill, or sometimes we were treated to music."

Changes in transportation created an opening for Campbell River's first major grocery store. Overwaitea, a Lower Mainland chain, opened a store in Campbellton in 1951, under the guidance of a young man destined to climb high on the corporate ladder. Clarence Heppell, or Hep, as he was known about town, transferred from Nanaimo to take over the new store and expanded the business in tandem with the community. The store doubled in size within two years of opening and by 1965 it was in a brand new downtown location. Impressed by his capable management, the executive brought Heppell into their circle, where he mentored the installation of new stores around the province and ultimately became president of Overwaitea.

In 1957 Campbell River's population figures lurched past Courtenay's for the first time. Between 1951 and 1957 there

Fire insurance street map of Campbell River, 1957.

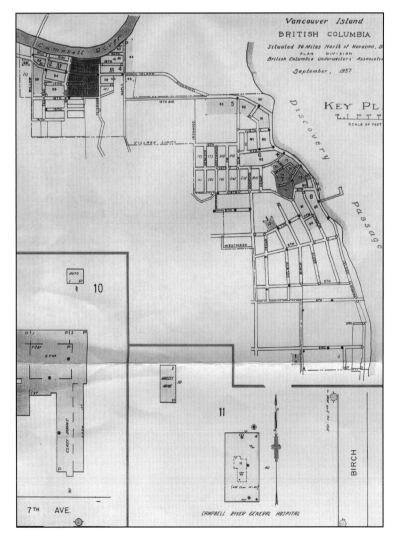

Tom Barnett, campaigning for re-election, 1965. Barnett was a Port Alberni millworker who represented north Vancouver Island (including Campbell River) for several terms as a CCF (later NDP) member of parliament. He was first elected in 1953. His wife Ruth, the daughter of the pioneering Pidcock family, had many connections in the Discovery Passage region. She was a champion of women's rights and environmental causes. *Courier-Upper Islander Collection, MCR*

was nearly a 40 percent increase, bringing the total to 3,069, compared with Courtenay's population of 3,025. The rising population inspired radical new thinking on the part of at least one businessman in town.

Tom Barnett, CCF (Cooperative Commonwealth Federation, renamed the New Democratic Party in 1961) Member of Parliament for the riding, had just settled into his new post in Ottawa when he received an intriguing telegram in 1956, sent from aboard an Ottawa-bound train. William Mullett of Campbell River requested the pleasure of the MP's company at lunch at the Chateau Laurier to discuss "a matter of great importance to your constituents." Mullett's plan was to "reclaim" the 14-acre (5.6-ha) tidal bay in front of the village of Campbell River, creating a shopping plaza and a small harbour. Barnett was intrigued by a unique aspect of Mullett's offer: he hadn't come to ask for money, but to offer turning over the harbour to the federal government upon completion of the project.[21]

Barnett thought the proposal had merit, but Mullett's plan fell flat with village leaders, erupting into one of the hottest debates to rock the town. The public were baffled as they attempted to follow a confusing volley of declarations by opponents and proponents. Commissioner Carl Thulin owned a portion of the affected foreshore, in use as a children's park. He was prepared to

The cenotaph at Willow Bay, before the bay was filled to create Tyee Plaza in the late 1950s, photographed by Godfrey Baldwin. *Baldwin Collection, MCR 392*

Aerial photo of Willow Bay, 1959, showing the newly filled area ready for the construction of Tyee Plaza. *Godfrey Baldwin photo, Baldwin Collection, MCR 18242*

turn the land over to the village, but only if the fill project was dedicated as a park and waterfront promenade. Others who were against the shopping plaza expressed a lack of faith in Mullett's ability to raise the necessary funds to complete the project. Some simply didn't like the man himself, an accountant who was dogged by rumours of a white-collar crime for which he had served time in jail.

After endless heated public meetings, hearings, debates and an unsuccessful slander suit brought against village officials, Mullett adroitly sidestepped local politicians. With the Quadra Island Ratepayers on side (hoping to gain a ferry berth out of the deal), Mullett went directly to the provincial Social Credit government. "At this juncture" Mullett was quoted as saying in the *Daily Free Press*, "we decided, reluctantly, to go over the head of village authority... As a result of Campbell's [the Socred MLA for this district] report we have been given carte blanche to go ahead, I am very happy to report. We believe that when the smoke clears, citizens will thank us for making the development possible."

With government support assured, Fraser Valley Lands Ltd. came in as financial backers and the plaza project was put to a local ballot. To the chagrin of some Campbell Riverites, residents of outlying districts such as Quadra Island were allowed to vote. While Campbell River voters were almost equally divided for and against the project (404 for, 372 opposed), a strong majority of Shelter Point and Quadra Island residents voted in favour. Fraser Valley Lands Ltd. allowed Mullett to complete the landfill, and then neatly sidelined him. His detractors, who still shake their heads over the whole project, chuckle about the fact that Mullett barely made a cent on the project. Nor was he successful in his bid for a seat as a Socred MP in the federal election of 1958.

Fraser Valley Lands Ltd. brought friends and foes together for a cocktail party launch of their shopping mall plan in 1959, and in August 1962, Tyee Plaza was open for business.

Quadra Islanders were jubilant when their new fifteen-car ferry slid into the dock at Tyee Plaza in 1960. The convenience of the location, in the minds of many, outweighed the dock's exposure to the blasting southeast storms, a situation demanding nerve and skill from the ferry's captains and crew to the present day.

In the late 1950s, while Campbell River folks were still deeply embroiled in the Tyee Plaza affair, a project on a much grander scale brought the district into the international spotlight. After years of discussion and several failed attempts, the federal government was ready once again to tackle Ripple Rock. Victoria interests made their last spirited plea for retaining the twin peaks as pilings for bridging the Passage to create a crossing to the mainland, but the chief engineer, Dr. Victor Dolmage of Vancouver, called for a network of tunnels to be drilled beneath Discovery Passage and up into Ripple Rock to create cavities for explosives. On April 5, 1958, after two years of grinding labour, the crew was ready for the world's largest non-nuclear explosion.

Engineers and explosives experts were reasonably confident there'd be no serious side effects, yet there were no guarantees the blast wouldn't trigger a tidal wave or an earthquake. As 1,375 tons (1,237 tonnes) of explosives and 370,000 tons (330,000 tonnes) of rock erupted into a giant cascade of water and rock in the middle of the narrows on that drizzly spring morning, some of the district's residents were ready for a fast escape. Cy and Lucy Trevett sat in their idling car at the water's edge, poised to flee, and Carl and Florence Thulin removed all the windows from their home. One hundred and fifty Rotarians and their guests, "pioneers and pensioners of the district," assembled at the community hall to watch the explosion on twelve television screens, later running outside to watch for an after-effect on the shore. But the decapitation of Ripple Rock proved an anticlimactic ending for this old foe. Down the Passage, in front of Campbell River, there was no hint of the gigantic explosion on the placid surface of the water.

Watching the blasting of Ripple Rock remains, for a generation of Canadians, their first recollection of a television broadcast. Film crews and photographers created a second-by-second record from a specially prepared bunker on Maud Island. They were joined by dignitaries and special guests like eighty-nine-year-old R.D. Merrill, who'd first purchased timber holdings in the district in the 1880s on the advice of the legendary timber cruiser Moses Ireland.

Some old-timers questioned the wisdom of going to the bother and expense of decapitating Ripple Rock, rightly pointing out that the Passage would still remain a tricky piece of water to navigate on the ebb tide. But the cruise ships, freighters, fishing boats and tugs that rely upon the inner coast route no longer have the additional menace of the jagged twin peaks of Ripple Rock, barely concealed by the water.

Volcano-like eruptions in the middle of the Passage don't seem to have bothered a sea monster that had long been resident there. Harry Assu of Cape Mudge wrote that a gigantic skate-like creature attended by circling birds was commonly sighted near Maud Island in ancient times. A monster with a somewhat different sounding name, dubbed Klamahtossaurus by the media (taking the name of the Weiwaikum Village), was reported cavorting around the waters of Discovery Passage and in Sutil Channel in numerous sightings throughout 1962 and 1963.

The first tentative public claim of a sighting brought others forward. Mrs. Durrant of Shelter Point said the creature she saw was "just like a big dragon." It was sandy coloured and appeared to be 20 to 25 feet (6–8 m) long. "The head seemed to swivel around like a snake and it gave a 'hissing' noise every now and then. There were three coils at the

The blasting of Ripple Rock, April 5, 1958. Workers dug tunnels under the twin peaks and set 1,375 tons (1,237 tonnes) of explosives, and the blast removed the top of the rock, a well-known marine hazard in the main shipping lane for the inner coast. *Bill Dennett Collection, MCR 19984-1, 19984-6 / R.E. Olsen photo, Vancouver Province Collection, MCR 12150*

back, that moved slowly up and down." As she watched, it suddenly slipped back into the sea and "vanished altogether."[22]

In 1963 a group enjoying a day at Rebecca Spit Provincial Park on Quadra Island reported watching a sea monster for several hours, a dramatic show that appears to be the last recorded sighting.

Transportation improvements in the late 1950s included the building of an airport in 1959, spearheaded by Don Corker and a group of volunteers. Dave Crawford, agreed to be paid at a later date and blew the stumps and cleared the runway at the site of today's Municipal Airport at the end of Erickson Road. An old building, last used as a library, was hauled up from town to become the airport office. Lloyd Watchorn was the first to land on the runway with his private plane, hours before Pacific Western Airlines inaugurated the town's first weekly connector flight to Vancouver on August 22, 1959.

The official opening of the new airport, 1959, on the site of what later became the municipal airport, at the end of Erickson Road. *Don Corker Collection, MCR 10601*

In 1959, when Bob Langdon opened Island Airlines, a rival seaplane base to BC Airlines, Campbell River was said to have the highest seaplane traffic in the world. These two airlines were soon joined by another newcomer, Trans Mountain Air, opened by Bill MacAdam. "There's nothing sleepy about this thriving community on Vancouver Island's east coast," said a Vancouver business journal. "It hums! Its very air throbs with beating airplane propellers lifting miners, exploration specialists, loggers and tourists into the northern part of the island...Aviation, according to Trans Mountain, is Campbell River's second largest industry, with a current annual payroll exceeding $750,000 and still growing."[23]

Highway and ferry improvements were also a hallmark of the post-war years. In 1965 the route to Sayward was paved, and in 1966 a new ferry service began, running vehicles and passengers between Kelsey Bay and Prince Rupert.

Few people in the district would have chosen to turn back the hands of time: the conveniences and comforts of post-war development had become the norm. But there were those who recognized the losses attached to the many gains. In 1958, the year BC celebrated its centennial, a historical society was formed in Campbell River to capture and preserve a few prized icons of a passing era. The magnificent art and culture of the First Nations people was evolving and changing with the times, and the determined individuality of the loggers and pioneers was giving way to a more controlled, regulated, mechanized lifestyle.

The society was formed under the inspiring leadership of Ed Meade, an accountant with a broad range of interests and the ability to captivate and entertain audiences with the fabulous coastal tales and artifacts he collected. Meade, acting as curator, displayed the collection in Painters Lodge and elsewhere around town until a museum was set up in the basement of the old Lourdes Hospital, which was by then the Municipal Hall.

On January 19, 1963, the town of Campbell River lost one of its most tangible links with the past, when Herman Quocksister checked into the Willows Hotel at 3:00 a.m. and reported smoke coming from beneath the door of Room 38. The grand old hotel had by this time slipped into seedy middle age, under a succession of owners from Gertrude and Stanley Isaac in the 1920s to Henri Dubeau in 1944, and finally to an Italian businessman, Joe Iaci, and his partner Bill Hollick.

The old Willows Hotel had become a seedy remnant of Campbell River's early years by the 1950s.
Godfrey Baldwin photo, Baldwin Collection, MCR 13364

The old place and its staff were ill-prepared for a fire, though this was the second major blaze for the Willows. The night clerk decided not to sound the alarm, thinking it would be mistaken for a burglar alarm. Fire doors were left gaping and at least one escape route was blocked. Four men died in the fast and furious inferno that ensued when the night clerk pried open the door of Room 38. One hotel guest, Michael Hamilton, had the agility to make a dramatic escape described in the *Courier*: "I went on my hands and knees to where I thought the stairway was, flames seemed to be coming up so I rolled down the stairs, I regained my feet at the bottom of the stairs and ran out."

The Willows Hotel, the business that founded the town of Campbell River, was destroyed by fire on January 19, 1963. Four people died; the building was not replaced. *Helen Mitchell Collection, MCR 18339*

During the cleanup after the fire, Ken Antonelli, a Rotary member, found the charred remains of the club's cherished dinner bell, a gift presented at the charter meeting on April 10, 1946. Another club member, Fire Chief Thulin, took the bent and burnt relic and lovingly restored it, giving it a new handle crafted from an overhead sprinkler.

The location once occupied by the Willows remained vacant for years, though the town was undergoing an unprecedented building boom. The editor of a new newspaper, *The Upper Islander*, reported in 1965 that building permits had reached an all-time high at $2 million and predicted they would reach $3 million before the year was out. Eighty-three new homes were built by September 1965, compared with twenty-four the previous year. An expansion at Elk Falls Mill, the announcement of a new paper mill at Gold River and the opening of a promising mine at Buttle Lake were the cause of this new wave of growth.

Western Mines (later called Westmin and eventually Boliden-Westmin) began developing their mine on Myra Creek, above Buttle Lake, in 1964. They bought claims first registered by James Cross when the Park Act was amended in 1918, allowing mining claims in Strathcona Park. Cross's claims had passed through a variety of hands over the decades, held in check by the want of capital and changing government views on mining in the park. When Westmin took over in the early 1960s they had both political will and capital backing on their side.

Western Mines shipped their first load of copper, lead, zinc, gold and silver in 1967. Ore was taken from an open pit mine at first and then milled on site to extract the raw minerals for shipping. As work progressed, and the full value of this tremendous ore-body was revealed, excitement flashed through the town. Thor Peterson recalled everyone started buying up shares which were steadily climbing. Loyalties were divided as some scrambled to get in on the profits while others spoke out against the eyesore of an open pit mine ripping open one of the province's finest parks. Some found themselves playing both ends at once.

The stalwart band of conservationists who had led the Battle of the Buttle once again rose to the cause. The writer Eric Sismey, who first saw the park during a 1912 survey, was among this group: "Since the mid-40s I have fished for tyee nearly every year and I still cannot reconcile the changes made to the lakes and the river. Those seeing it now, for the first time, may find some beauty in the waters, the surrounding hills and mountains even though they cannot enjoy the barren land. But those who knew the old river, poled a canoe through its rapids and fished its pools, those who may have paddled a canoe along Buttle's rugged and timbered shore, stopped, perhaps to toss a fly in the little bay at Wolf Creek, will know that the people's right to natural beauty

Cliff Lin, a Western Mines shift boss, taking a break with several other miners. The mine generated a spinoff economy, creating secondary jobs in the district, but a vocal minority raised environmental questions about the dumping of mine tailings in Buttle Lake. The government of the day turned a blind eye to their concerns.
Courier-Upper Islander Collection, MCR 10734

in a park which was once solemnly dedicated to the people of the province has been sacrificed to what many choose to call progress."[24]

Roderick Haig-Brown was joined by people like Dr. Bob Gordon and a biology teacher, Van Egan, who spoke out against the mine in 1965, not simply because of its effect on Strathcona Park but because of Buttle Lake's importance as a watershed. Once again it was hunters, fishermen, hikers and boaters who were at the vocal forefront.

The greatest hurdle was a government set on generating profits, and unable or unwilling to see any value in preserving pristine wilderness. The Social Credit party sanctioned both logging and mining in the park. In the mind of Ray Williston, a Socred MLA, "people-use" parks were a priority. "You can't argue this to any park lover," said Williston in a taped reminiscence, "because whether he's going to use it or not...if you touch it you're damned." One of Williston's proudest political accomplishments, for which he received the tacit support of an Alberni NDP colleague, involved the exchange of first-growth timber in Strathcona Park for what became Rathtrevor Park at Parksville. "I was trying to get hold of this property—fair means or foul—because [we] used to camp there as kids."[25]

Social Credit MLA Ken Kiernan was the minister responsible for mines and later for parks at various times through the Western Mines debate. He held firm to his government's position that they were duty-bound to honour mining claims allowed in 1918. Haig-Brown reflected on what he considered a lack of foresight by Kiernan in his dual role as minister for parks and mines: "One of his first proposals was that the Class A parks should be opened to mining and logging. This was a most opportune proposal since Western Mines, amongst others, was anxiously waiting up on Myra Creek, above Buttle Lake, for something of the sort. Their first ideas were disarmingly simple. Certainly the mine would be in a park, but it would be just a little mine, just a little hole confined to a few acres that wouldn't bother anyone."[26]

The unsettling hint that surfaced in 1965, that the mine might include a townsite (not just single men's quarters), drew the ire of both conservationists and business people in Campbell River. The details of Western Mines' application for housing included "houses, apartments, hotels, motor courts, rooming and boarding houses, education, recreational and community facilities, stores and business accommodations."

Housing in the park was the final straw for Haig-Brown. "It is impossible to blame the mining company for taking advantage of the weakness and indecision they are faced with. That, after all, is their business. But there can be no conceivable excuse for a government...that accepts arguments presented with such contemptuous disregard for fact and such obviously self-seeking purpose."[27] Following a flurry of discussion between mine management and the government over the location of the proposed village (each having preferred sites), and difficulties over road access, Western Mines quietly dropped the housing project.

Yet another threat from the mine united various factions around town in 1966, when the Social Credit government approved Western Mines' application to discharge waste from their mine and mill, and "domestic sewage," into Myra Creek and Buttle Lake, which remains the source of Campbell River's drinking water. Provincial officials insisted they would take responsibility for monitoring water quality, edging the Upper Island Health Unit out of the process. With Western Mines dumping 325,000 cubic feet (9,750 m³) of tailings per month into the lake, municipal Councillor Isabel Sandberg took a stand. "It is our water, and we should be allowed to continue to take samples for our own information. Sounds like the Pollution Control Board wants to be both judge and jury."

As a result, tests were commissioned at the behest of the province, the Campbell River Water Board and Western Mines. The results demonstrated an increased level of heavy metals in the water, but according to the report there was no cause for worry. A local group disagreed. The abundantly apparent degradation of fish stocks in the watershed was ample cause for concern for the salmon fishery and the health of residents. A lobby group took up the slogan "Come to Campbell River and Drink Tailings," but nothing they could do or say, for the present, had any impact on those in power.

Tony Dolan, supporting the campaign to stop Western Mines from dumping tailings into Buttle Lake, 1966. *Courier-Upper Islander Collection, MCR 12000*

By the end of the decade Roderick Haig-Brown was becoming impatient for a new generation to champion a large-scale environmental movement. And indeed, the "baby boomers," raised in the lush economy of the post-war years, were already beginning to explore the full meaning and entitlement of their democratic rights. Though the process was to take longer than Haig-Brown may have wished, the baby-boomers would rise to the cause. Meanwhile, there were many things for them to learn and experience in the coming decade.

CHAPTER 9

A Fresh New World
1969–1981

Why can't we secure parks and wilderness areas and wild rivers and the other spectacular things of the continent hard and fast in the heart of the Constitution, so that they will be safe from violation even if the biggest goddammed diamond mine or oil well or underground facsimile of the whole General Motors complex is found in one of them? Why not? Has industry some inalienable right to invade public lands wherever found and destroy them?

Were I a man in power I should be a man in a hurry—in an awful hurry—to make full use of [a] new spirit [amongst conservation-minded youths] and bring it to its triumph in the shortest possible time.[1]

—Roderick Haig-Brown, 1966

The beauty and solitude of the Discovery Islands held a compelling attraction for a new social entity in the late 1960s, a youth movement vehemently opposed to US involvement in the Vietnam War, pollution, big business and the "establishment"—the institutions that supported all of these. There were essentially two types of people in the movement—peace-loving idealists who, like Wendy Terral Balatti, "wanted to take the best [ideas] of the olden times and bring them up into the fresh new world," and those who simply wanted a good time, at a safe distance from the mores and soap suds of their parents' generation. But long-time residents of this "coastal paradise" saw no virtues, style or integrity in either type of long-haired youth. By the early 1970s the words "dirty," "filthy" and "lazy" were synonymous with "hippies."

Communal living, which allowed for the pooling of energy and resources, was a popular way of going back to the land. An artists' cooperative on Quadra Island was sponsored by an American woman who owned an old homestead on bluffs overlooking the Strait of Georgia. On a soft, golden day in August 1970, Peggy Rowand, a reporter for the *Campbell River Courier*, stepped into the foreign world of hippiedom to write a story about this new phenomenon. "Amid the sights, sounds and scents of summer the place had a leisurely, yet purposeful air." Everyone was at work, even a new arrival, a pretty young woman who dandled a baby while peeling and coring apples. A fair-haired, blue-eyed beekeeper with a "lazy smile" pointed toward a newly planted field of clover, a potter methodically sorted pots for a second firing and a girl toiled in a neat vegetable garden, while nearby a young man pumped water from a well.

The philosophy of these people, who asked to remain anonymous, was shaped around non-aggression, a rejection of materialism and a wish for freedom. Many had moved from the United States to Canada, where they found greater tolerance and sympathy for their views. "We are different from your generation," said one fellow. "We have learned to get along well with our peer groups because we have studied psychology and instinctively understand one another. If I'd been born in the thirties...I would have been looking for economic security. Now I'm seeking a more meaningful way of life."[2]

Beach stone cottage, Jones Farm artists' commune on Quadra Island, c. 1972. *Courier-Upper Islander, MCR*

Another "nomadic group of young people" as the *Campbell River Courier* described them, were not so lucky. Without a land-owning benefactor they were chased from island to island. From Galiano they moved to Thurlow Island, where they got jobs cutting shakes for an outfit called Cosmic Logging. Then the group of twelve moved to a ghost town of derelict buildings at Rock Bay. Within months they were once again packing their bags when the new property owners, Merrill and Ring, served them with an eviction notice. Their quest was "peace and quiet in the countryside away from the rat race of the metropolis" and they were incredulous at their inability to find a safe haven anywhere on the coast.

The company, Cosmic Logging, was the brainchild of Ken Drushka and Brian Lewis, dropouts from mainstream society who were trying to establish themselves on the islands. Drushka discovered Sonora and Thurlow Islands in 1968, following the "summer of love," in the year of the Chicago riots and the assassination of both Robert Kennedy and Martin Luther King Jr. For Drushka, a Toronto journalist, it seemed conceivable that the United States might be moving toward a fascist-style totalitarian government. "This is the climate, the context, in which I came to the coast," recalls Drushka. "I thought, if that's what's happening then it's probably a good idea to know how to survive outside of cities."

What Drushka found on the Discovery Islands was a fabulously wealthy environment in which the second-growth forest was beginning to reach maturity. But the flipside was that much of the land (and work) was entirely in the control of Crown Zellerbach and the BC Forest Service. From mid-century onward, the hardy souls who had lived and worked on the islands and up the adjacent inlets had largely moved on. By pounding on a few bureaucrats' desks Drushka managed to eke out a marginal living on shake bolt claims, after trying handlining for fish from a small boat and working for a gyppo logging outfit—which didn't end up paying wages.

Ken Drushka was one of many people drawn to the Discovery Islands in the 1970s. He tried to achieve an independent lifestyle and revive the coastal economy, which had fallen flat after large corporations such as Crown Zellerbach were granted massive forest management licences in the 1950s. Drushka went on to become an outspoken critic of forest policy.
Courier-Upper Islander Collection, MCR 15150

Cosmic Logging was not just another company, says Drushka, it was a "state of mind." They saw themselves as a happy blend of the best of the ideas of Nietzsche, Ken Kesey and the Beatles—wedded to the rugged adaptability of the old-time gyppo logger and the pioneer spirit of the mid-coast: "I remember once when we first went up to Thurlow to look at the cedar up there, Brian Lewis and I were walking up the old Camp O Hastings Outfit road one morning, stoned on acid. Brian said to me, 'What would a Cosmic logger do if there was a bear suddenly charging at him?' I said, 'Well, you know, just make a lot of noise,' and he said, 'Well, you better start doing it because here comes the bear!' So I looked up and there's a bear just running straight at us. We made lots of noise and the bear took off. So we thought, yeah, this is what cosmic loggers are; this is the state of mind. It's the gyppo logger idea—whatever happens, you deal with it as best you are able to do under the circumstances."[3]

When Drushka and Lewis secured a fairly large timber sale in 1969 they set about outfitting themselves in Vancouver. Lewis found some wilderness-bound California bikers who unwittingly accepted his ancient and rotting gillnet boat in trade for some cash and a newly restored panel van painted a vibrant yellow with fire streaks adorning its sides. Drushka and Lewis bought a can of spray paint, added "Cosmic Logging" to the door of the van and placed an ad in the *Georgia Straight*, an alternative Lower Mainland newspaper: "earn from $0 to $35 a day." Drushka was taken aback by the response: "By then the hippie thing was happening. I'd never encountered hippies before [but] these were the only ones who answered the ad." They loaded up their fire-streaked van with supplies and an "improbable" crew of freaks from all over North America and headed up to Rock Bay, where they were barged across to Thurlow Island to pursue a short but memorable career as cosmic loggers.

Ken Drushka and Brian Lewis started the Cosmic Logging Company—more a state of mind than a business entity, but they did put young people to work on shake bolt claims on the Discovery Islands in the 1970s. Drushka and Lewis bought a vibrant yellow and red van, photographed by Joe Ziner, to transport their crew and gear to Thurlow Island. *Photo courtesy Joe Ziner*

Jimmie King, a flamboyant First Nations elder of the Kingcome Band, experienced hippie life first-hand in the late 1960s. King was a well-known figure around Campbell River, a man of heavy girth, with an expansive personality to match. "I think of him proudly pushing a battered baby pram down Campbell River's main street stuffed full with plump, serious-faced babies and calling out to anyone he recognized... "Hey! You seen my grandchildren?" wrote Morgan MacGregor (later Ostler) of the *Upper Islander*. "I first remember Jimmie several years ago," she wrote in 1969, "when he was carving a pole outside the Discovery Inn. It was a great tourist attraction but Jimmie spent more time being convivial with tourists and friends than he did carving." This slow style of

Jimmie King (at centre), 1965. King was a flamboyant First Nations elder who hopped aboard a VW van with a hippie couple to make a wild trek to California, where he carved a pole for a wealthy patron. Months later he returned to Campbell River, full of tales of his adventures. *Courier-Upper Islander Collection, CRM*

working was a source of frustration for a hip couple hired by a California collector. They loaded King and his roughed-out pole into their rainbow-hued van and whisked him off to California for the trip of his life. He didn't resurface again for eighteen months.

"There was a lot of innocence and excitement about freedom," says Wendy Terral Balatti, a former college instructor. There was also a certain blindness about the insidiously entrapping quality of constantly living on a high. "We thought pot was just a friendly herb. We were turning dirt into euphoria with a little sunshine." A Campbell River newspaper reporter visited this euphoric world in September 1970:

> People sit in a circle crosslegged and solemnly puff on the hooka pipe. The aim is to inhale deeply, drawing the smoke down into the lungs and holding it there for as long as possible. To have the desired effect it is essential to do this. Those experienced in the art of inhaling get "under-way" quicker than the novice. The whole performance looks silly and there is a certain amount of self-consciousness in the newly initiated.
>
> Effects last from six to 12 hours, according to the strength of the drug. With hashish there's a peculiar effect on time. A six-hour conversation can seem as short as 30 minutes. Driving ability does not seem to be impaired, but the time factor, in reverse this time, can make a two minute journey seem never ending.[4]

It wasn't just hippies who were smoking pot and popping pills. Loggers, fishermen, miners and millworkers, many of them transient residents, began experimenting with drugs long before the hippie era. The men would arrive in town after a stint of work and, according to Dr. Dick Murphy, some of them would head for the nearest beer parlour. "After the first night they'd say, 'to hell with this swill, let's go get a fix.'" Their loneliness, combined with their relative affluence, led to self-destructive behaviour. By the late 1950s Campbell River was topping BC's list of heroin addiction centres, just behind Vancouver and Nanaimo.

Statistics released by the provincial attorney general's department in April 1972 revealed that three out of every 100 people living in Campbell River used heroin, for a total of approximately 280 known addicts.[5] In a bust that same year, four Vancouver men in possession of 800 caps of heroin valued at over $20,000 were apprehended in a Campbell River motel room.

Though loggers and fishermen were the main users of heroin, hippies on the islands, with their long hair and casual clothes, stuck out as a target for those concerned about the rising drug trade. In fact the lifestyle of most of these young people barely kept them in beer and pot, but by the mid-1970s things were starting to heat up between established residents and the "newcomers."

In the hottest part of the summer of 1975, several transient youths were routed out of their makeshift shelters on an abandoned homestead on Quadra Island by a group the *Courier* described as "vigilantes." After pushing over the flimsy shelters, Sam Hooley recalls that "a few young bucks" hung nooses in the trees as an aggressive warning to the hippies to stay away. He says it was concern over the squatters' badly managed campfires that propelled them into action, but the youths were convinced the vigilantes wanted to clear the place so they could use it as a rifle range (which did not come to pass). When the story of the nooses hit national television, the incident took on much larger meaning. Sam Hooley, who had been part of the crowd ousting the squatters, got a telephone call from a sister living in Winnipeg: "Sam, what the hell are you people doing out there!"

Ted Mather recalled that the whole situation was blown out of proportion but it did start a process of reconciliation. "Suddenly all the rednecks were really nice to me, going out of their way to show they were not like they were portrayed on television."

Between the two extremes of rednecks and hippies was an ambiguous middle ground where pale pink lipstick, beehive hairdos and miniskirts were in vogue. Taking in this innocuous fun were people like the Pelletier family, who opened Campbell River's first drive-in restaurant, Del's Drive-In. Yvonne Pelletier started carhopping (waiting on customers parked in the Del's lot) when she was thirteen, wearing a lime green miniskirt, a white blouse, a little green and white cap and white go-go boots.

Sam Hooley was one of a vigilante group determined to remove squatters from their makeshift shacks on a long-abandoned homestead on Quadra Island. The appearance of this photograph on the national news brought negative attention to Hooley and others, and served as a catalyst for improved relations between "hippies" and "rednecks." *Courier-Upper Islander Collection, MCR*

Hair took on enormous importance in the late 1960s. There were those around town who waged a silent competition over the height and mass of their lacquered beehive hairdos. Even in the most conservative business circles, buzz cuts were abandoned as men's locks slipped down over their ears to join heavy mutton-chop sideburns. Rock groups like the Beatles and The Rolling Stones set the trends for male fashion and their music infiltrated the groovy social scene at cocktail parties given by the likes of Dale Young, the wife of Campbell River's new high school principal.

Bruce Saunders was chairman of the school board when John Young was hired in 1965 to take charge of a new senior high school, then in the planning stages. Saunders recalls that the board was looking for a strong focus on discipline and vocational training. That is not, in the end, exactly what they got.

Young's striking physical and intellectual presence might have suggested right from the start that this was a different sort of man. He's been characterized as "a driver," someone who exuded energy and confidence from every pore of his short frame. His contemporaries described him as a dapper dresser with a flair for style, which one newspaperman decided was more in keeping with a "Paris boulevardier than an educator." His personal expression extended to his cars, including a powder blue Cadillac and later a little Morris Minor painted psychedelic colours.

Joseph Aurele (John) Young was the eldest of nine children, raised in a family of mixed French- and English-speaking Micmac, Acadian and Scottish ancestry. While his cultural heritage was rich, his family's circumstances were not: "My father [who worked for Bathurst Pulp and Paper] had been active in the union in New Brunswick in those days, from which he was fired for union activity at the height of the Depression. You can imagine the kind of life we had."[6]

At the age of eighteen, Young enlisted for World War II service, where he enjoyed his first experience of regular meals. "My God, I thought that was wonderful! I'd never had such good clothes, nice boots, nice clean underwear and a suit and warm coat. And the food was so good! Everyone else was complaining about the food and I thought it was just marvellous."

At war's end a buddy who was enrolling at the University of British Columbia on a veteran's pension encouraged Young to join him. "I didn't even know, really, what university was—all I knew was that just rich kids went there." Young persevered through the first difficult year, graduating in 1949 with first-class honours. Between teaching stints he augmented his first degree with a year in France at the Sorbonne, and further studies at UBC, where he got his Master's degree in teaching and sociology. He also served as a Canadian-sponsored advisor to the Minister of Education in Borneo. His work with aboriginal people proved a galvanizing and rewarding experience. "I was treated like I was a god over there, which maybe suited my Napoleonic complex; I've been accused of having a Napoleonic complex."

On his return home, Young joined forces with Keith Spicer to help found the Canadian organization CUSO, and dabbled in left-wing politics while working as a principal in Greenwood and Keremeos. His involvement with the New Democratic Party led Young into a friendship with a young man destined to be a long-term MLA for the Campbell River district. "He became a mentor," recalls Colin Gabelmann, "[who] steered me towards university."

During his first year at Campbell River, 1965, junior and senior high school students shared cramped quarters, taking shifts in a school that was later replaced by the current Phoenix Middle School. On a cold January day in 1966, Young led his staff and the entire student body of 213 teenagers through the snow to the bright, fresh new high school, which they dubbed Carihi.

John Young touching up the paint job on his new car, early 1970s. Young was the first principal of Campbell River's new senior high school, Carihi. He implemented controversial teaching methods designed to allow students and teachers greater freedom and responsibility. Some thirty years after he left Campbell River, the mention of John Young's name could still evoke a mixture of impassioned responses. *Courier-Upper Islander Collection, MCR*

Young had the pick of the junior/senior school staff, whom he involved in the design of the facility—a first, according to one of his former teachers, May Tunningly. Biology labs were built to teacher specifications, and the extra-wide hallways and student lounges gave the place a less institutional feel. Van Egan, a biology and oceanography teacher, recalls that together they slowly forged a new philosophy of student empowerment which was to build and develop over the eight years Young worked in Campbell River.

In an era when teachers were not invited to participate in the management of schools, Young encouraged their involvement at weekly—sometimes daily—staff meetings. Teachers took part in the selection of new staff and specialist teachers were no longer required to teach outside their disciplines. "It was the most stimulating time of my career," recalls May Tunningly, who thoroughly enjoyed the high-calibre teachers Carihi began attracting. "They were . . . open to new ideas, open to change. It was a marvellous way to end my career." Van Egan echoes that sentiment, saying, "Those were the best years of my teaching career and also the hardest I've ever worked."

High morale amongst the teachers had a positive effect on the students, according to a writer for the *Victoria Colonist* in 1967, who said "an observer soon senses that the relationship between the teacher and students is unusual. If the school is revolutionary, this is the revolution."

Their first major departure from tradition came about when Young and his staff decided to allow ten or fifteen straight-A students the freedom to choose whether or not to attend class. These "scholars" could work at an accelerated pace in the student lounge, or in the library with the assistance of librarian Ann (Elmore) Haig-Brown. As other students began clamouring for this privilege, what came to be called the "responsibility plan" was gradually extended to all.

Campbell Riverites are still strongly divided in their views about whether this freedom was a boon or a hindrance to education. The teachers agreed there'd always been kids who did not succeed and, as Van Egan recalls, these were the very people they thought needed the opportunity to learn self-motivation. They were, after all, no matter their academic standing, about to enter the adult world.

Rules were pared down to four basics: no truancy, no smoking in undesignated areas, no loafing and no irresponsible behaviour. Grades eleven and twelve could be completed at an individual's own pace. Some graduated in eighteen months and others took over two years. The custodian kept the school open until 11:00 at night, and it was common to find students at work in the labs and library after hours. Students could dress as they pleased, from long hair and miniskirts to jeans, and they were allowed to choose their teachers and their range of courses.

No one failed at Carihi; their reports were simply marked incomplete and they were encouraged to try again. Pregnant girls, adults (who graduated alongside their sons and daughters), and disaffected youths from other districts were welcomed into the school. There were no punitive disciplinary measures and teachers were not allowed to yell at students. Many of the rights students gained are now widely taken for granted, but in the late 1960s and early '70s these departures from the norm were considered radical.

Young continually monitored the success of the school in a variety of ways. A former teacher, Jean Purcell, admired "the tremendous dedication of this man and the constant evaluation to which he subjects his work." According to Young, in-school surveys gave the system a 90 percent approval rating. In addition there was virtually no vandalism during the seven years Young was at Carihi,[7] though it was a growing problem elsewhere.

Some former students look back on their years at Carihi during the "John Young era" as a fantastic experience and others say it was a giant flop. Alvin "Bear" Scow (now a Wewaikai Band Council member and businessman), says freedom came too quickly for him. He would have preferred a gradual preparation in his junior years. Al Thulin (co-owner of the Willows Pub) and Dan Samson (co-owner of Remax Check Realty) express a common view that too many students came out of Young's laissez-faire system with a substandard education, which continues to have a negative impact upon them.

On the flipside, Bob Duncan, manager of the Discovery Harbour Shopping Centre, thoroughly enjoyed his senior high years during Young's tenure. He concurs with a student interviewed at the time who said, "Most of us skipped a lot of classes when we first came here—I suppose because we weren't used to it. You soon realize there's no point in skipping classes and wasting time."[8] Linda (Burnard) Hogarth, curator at the Museum at Campbell River, feels lucky to have studied under the "enthusiastic and dynamic" staff Young assembled because "they created a really stimulating environment."

Young sought and received a tremendous amount of media attention for his views on educational reform and the performance of his school. As his system began to show results, he pumped out a steady stream of articles, papers and reports, accepting speaking engagements across the country. The theories and ideas he and his staff practised were not unique: for the most part they were following intellectual debate of the day, some of which was being tried in avant-garde private schools. It was the fact that they were experimenting with cutting edge ideas in a public school in a small, one-senior-high, working-class town that was unparalleled. As the experiment unfolded, film crews, reporters and interested spectators became a common sight in the halls of Carihi. Everyone, it seemed, was keeping an eye on Campbell River—some with marked enthusiasm and others with fascinated skepticism. People considering a move to the district, like Heather Stewart and Rolf Kellerhals, were heartened to read that *Maclean's* magazine ranked Carihi as one of the top ten schools in Canada. In fact the magazine called Carihi "the most impressive high school in the country."

While many of his colleagues were enthused, a growing number of residents were becoming alarmed, a situation intensified when Young expressed his views on public education in a non-stop media campaign: "Schools should be institutions where concepts like freedom, responsibility and independence are not talked about but are put into practice. We cannot expect such schools to approach perfection, but we can expect them to be much more in harmony with the needs and aspirations of free men. Freedom *is* worth far more than it costs."[9]

For some this sounded like anarchy. Joan Bunting, a former Carihi teacher, says "John Young completely divided this town!" She feels that by attracting so much media attention to the school Young intensified the debate and the divisions.

Young's teachers and board chair, Bruce Saunders, cautioned him to move out of the limelight and take a more personal approach to gain parent and community support: "The Board does not have serious reservations about the educational program of the school," wrote Saunders in a memo to Young's vice-principal in 1970, "but it is totally convinced that its continuance is contingent on the development of understanding and support from the community."[10]

Some who checked out the school for themselves were entirely happy. "I was very impressed by the maturity of the students..." said Penny Liebel. "It seemed to me that the students have a good feeling about their school; they feel that the teachers care about them."[11]

Others, like Ed Olive, were anything but happy with what they found. Ed recalls not being able to get a "straight" answer to his expressions of concern, so he wrote a letter to the editor of the local newspaper. He received numerous calls from similarly concerned parents. John Young also called. "What started out to be a discussion about the school system soon became a very heated argument," recalls Olive. "This fellow said to me that as a parent, or as a taxpayer, I had no right to criticize 'his school.'"[12]

Olive was a long-time resident and an Elk Falls Mill employee, who had achieved a responsible position in spite of a limited education. As well as raising his own children, Olive and his wife took in a number of foster children. At issue for him, in part, was his thirteen-year-old foster child. Olive was proud of the fact that the girl had managed to pull up her grades while attending the junior high school, but at Carihi she was losing ground, a fact that was not communicated to Ed for some months.

Ed responded by forming a group, including professionals and tradespeople, bent on taking John Young to task. They collected 1,463 names on a petition and in 1970 they took out shares to start a newspaper, *The Freelancer* (which took on a life of its own, becoming *The Mirror* a year later). According to Olive the other papers had a pro-Young bias; *The Freelancer* "reported things a lot more truthfully. When the truth started coming out the other papers had to print the truth." What "the Olive Group" wanted was a return to daily attendance taking, notification of absenteeism, and restriction of the "freedom plan" to those achieving high marks.

But Young was not prepared to budge; nor was he willing to give up his public attacks on the whole education system, ministry officials and the minister of education. As far as Young was concerned, change elsewhere in the province was moving far too slowly. In the 1990s, reflecting on the experience, Young admitted to a degree of arrogance in his stance. He thought his academic standing and acclaim as one of Canada's foremost educators shielded him from being fired.

Ed Olive and his colleagues increased their pressure by taking their complaints to Social Credit MLA Dan Campbell, the ministry, and the local school board. Olive went from being a man of limited writing and public speaking experience to a media maven, championing a cause that had become his central focus. Looking back in the 1990s, Ed says it was one of the most rewarding times in his life. He appeared on radio and television, and wrote over seventy letters to the editor. One of his articles appeared in the *Christian Science Monitor*, winning his group support from across the country.

During the first few years the more liberal school board members were generally in favour of the changes taking place at Carihi. But as criticism began to build, the loyalties and interests of the board split into two camps, dubbed by Young "the four black hats and the three white hats." Bruce Saunders, who lost his seat as trustee in the 1970 election, remained firm in his belief that if you "pay a guy to do a job, you don't stand in his way."[13] Quotes in the media demonstrate Saunders's approval of Young's capability as an educator, as well as his general approach, but Young's intransigence and egotism mitigated against his success. "He was the most amazing man," recalls Saunders, "but a real pain in the butt."

John Young found his most powerful adversary when he began taking public shots at the "antiquated" views of the ministry of education. When District Superintendent Jim Logie retired, the ministry sent in a successor whose mandate was to quell John Young. In 1971 the ministry revoked the school's accreditation, a stinging chastisement reserved for schools performing at below-standard levels. In the eyes of some the move was clearly a political tactic. The Carihi teaching staff was widely acknowledged to be among the best in the country and UBC ratings showed that Campbell River students were achieving 17 percent higher grades than the provincial average.[14]

In early August 1972 the *Courier* reported that the school board had "adopted stringent new rules and regulations for the operation of the senior secondary school," by a vote of four to three. "Rules for students at Carihi stress attendance and absence for a consecutive period of two weeks without a medical certificate could mean expulsion."

The air had the golden stillness of late summer as John Young put his personal cares aside to join the party faithful working at New Democratic Party headquarters on August 30, 1972. It was provincial election day and it was becoming apparent the NDP candidate, Karen Sanford, might top the polls. The education ministry foresaw an even bigger victory for the NDP across the province, and escalated their plans to oust Young. "The education minister, Donald Brothers, phoned Campbell River and [the board] held a meeting around noon," says Young. "Phil Sampson, the secretary treasurer, he phoned me, tracked me down in the committee rooms. He said, 'John, I have an extremely important letter to give to you. Should I deliver it down there or would you rather come up to my office?' I said, 'I think I know what it is. I'll [come] up to your office.'"[15]

When school opened in September the newly appointed interim principal, Walter Fogg, faced a crowd of about 1,000 people—students, parents and "agitators"—in the school gymnasium. Fogg's demands that protesters leave were ineffectual. "I did not ask for this job and I do not want it," declared Fogg. The protest had started out peaceably enough when 200 parents, teachers and students gathered outside the school with placards and pro-John Young songs, but when they overtook the registration process in the gym, Fogg called in the RCMP. A parent, Mary Hay, and a seventeen-year-old student, Robert Baskin, were arrested as a warning for the crowd to disperse.

Reflecting on the situation a few days later, Bob Blakey, editor of the *Courier*, called upon the electorate to consider carefully when making their choice for three new trustees in the upcoming election. "Voters would do well to reject any candidate who is strongly pro-Young or anti-Young." It was time to find a peaceful middle ground.

Only one of the litany of charges against Young was deemed sufficient grounds for dismissal: insubordination.[16] His public criticism of his board and ministry were Young's undoing. Though the board gave Young a year's salary as severance, he was unable to get further work in the education field in Canada. Teachers who supported Young, people with top academic and teaching records, feel they were overlooked for career advancement in District 72 for decades to follow.

Young went on to become a businessman and educator in China, and now works as an advocate for the poor, as well as serving as an outspoken trustee on the Victoria School Board. Over the intervening years he has gained and lost several fortunes but never his indomitable spirit. "The flame of freedom burns with an intense heat even to this very day in my guts and I won't allow anybody to encroach on my freedom," said Young in a 1998 interview. With his long grey hair and full beard as an enduring symbol of defiance, Young continues his crusade. "I'm going to keep working forever. I have no intention of leaving this world; there's too much work to do."

John Young shared the headlines with Karen Sanford on August 30, when her landslide provincial election victory was emblazoned across the front page of the *Courier*. Sanford was prepared for the possibility she might unseat the long-time incumbent, Dan Campbell, but her 4,000-vote majority took everyone by surprise. The real surprise, though, was the NDP's standing in the province as a whole, where they won a solid majority. It was a fresh new world—British Columbians had tired of the Social Credit.

Dan Campbell took his defeat with grace. Sitting in the back of Social Credit headquarters with a Styrofoam cup of rye and water, Campbell watched the radiant Premier-elect Dave Barrett on a portable TV. Ending a seventeen-year political career, he and his wife Jeannie walked across to the NDP headquarters to congratulate Sanford on her "well-earned" victory.

Sanford was one of a growing number of women entering politics in the early 1970s. Nineteen female candidates had run for office in the election of 1972. "I think that the attitudes are changing," said Sanford during her campaign. "There are some women who are finally realizing that things are not all what they might be as far as women's rights in this country are concerned."

One of the NDP's election promises was to do something about lax pollution laws. Sanford took the Socreds to task for extending their deadline by over twelve months for new pollution control requirements for mills. "Nothing could be more hypocritical than this policy of talking tough for the benefit of the voters and acting soft for the benefit of the owners," charged Sanford in the *Courier*. She also took a shot at the Socreds' soft touch with multinational logging companies. "We say that people who argue that economics rate ahead of environmental protection have a death-wish for mankind."

Logging and mining in Strathcona Park came under serious scrutiny by the new government. A newspaper headline of the day announced, "Western Mines faces closure," and while this did not come to pass, the NDP government enacted a moratorium on any further resource extraction in the park as of 1973.

A young couple who were to play a vital role in ensuring the preservation of Strathcona Park made a full-time business of their lodge on the shores of Upper Campbell Lake in 1972. Myrna (Baikie) Boulding and Jim Boulding gave up their teaching jobs (Myrna taught under John Young and Jim taught at the junior high school) to fulfill Jim's long-held dream of a wilderness lodge for young people. Jim Boulding was described by his contemporaries as a giant of a man, a fine athlete and a superb outdoorsman—a rugged individual in the Hemingway tradition. His devoted friend and colleague, Rob Wood, said Boulding's philosophical approach and love for the natural world were his great strengths. He believed exposing people to nature could (and often did) transform their lives.

The basis for their business was a beautifully crafted log building erected on Upper Campbell Lake in 1930, which the Bouldings purchased in 1958 from Myrna's family, Baikie Brothers Logging.

For the first few years Jim and Myrna used the lodge as their summer residence. The place seemed to attract business on its own. "We had people coming by who wanted to stay with us," recalls Myrna. "So we began charging them and that's how we got started."

Baikie Brothers bought Strathcona Lodge, built on upper Campbell Lake in 1930. In 1958 Myrna and Jim Boulding purchased the property and started a wilderness lodge for young people. Strathcona Park Lodge & Outdoor Education Centre has become a leader in wilderness training and programming. *Bill Chambers Collection, MCR 13041*

As life will sometimes have it, the same year the Bouldings gave up their teaching jobs to add a non-profit outdoor education centre to their resort, their main lodge was destroyed by fire. Within hours the cedar building, with its recent additions and refurbishment, was a complete loss. Interviewed on the scene, Boulding told an *Upper Islander* reporter he was far from defeated. "If I have to [rebuild] it by myself, I'll do it. Whatever it takes, I'll give it. I won't let it die." A few days later, when asked if the loss of the main lodge would affect his business, Boulding said: "Perhaps, but only slightly. We had sixty kids up here from Vancouver the day after the fire and we managed to put them all up and feed them." Within three weeks they had a new chalet-style lodge under construction.

Inspired by a year studying wilderness education in England, the Bouldings sidelined the tourist resort business in 1974 to offer training for young people and teachers. Their programming utilized much of the mid-Vancouver Island region, from coast to coast. They offered courses in mountaineering, boating and wilderness survival. On-site programs included music, writing, crafts and cooking. A special feature for young people was an in-depth wilderness leadership program, which ended with a stint of teaching school groups.

Over a four-year period from 1974 to 1978 they ran courses for 1,000 teachers and 20,000 students from around the province. "Customized programs are a specialty and we've been lucky to have some really excellent people leading programs and shaping the direction we've taken," said Myrna Boulding in a 1998 interview. Myrna credits Roderick Haig-Brown; the Native leader and writer George Clutesi; John Jackson, who started three outdoor schools in Britain; and mountaineer Doug Scott as having played particularly inspirational roles.

The Bouldings' staff were an international mix of mountaineers, hikers and kayakers. Many of them had a decidedly countercultural appearance that didn't sit well with a few locals. "There were people in Campbell River who thought we were just a bunch of environmentalists, tree huggers," recalled Myrna. This and a continuing linkage in the minds of some between the Bouldings and John Young strongly affected their local business. In 1976 the school board announced that no classes would be granted permission to attend programs at Strathcona Lodge, which was hosting a UNESCO conference that year. The school board claimed they didn't need the Bouldings' services because they were covering environmental studies in-house, but Jim Boulding saw the decision as a punitive action stemming from the days when, as a BC Teachers Federation representative, he supported John Young.

No matter the setbacks, the Bouldings fulfilled their vision. They were among the first to offer activities based upon the full range of outdoor pursuits available in this region of mountains, lakes, forests, streams and ocean.

Ken Drushka shared the Bouldings' understanding that children raised in urban environments need hands-on opportunities to learn about the natural world. Drushka's vision was to groom young people as "resource stewards." He also saw the need to re-establish jobs for small independent contractors on the coast. In 1971 Drushka secured funding from the new Opportunities for Youth Program to undertake a study of watershed rehabilitation on East Thurlow Island. The aim of the pilot project was to demonstrate the potential for creating jobs by enhancing the regeneration of trees and fish.

The "Synergistic Salmon Systems" report led to a $300,000 program to train young people in salmon stream rehabilitation. But within months the project was stalled when it became hopelessly enmeshed in a nightmare of bureaucracy. And worse, while Crown Zellerbach foresters generally supported the program, the crew working on the island determinedly opposed it. Not only did the loggers refuse to reroute roads away from the stream, but they removed barriers meant to block runoff from entering the stream. Drushka's response was to intensify goodwill efforts to bring the loggers on side, but when members of his crew pushed for a more combative approach, bringing in Greenpeace and the media, the project fell apart.

The problem of declining fish stocks had also been under discussion for decades by organizations like the Native Brotherhood. The Kwakiutl District Council (representing eleven Kwakwa̱ka'wakw bands) and other First Nations groups began pressing for a greater say in the management of their traditional livelihood. The KDC noted a sharp decline in Native participation in the fishery between 1954 and 1971, when the number of Native-owned vessels dropped from 1,275 to 600. "It is . . . our belief that we are one with the land and sea we own," stated a KDC pamphlet, "and that we must live in delicate balance and harmony with the world around us if we are to survive as a people."

The Homalco people of Church House, at the mouth of Bute Inlet, lost twenty licences, affecting nearly their entire population from 1960 to 1970, when a new rationing system for commercial fishing licences required a specific catchment size. Many, if not all, Homalco fishermen fell below the quota and were no longer eligible for licences.[17] This was a final blow to their economic independence, which had already suffered as the canneries and small logging operations of the northern Discovery Islands were displaced in the post-war years. Many Homalco people relocated to Campbell River and elsewhere, leaving their former village to become a virtual ghost town. The circumstances of the Homalco people went from bad to worse. They had faced the adverse effects of alcohol abuse (dating back to the early trading and settlement days), isolation, residential schooling and a gradually declining local economy. Now, as they scattered to various points, they faced the loss of their unique cultural identity.

The federal government had a solution for declining fish stocks: the construction of a major hatchery on the Quinsam River. When the program was announced in 1972 it came in for criticism from some quarters. Norm Lysne, a fisherman serving on the regional district board, thought the idea was basically sound but questioned the wisdom of spending millions of dollars on a hatchery without cleaning up industrial activity downstream. "The estuary," said Lysne, "is as important as the breeding ponds in the life cycle of the salmon." Roderick Haig-Brown shared Lysne's view. Log booms, sawmills, heavy metals from Western Mines and a cement plant dredging its gravel from the river had to be cleaned up to ensure the survival of Campbell River's fish stocks.

"Nature does a far better job of producing salmon than a hatchery does," Haig-Brown was quoted as saying to the press. "In my opinion it is more economical in the long run to repair a damaged salmon river than to build a hatchery." He went on to explain that salmon lose their genetic variation when raised in hatcheries, resulting in changes to behaviour, weight and size.

The Quinsam Hatchery went ahead, informed but not blocked by these criticisms. Pollution continued unabated on the estuary for a further two decades, while hatchery employees and conservationists like Dr. Dick Murphy and Mike Gage continued pressing government and industry to bear the expense of relocation and cleanup. But the prevailing sentiment of the day, expressed by community leaders like Ken Forde, was that boaters and manufacturers had a historic right to continue using the estuary.

Meanwhile the hatchery, which opened in 1974, kept the coho run alive. "The hatchery became the last line of defence for the survival of salmon and trout—and the culture surrounding it," said Rob Bell-Irving, a Quinsam Hatchery employee. The returns have increased steadily, starting with 2,000 coho in the first few years to 28,500 by 1985.[18]

This was not the first time Haig-Brown's astute observations provoked a painfully slow awakening on the part of the general public. As always, no matter the obstacles, he was willing to champion his causes to the end, following an underlying philosophy he described in 1950: "I have been, all my life, what is known as a conservationist. I am not at all sure that this has done myself or anyone else any good, but I am quite sure that no intelligent man, least of all a countryman, has any alternative. It seems clear beyond possibility of argument that any given generation of men can have only a lease, not ownership, of the earth; and one essential term of the lease is that the earth be handed on to the next generation with unimpaired potentialities. This is the conservationist's concern."[19]

On the Thanksgiving weekend of October 9, 1976, as the salmon spawned up the Campbell and the apple trees hung heavy with fruit at Above Tide, Roderick Haig-Brown gave the lawn a final trim for the season. Turning from the tractor shed, he looked up in response to Ann's call to lunch, and collapsed on the lawn. He passed away within hours. The shock of Haig-Brown's early death at age sixty-eight reverberated throughout his extensive network of friends and colleagues in the community and across North America. Losing a man still in his prime, with so much brilliance, integrity and wisdom to share, affected his friends and family for years. "The meaning of such an early death," wrote his daughter, Valerie Haig-Brown, several decades later, "when it seems he could still have accomplished so much still escapes me."[20]

Ann Haig-Brown, though she had retired some years earlier from her job as the Carihi librarian, was able to continue living in her house by the river. In 1976 she and Roderick had sold their property into a provincial trust which ensured its preservation and allowed them the right to remain at Above Tide, tax free, through their lives.

The corner bench in the tiny kitchen of the Haig-Browns' house continued to be a popular spot for a stream of people seeking personal and professional advice. Ann's solid and caring personality, together with her broad intellect, ensured her a wide range of friends and community involvement. A naturalist, Howard Telosky, was one of many inspired by Ann's optimism and her fascination with the world around her. She "always had that special way of making others feel important."

This attitude made Ann the logical sponsor when a Parents in Crisis chapter was formed in Campbell River. For years Ann had provided a safe haven for people in need. Soon Above Tide became a semi-official transition house for women fleeing abusive relationships. "Often women came for repeat visits and I wondered if an angry husband might come looking for them and possibly get rough," recalls her daughter, Mary (Haig-Brown) Bowker. "This never happened, possibly a sign of the esteem in which my mother was held. I was glad when the doors of the [Ann Elmore] Transition House opened [in 1987]. Mother was very honoured when they named it after her, using her birth name." Ann was also a strong supporter of other social service organizations that emerged in the 1970s, like a women's centre, the Adult Care Society and the John Howard Society.

Skip McDonald became Campbell River's first official mayor when municipal boundaries were expanded in 1969, bringing Elk Falls Mill within the town's tax base. Some outspoken members

Ann (Elmore) Haig-Brown outside her family home, now a heritage site on the banks of the Campbell River. Her husband Roderick died prematurely in 1976; she outlived him by many years, continuing her work as a community activist and champion of battered women. *Courier-Upper Islander Collection, MCR 15191*

of the Willow Point district, which narrowly voted to join the municipality, didn't care what new amenities might come their way with the large mill tax—for them, the change simply spelled more taxes. At the helm of this group was Ken Forde, who operated a car garage in Willow Point.

Ken Forde's determined and outspoken views led him to a seat on municipal council in 1966 and a five-year stint as mayor, starting in 1971. The *Courier* newspaper described Forde as a born crusader and an occasional hothead who was admired for his honesty and integrity. Forde's platform remained firmly focussed upon fiscal restraint and representation for Willow Point. Some accused him of being old-fashioned, a man still representing frontier values at a time when progressive people were looking for an investment in civic planning

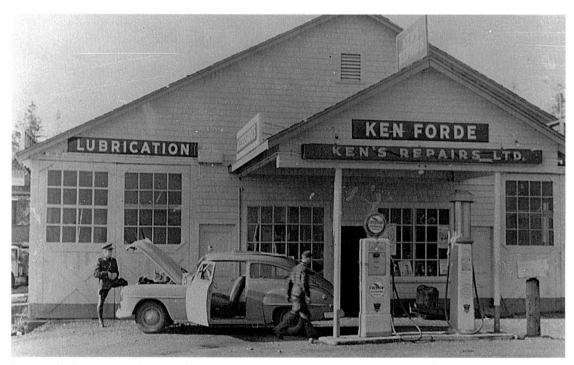

Ken Forde (not in this photograph) operated a garage in Willow Point and served as mayor for Campbell River starting in 1971. He earned a reputation as an occasional hothead, but he was admired for his honesty and integrity. *Wieshlow Collection, MCR 19770*

and development. While Forde was at the helm, the municipality built a sewage treatment plant. It was erected on the town's otherwise enviable waterfront, as a cost-saving measure. Questions about the economy of this choice increased over the years, as did the noxious fumes the plant exhaled across the main entrance to the town.

In 1972 another contentious issue arose when a merchant decided to buck a 1960 bylaw requiring that all businesses except essential services remain closed on Sundays and on Monday afternoons. The co-owners of Gordon's Men's Wear set a trap for a law-breaking neighbouring merchant, sending an emissary to make a purchase on a Monday afternoon. Triumphantly waving a pair of Stanfield's underwear and a bill of sale, the lad precipitated some serious questioning by his action. Was Campbell River ready for a six-day week? It seems so, for the offender, guilty as accused, was given the ridiculously low fine of $3.

During Skip McDonald's term as mayor, the waterfront south of Tyee Plaza was filled to create Foreshore Park—following a lively debate over its potential for commercial development. In 1972 Thor Peterson and Dr. Bob Gordon co-ordinated the construction of a First Nations-style "big house" as an architectural feature for the park, which has become a lasting tribute to Kwakwaka'wakw art. The monumental posts and beams of the Heritage Pavilion were carved by Sam Henderson and his sons, Ernie and Bill, along with Bob Neel, Ben Dick, Eugene Alfred and Dora Cook. The Heritage Pavilion was officially opened at the Salmon Festival, Campbell River's annual July 1st celebration, and dedicated "to the people of all nations that find enlightenment in the rich cultural heritage of our community."

Pat Martin and Jim Luckhurst paid off the financing of their mill in 1973. Naming it the Raven Lumber Company, they'd purchased it from Baikie Brothers (their former employers) in 1962. Within just over a decade they'd boosted production significantly, going from 25 employees to 250 in the peak years, while branching into logging and property development as Raven Industries.

A significant number of Raven Lumber's employees were Sikhs. By 1970 there were twenty Sikh families in Campbell River. For the first few decades a spiritual leader, Mrs. Sangha, read the sacred texts in temporary facilities, until they were able to build a temple on Pinecrest Road. Sometimes encountering insidious racism, the Sikh community has made significant contributions to many civic institutions such as the hospital and museum.

Campbell River was declared the fastest growing town in the province in 1973,[21] but there was an absence of grace in its architecture and streets. Cod Fish Flats, a soggy marsh backing the main drag, was still a scatter of scruffy war-era bungalows—some of which had been taken over by vagrants. New homes were being built on the ridge south of town, taking advantage of the view of Discovery Passage and the mainland mountains. In the minds of a growing number of people, who planned to spend their lives in Campbell River, it was time to update the town and acquire some of the amenities and polish of a settled community.

Tom Barnett, a recently retired CCF/NDP Member of Parliament for the riding, was approached in 1977 by municipal Councillor Joan Stephens, who urged him to run for mayor. Though Joan and Tom were not of the same political stripe they were in full agreement about the pressing need for planning, improved services and a larger vision for Campbell River. During Barnett's three-year term as mayor, the economy experienced yet another soaring upsurge, but for the first time there was an Official Community Plan to direct development. There were a record number of housing starts in the late 1970s (especially in Rockland and Willow Point), which council surcharged to create a long-term fund for purchasing waterfront properties along the highway leading into town.

During this economic boom many new services and businesses appeared. North Island College opened in temporary quarters in 1975, and Ironwood Mall became the town's first enclosed shopping complex in 1977. Two years later an indoor swimming pool was added to the ice arena on Pinecrest Street; Quinsam Medical Clinic moved to a new location near the hospital and the Yaculta Lodge seniors' complex opened. Many more projects were being planned by an amazingly active group of volunteer organizations who were fundraising, planning and lobbying for such things as a new library, museum, art gallery, performing arts theatre, and more sports and recreation facilities.

The completion of a paved highway to Port Hardy in 1979 linked north Vancouver Island communities together, enhancing Campbell River's role as a supply centre for the region. Premier Bill Bennett was on hand to celebrate the opening, posing for one last round of "pothole golf," a media appeal used by a north Island resident named Gerry Furney to draw attention to the need for a paved road.

The electorate was thrilled with the new highway, its spacious lanes curving through the dramatic mountain and lakeside scenery of the north Island, but not enough to put a member of the then-governing Social Credit party in charge of the newly formed North Island riding. Colin Gabelmann had just been selected as the NDP candidate for the riding when, one week later, the government called a snap election in 1979. Gabelmann took the seat and held it for seventeen years.

Colin Gabelmann was raised in a politically charged household, where his loyalties were divided between the views of his Tory mother and his CCF stepfather. Gabelmann's stepfather shared much in common with the hippie movement of the 1970s. He left Germany in 1928, fearing the advent of a fascist government, and settled in the Okanagan Valley with a vegetarian commune. When the Depression hit, the community scattered, but Fritz Gabelmann established himself as a orchardist in Osoyoos. There he met and married an Englishwoman, and adopted her son Colin. "Eventually," says Colin, "I chose his politics over my mother's and she finally did too."

Gabelmann joined the celebrations when the Kwakwaka'wakw people opened two museums (the Kwagiulth Museum at Cape Mudge and the U'Mista Cultural Centre at Alert Bay) to house their treasured ceremonial regalia. The basis of these collections were repatriated masks and dance pieces taken by the federal government when anti-potlatching laws were enforced in 1922. The opening ceremonies were emotionally charged events, as elders recalled the pain inflicted upon them, and rejoiced in their hopes for the future. Harry Assu of Cape Mudge described

Colin Gabelmann at the Elk Falls Mill, 1983. He served the Campbell River area riding as an NDP MLA for seventeen years, starting in 1979. During his last term, Gabelmann served as attorney general. *Photo courtesy Colin Gabelmann*

the opening of the Kwagiulth Museum on June 29, 1979 in his autobiography, co-authored with Joy Inglis: "My son Don brought his seiner around to the beach in front of the museum. Chiefs of all our Kwagiulth villages were on board, drumming and singing. Jim Sewid was our speaker. He welcomed everybody from the beach. There were about five hundred people. He called to the chiefs of each band in our language, welcoming the people from that village. That's when they threw 'Klassila,' the spirit of dancing, from the boat to the shore, where it was caught by a fellow who started up dancing. Then he threw it up and into the museum."[22]

Bill Roberts, the Chief of the Campbell River Band, began making plans to develop the waterfront in the late 1970s. Roberts' initial idea was to create a source of income and employment for the band by building a recreation marina as well as a commercial facility to accommodate the commercial fleet.

When Raven Industries built a new office block in 1979 (the Royal Bank building), across from Tyee Plaza, they were among the first to inject new life into the sagging downtown core. Some of the smaller merchants, who could afford neither mall rents nor competition, had closed their doors, leaving "missing teeth" along the town's main thoroughfare. Those that remained viable, like Seymour Pharmasave and Page 11 Books, survived on their established reputations for specialization and customer service.

Greg Culbert, a businessman, was among the first to consider refurbishing one of the town's older buildings. In the sodden damp of the late fall of 1976, Culbert pushed open the door of what had been the old Dawson family home, across from the government dock. The roof leaked a steady stream in this dank and dreary nest for birds and rodents. Undeterred, the Culberts remodelled the place into a seafood shop and packing plant. "We felt that rather than put up an ugly, concrete square building, let's have a little bit of style and pizzazz," Culbert told a reporter when he received a Chamber of Commerce award for his work.

Another favourite hangout for bats, mice and pigeons was the upper storey of the municipal hall, the former Lourdes Hospital building, an interesting remnant from the old days of "Thulinville." The place, on a slope overlooking the centre of town and beyond to Discovery Passage, had been awkwardly adapted as municipal offices after 1957. By the early 1980s the staff and council had no thoughts of winning prizes for heritage restoration; they were desperate for a new building. The old hospital-cum-municipal hall was demolished in stages as a new textured-concrete replacement took shape behind it. At the official opening ceremonies in June 1982, Mayor Hugh Campbell honoured his predecessor, Tom Barnett, by naming him the city's first freeman. Tom's wife, Ruth (Pidcock) Barnett, was also praised for her work on environmental concerns and for her tireless service on the historical society board.

While most downtown merchants were simply holding on, looking askance at the profit-robbing Ironwood Mall, Clair Hamilton took action to save the downtown. He'd been through a similar experience when the Tyee Plaza was created and a curtain of isolationism fell between the old merchants and the new. After reading about how other cities were surviving the "chain store age," Hamilton attended a week-long seminar in Toronto in 1979. The enormous enthusiasm he brought home radiated among his colleagues immediately.

Tapping into a downtown revitalization incentive program offered by the government, Hamilton's group spruced up the streets, facades and focal points of the town. But just as this project got underway the global economy went flat, spiralling into yet another recession. Within the district the unemployment rate skyrocketed by 73 percent (other areas of the province were similarly affected) and lineups formed outside a soup kitchen/food bank organized to deal with the crisis. By 1981, says Bruce Baikie, "it felt like someone had just turned the taps off."

Roderick Haig-Brown had always feared these times of recession, when political will weakened and public financial need mitigated against environmental protection. Witnessing how quickly industry and development were encroaching upon the land and sea, Haig-Brown's writing took on an urgent tone toward the end of his life. In his last years he pinned his hopes for the future upon the post-war generation. By the 1980s, that generation had mellowed and matured. Having learned the lessons of the 1960s and '70s, they were ready to take up the gauntlet Haig-Brown had tossed at their feet.

CHAPTER 10
The Trump Card
1981–1999

The adventure lies in the acceptance of the unknown and the willingness to adapt and tune in...This is exactly what I had in mind when I turned my back on the scheduled professional life in the big city. Going climbing or escaping to the mountains at week ends, refreshing as it may be, can no longer be enough once you've had the experience of constant exposure to the beauty and magical power of the wilderness. The variety of the changing mood and personality of the landscape becomes so energizing and inspiring that it is hard to comprehend why so many people choose to live in the city.

—Rob Wood, 1991[1]

Fred Nunns and Captain John Kwaksistala, Campbell River men of the 1890s, both knew coal seams lay beneath their feet. For Nunns the sustaining hope that Canadian Collieries would establish a mine on or near his property kept him rooted on the banks of the Campbell through most of his lonely life. Captain John no doubt had mixed feelings. He had seen how coal mines at Cumberland had produced a spinoff economy for his people, but involvement with non-Native people had always taken a toll on the health and culture of the First Nations. For better or worse, the expected coal mines did not become a reality during their lifetimes.

Capt. John and Fred also shared a delight in the fantastic fishing in Discovery Passage. Their enthusiasm, whether for sport or income, was far more complex than a simple need to fill larders or to make a living. They watched the play of seasons on the river and ocean and knew the intricacies of the weather, tides and habits of their prey. They were fully involved members of a magnificent coastal environment.

The depth of these feelings might have neutralized any ambitions they had for a share in coal mining wealth, had they lived to see the negative impact mines would inflict upon fish habitats in the twentieth century. Certainly that was the case for a new generation of fishers, men like Rob Bell-Irving, Thor Peterson, Dick Murphy, Don McIvor, Mike Gage and Van Egan, ready to stand up when Quinsam Coal tried to fast-track an application to establish a mine at Middle Quinsam Lake in the late 1970s.

Quinsam Coal was formed by a partnership between Weldwood of Canada (a logging company that took over the old Canadian Collieries holdings) and Luscar Mining. Their first proposal included an open-pit mine on the Campbell River watershed, upriver from the hatchery, with a shipping dock on Tyee Spit, at the mouth of the river.

For conservationists the possibility of an open-pit mine upriver from a multi-million-dollar hatchery was an outrage, the culminating event of years of pollution in the Campbell River watershed. It was time to take an immediate stand, warned MLA Colin Gabelmann, as conservationists predicted the devastation from further mining. Once the company passed the second stage of a three-part approval process, the mine could not be stopped.

People representing commercial and sport fishing groups were at the heart of the protest, along with two new groups formed as a result of the Quinsam Coal proposal. Dr. Dick Murphy organized the Campbell River Estuary and Watershed Society in 1979 to lobby for a full cleanup of pollution in the river. According to a writer for *The Northern Miner*, the "loudest and most articulate" objections to the Quinsam Coal project came from Save Our Salmon (SOS), a group spearheaded by Thor Peterson, a real estate agent.

Peterson's ideas and sensibilities are deeply rooted in this coastal environment of big fish, wild characters, rough tides and high stakes investments. From his youthful days working at April Point Lodge, his family's sport fishing resort on Quadra Island, to his water taxi service and a real estate business covering much of northern Vancouver Island, Peterson has come to know this region better than most. "Campbell River has been good to me," he said in 1998. "When the Quinsam Coal thing came up it felt like it was payback time."

Plunging into an all-consuming battle, Peterson found himself overwhelmed by a multiplicity of side issues. It was only in later years that he remembered Roderick Haig-Brown's sage advice to stay focussed upon the central issue, for fear of losing yourself and your cause in a maze of side issues.

As the SOS campaign intensified, some of Peterson's friends decided to inject a little humour into the situation by erecting a professionally made sign on one of Peterson's downtown development properties, reading Future Site of Quinsam Coal Docking Facilities. While Peterson and his friend Alec Wood sat laughing over the prank, a scenario unfolded that in the end served to heighten Peterson's determination:

> This big burly guy who happened to be the manager up at the mine came roaring up and he's glaring at [the sign] and he's taking pictures of it. He comes over to my car and he says, "Are you responsible for that sign?" I said, "No, I'm not, interesting eh." He says, "I'm so and so, manager of Quinsam Mines." He says, "Do you own that land? Is your name Thor Peterson?" And I said, "Yeah, my name's Thor Peterson and I do happen to own that land." He says, "You get that goddamn sign down right away!" I said, "You get your goddamn hands off my car," and I opened the door up and he backed off.

He went over to his car and sat [there] for a few minutes; then he walked over
to the sign and pushed it down. Alec and I looked at one another, and holy
smokes, the gloves were off! This was not Kentucky, man.[2]

With the province taking a passive back seat, conservationists persuaded the municipality to
assume the cost of an environmental impact study. The rationality and intensity of their opposition and a weakening market combined to discourage Luscar, who pulled out of their partnership
with Weldwood. At the same time government officials received a flood of letters, a petition
signed by 5,000 people and delegations, and eventually the government said no to Quinsam Coal's
fast-track stage-two application in 1981.

But Rob Bell-Irving of Save our Salmon warned people to remain alert: "I don't think people
should be lulled into thinking this thing is dead." It was not. Weldwood returned with a new partner, Brinco Mining, who opened a local office and launched a slick campaign to sell the mine's
high points—jobs and economic spinoff for the community. Bell-Irving recalls how this well-pro-
moted tactic divided the town, making inroads into power bastions like the Rotary Club, and pit-
ting neighbours against each other.

With the required tests complete, Quinsam Coal once again submitted their stage-two application in November 1982 and were quickly granted approval, but with one conciliatory proviso.
The company was required to hold a public inquiry—a first in the mining approval process, now
a standard procedure.

The goal of the inquiry was to arrive at a compromise. Mine officials and forty concerned individuals and representatives of groups made presentations to a three-person panel, with the end
result that Quinsam Coal was ordered to comply with stringent recommendations made by the
board of inquiry. Bell-Irving and others continue to monitor the terms of the agreement, noting
their disappointment over backsliding on some issues, but in general the inquiry converted ran-
corous debate into concessions that ensured both jobs and protective measures for the Campbell
River watershed.

A side benefit of the controversy was that Western Mines' role in the increasing heavy metal
count in the Campbell River watershed came into sharp focus during the "Hell NO, Quinsam
Coal" campaign.

In the late 1970s Western Mines thought they had only a few years of ore left, but just as the
recession began in the '80s they discovered a rich new ore body, the H-W Mine, which was
expected to add fifteen years or more to the life of the operation. It was time for the company to
prove their longstanding assertion they were not the cause of steadily increasing heavy metals in
the Campbell system.

The study Western Mines commissioned, as Dick Murphy recalls with a chuckle, appeared to
prove the company's point. It was, the company contended, erosion from all the side streams
(flooded by hydro dams) feeding into Buttle Lake that was the problem, not the mine. But when
Murphy and others looked at the report they discovered an interesting omission. Myra Creek,
flowing from the mine site into the lake, was the only stream not included in their study.

Peterson and a group of concerned citizens, along with the municipality, contributed in excess of
$200,000 to hire "the best lawyer in the country" for a public action suit. Then Peterson called upon
an old political connection with a northern NDP MLA who was willing to contrive a meeting with

It was ardent sport fishers like Dr. Dick Murphy who led the fight to have sources of pollution removed from the Campbell River watershed.

the federal fisheries minister. The results were dramatic. Four tests on Myra Creek resulted in four charges of pollution. However, when the case appeared in court it was thrown out on a technicality: in the intervening months company officials had changed the name from Western Mines to Westmin. They were off the hook for the present, but Peterson recalls that just bringing them to court had the desired effect. From that point on Westmin began installing a land-based disposal system.

It was four and a half years before conservationists were able to get the case back into court in 1985, and the judge handed down a conviction and an $80,000 fine. "Judge Davis said he was satisfied beyond any reasonable doubt that Westmin Resources had allowed heavy metals such as zinc and copper to flow into Myra Creek," reported the *Upper Islander* newspaper. "After looking at pictures of the settling ponds as they were in 1981 Davis said anyone would have been aware there was a problem...the situation was obviously deleterious to fish. Their casual disregard in the matter was 'tantamount to willful blindness.'" The judge also went on to congratulate Westmin on the fact that since charges were laid in 1981 they had invested $14 million to develop a new land-based tailings disposal system.[3]

A few years later Ernie Poepperl, an ardent steelhead fisherman went to Dick Murphy with interesting news. "He said, 'Dick, the river is alive again!' I said, 'How do you know that, Ernie?' and he said, 'The algae is coming back.'"

In 1986, yet another environmental threat emerged when the government lifted the ban on mining in parts of Strathcona Park.

Cream Silver Company may have played a role in the Social Credit government's decision to reopen the park for mining. In the early 1980s the company was in financial trouble, having accrued a deficit. They contained it by offering shares on their long-held claims in the park. "We have to believe that, considering the state of unemployment on Vancouver Island," Frank Lang, the company president, told his shareholders, "the government would be most anxious to expedite the return of these claims, and allow the commencement of a multi-million dollar exploration program which, if successful, could ultimately provide 300 to 500 direct and indirect jobs."[4]

It had significant potential. The ore body surrounding Cream Lake is contained in the same mineral band as Westmin's abundant H-W Mine, which is considered a world class mine. When Cream Silver Company got the green light in 1986 they started exploratory work in the park and launched a promotion campaign. But what they had not anticipated was the number of people passionately attached to the pristine beauty of Strathcona Park.

Jim Boulding of Strathcona Park Lodge & Outdoor Education Centre was among that contingent, having played a vital role in the environmental campaigns of the 1970s and early '80s, especially as they affected his beloved park. However, by 1985, when discussion of lifting the mining ban became public, Jim Boulding could only watch from the sidelines. As he struggled to overcome life-threatening cancer, young people Boulding had imbued with his love of the wilderness came forward. The baby boom generation that Haig-Brown noted in its infancy, and Boulding nurtured through their wild years, had matured and was ready for the challenge.

Marlene and Steve Smith formed a lobby group, Friends of Strathcona Park, to act as a linchpin for various outdoor groups working together in a campaign that adopted the slogan "Don't Cut the Heart Out of Strathcona Park." Branches were established in Campbell River, Courtenay and Parksville, with a growing involvement from mountaineers like Rob Wood, Dr. Bruce Wood and Ruth Masters.

In the face of steadily mounting opposition, Cream Silver Company borrowed inspiration and rhetoric from Westmin, claiming they would just put a small scar on the terrain and enhance access to the park. What use was a park without roads? "The main road in the centre of Strathcona Park...was built by Westmin Resources," said Frank Lang of Cream Silver, "which provides thousands of dollars annually for park development and campsites."

Cream Silver protestors, 1988, were determined to stop mine exploration work in Strathcona Park. They maintained a blockade in the park for several months, until a television survey determined that 70 percent of the electorate were against mining in the park. This resulted in a provincial government ban on further mining. *Courier-Upper Islander Collection, MCR*

While hundreds of people attended rallies in Campbell River and Courtenay, Cream Silver forged ahead with exploratory work. When test drilling began in 1988, the Friends of Strathcona quickly organized roadblocks described by Rob Wood in his book, *Towards the Unknown Mountains*: "Word got around quickly and soon there were enough blockaders camping across the access road to cause Cream Silver to back off and seek a court injunction. This took several days, enough time for us to get more people and camp supplies to the site. This was not easy, considering the winter conditions and the remote location."

The protestors kept up their vigil for two months, joined by newspaper reporters, television crews and nearly 2,000 visitors. More than sixty people allowed themselves to be arrested, including elderly men and women who were prepared to face the consequences of a criminal record: "Suddenly, we were among the main news items and support came rolling in as the protest escalated beyond our wildest dreams," wrote Rob Wood. "Coalitions with unions and Native groups were formed as people could see we were sincere enough to go to jail."

Early in the campaign the Social Credit government had skated through a conflict-of-interest scandal when it was discovered that minister of mines, Stephen Rogers, was a shareholder in the parent company backing Cream Silver. Now, with support for the Social Credit government flagging, the politicians could not afford to ignore the massive reaction against mining in the park. When a television station survey demonstrated that 70 percent of the electorate was against mining in provincial parks the government was compelled to hold public hearings.

At this juncture Wood, exhausted by his long months of work, returned to his home on Maurelle Island to discover that his wife Laurie had purchased a television set during his absence: "When she suggested gleefully that we watch the six o'clock news I groaned a bit but gave in. As she switched it on, an amazing synchronicity occurred. The very first thing I ever saw on the TV in my own house was the news commentator announcing, 'There will be no more logging or mining in Strathcona Park, forever!'"[5]

Only the first of those arrested and charged with mischief were convicted; the rest were acquitted on a technicality. Frank Lang set up a hue and cry, as he rejected the government's offer to pay his company's exploration expenses that, according to the *Upper Islander*, had already been subsidized through government grants. For years afterward he threatened to take the government to court for $72 million, a "portion" of his company's expected profits. "I think the shareholders have had a really dirty shake," Lang told the *Courier-Islander* in 1989. "It's bad enough when you're exploring—at best it's a high risk—but when the government kicks you out and offers you your money back it's an insult."[6]

Jim Boulding did not live to enjoy this victory. The big man passed away in May 1986, two days before he and his wife Myrna were to be presented with a prestigious United Nations Environmental Stewardship award at UBC. The award ceremony became both a wake and a celebration of Boulding's many accomplishments in his fifty-four years.

The ability of Campbell Riverites to rally together was called upon in a short but intense drama of another sort on a summer night in 1984, when they were roused from their beds to evacuate 787 stranded cruise ship passengers.

Watching the boats in Discovery Passage is a favourite pastime of Riverites, who track the movement of seiners, trollers, sport boats and tugs pulling strings of barges against wind and tides. Most prized in this parade are the giant cruise ships that slide through the Passage on summer evenings, lit from stem to stern like glamorous holiday castles.

Those awake near midnight on June 29, 1984, watching the city-like *Sundancer*—with its swimming pool, lounges, casino and ballroom—sent envious thoughts following in its wake. A little farther up the Passage, just off Menzies Bay, Dorothy Holland was jolted from such reveries when she noted the ship's erratic behaviour and sounded the alarm.

A passenger aboard ship, Lucille Goodlive, was in the bathroom preparing for bed when she felt a sharp jolt and a "collision-type sound followed by a series of thumps and bumps." Lucille's husband put down his book and chased up the stairs to investigate, coming back within minutes to report there were people running about, crew members in life jackets and someone yelling "abandon ship." Heeding advice received only hours before during an emergency drill, the Goodlives dressed warmly and made their way to their assigned lifeboat. Others, not so well prepared, were to spend hours in their pajamas and slippers.

The *Sundancer* was barely seven hours into a cruise from Seattle to Alaska, its passenger roster dominated by elderly people from various points in the US. The Canadian pilot, a seasoned veteran of the Inside Passage, had asked for increased speed to run the force of an ebbing tide in Seymour Narrows, but in so doing the ship struck Maud Island.

The MV *Sundancer* struck Maud Island on a summer night in 1984. Many hours later her 787 passengers and crew were safely evacuated from the ship, which was docked at Elk Falls Mill. *Courier-Upper Islander Collection, MCR 14205*

The pilot ordered the ship to the nearby Elk Falls Mill dock, where a gangplank was lowered from the high side of the heavily listing ship. On the low side passengers like Lucille Goodlive could see nothing of the careful rescue mission taking place on the giant ship. Goodlive, a retired high school counsellor, found herself comforting a panicky youth whose parents had been unable to cope with his mounting anxiety and had left him to his own devices. Standing by their assigned lifeboat for over an hour, they caught only vague drifts of information from a muffled PA system and scurrying crew members.

Finally instructions came to leave their lifeboat and make their way down a flight of stairs to an exit point. Goodlive recalls her mounting fear as she inched her way down a packed stairwell. "We could hear pots, pans and dishes falling on the floor as the listing of the ship increased," wrote Goodlive in her memoirs. Another sharp bump, which they later learned was the gangplank breaking away from the dock as the ship sank deeper, was followed by an order to about-face and head back up the stairs to an alternate exit point.

After squeezing up the stairwell once again, they crawled along the dangerously tipped deck to reach a portal. From there all but the most disabled (who were removed by a crane) dropped from rope ladders into the waiting arms of Search and Rescue staff and volunteers.

Just as their predecessors had done in 1927 when SS *Northwestern* of Seattle ran aground off Cape Mudge, Campbell Riverites gave their all to the rescue mission. "The people of Campbell River can justifiably be proud," announced the town's new Mayor, Bob Ostler, "of the individuals and organizations who responded so magnificently. The municipal office has received many letters from passengers of the *Sundancer*, describing in glowing terms the care, concern and efficiency of all who were involved..."

Bob Ostler came into office in 1983 during a time of wildly divisive environmental battles and a recession just beginning to show signs of recovery. Though he was new to municipal politics, Ostler's business and leadership skills, honed during his years as a BC Tel executive, proved a match with the aspirations and drive fuelling a new vision for the town.

Ostler's first move was to call for a staff and council retreat to create a long-term plan for the municipality. The result was an energetic vision to reorient the town to its waterfront. Collaborating with the Downtown Revitalization project then underway, civic leaders fostered a transformation that was to give the town a polished new look. Trees were planted along the newly styled Shoppers Row where decorative lamp standards and brick sidewalks were also installed. Shop fronts were refurbished and Tyee Plaza was dressed up with a bus shelter surmounted by a spar tree, where the carved figure of a high rigger named Big Mike became the focal point of the town's core. The municipality collaborated with this work by constructing a sport fishing pier linked to waterfront footpaths, a first in Canada.

By the time the economy improved in the late 1980s the town was ready for a new generation of merchants and residents.

Part of the municipality's master plan was to consolidate business into the area between Shoppers Row and the new Ironwood Mall. A variety of lures were used to attract commercial development to that tattered old residential area, Cod Fish Flats. The plan snowballed when the municipality eased bylaws to encourage Overwaitea to open Elmwood Park in the Flats in 1987.

Some heritage buildings were refurbished and others demolished. In 1986 Patricia Young and Peter Dwillies remodelled the former police station/courthouse across from the government dock to become the Pier House Bed and Breakfast. That same year Bruce Baikie, Lauren Miller and Dan Samson bought a boarded-over eyesore at the corner of St. Ann's and the Island Highway and restored its original 1950s art deco styling.

Lavers and the Bee Hive did not enjoy the same kind fate. Both these former Thulin family business blocks were torn down in 1988. Skip McDonald built a modern version of the Bee Hive with more emphasis on the sea view. A new multi-purpose building, the Georgia Quay, was built on the Laver's site in 1989.

The fourth generation of the Thulin family continues to be part of the town's business scene. Glen, Gary and Dean Thulin are the current owner-operators of the Pioneer Hardware started by their grandfather in 1937. Sue and Al Thulin opened a neighbourhood pub on the edge of the Beaver Lodge Lands in 1986, naming it the Willows in memory of Al's great-grandparents and Campbell River's first business.

A fire at Painters Lodge in 1985, originally thought to be accidental, robbed the community of a prized heritage gem. By the time Joe Painter, who retained property next door to the lodge, was awakened by his barking dog at 4:00 a.m. on Christmas Eve, the lodge was engulfed in flames. Years of memories and mementos, including photos of famous guests like Bob Hope and Bing Crosby, went up in smoke. "Christmases there," said Joe Painter following the fire, "were spectacular. It was the centre of social life around here." Painter's eighty-six-year-old mother, June, took the loss especially hard. "She didn't think she'd outlive that lodge," her son told reporters.

The current owners, Bryon Armstrong and Ted Arbour, sold the remaining cabins and grounds to Bob Wright of Oak Bay Marine Group, who built a new and vastly enlarged version of the old Painters Lodge

Mayor Bob Ostler, 1982. He brought energized vision and leadership to the reshaping of the rapidly growing town of Campbell River. *Courier-Upper Islander Collection, MCR*

Patricia Young and Peter Dwillies purchased the old courthouse on what is now Pier Street and restored it to establish a bed and breakfast, preserving one of the few heritage structures remaining in downtown Campbell River. *Courier-Upper Islander Collection, MCR*

Painters Lodge, a name that has become synonymous with Campbell River, was destroyed by fire on Christmas Eve 1985. The fire is thought to have been the work of an arsonist. *MCR 18477*

Bob Wright of the Oak Bay Marine Group bought the Painters Lodge property and the remaining cabins following the 1985 fire. He then built a new and vastly enlarged version of the resort. *Courtesy Oak Bay Marine Group*

in 1988. Nearly a decade later the drink-loosened mutterings of a former employee, Simon Wydenes, brought about arson charges, which have yet to be resolved.

Fire destroyed another landmark in 1992 when the former Anglican church at the north end of town went up in smoke. The old structure held a special place within the community as the town's first official church, though it had been deconsecrated and turned into an antique shop and furniture store six years prior to the fire.

A vital component to Campbell River's transformation into a settled community was the blossoming of recreational, sporting and cultural facilities. The accomplishments of the 1980s and early 1990s were truly impressive, starting with the construction of a large new library in 1986, painted a controversial shade of deep pink. The structural detailing of the library echoed the art deco style of the adjacent Van Isle Theatre, which the municipality purchased in 1985 to convert to a performing arts theatre. The patience of theatre-goers had been tried beyond endurance by the folding chairs of the school gym and the restricted view of a makeshift stage. When Jacquie (Glover) Gordon saw a notice in a local paper calling for a volunteer committee to convert the Van Isle to a performing arts theatre, she immediately submitted her name. Her years of hands-on experience with plays, musicals and operas proved vital to the project.

Jacquie's lifelong interest in the arts was nurtured by three generations of her Union Bay coal mining family. Her great-grandmother's devotion to music earned her the title of "the merry widow," and her father, a mine mechanic with a passion for opera and literature, was still quoting Shakespeare on his deathbed.

After several years of exacting work the newly styled Tidemark Theatre opened with a ten-day celebration in October 1987. It was one of the most exciting events of the 1980s, a terrific showcase of local talent, including an exhibition of works by the internationally renowned local artist Sybil Andrews Morgan, along with choral, dance and operatic performances.

The drive to construct a new building for the Museum at Campbell River is another example of the community's will to achieve polish, and a diversity of attractions. Stephanie Tipple, president of the museum society, and a tightly aligned board of political and business leaders, along with the executive director, Jay Stewart, were determined to build one of the finest community museums in the province. They stubbornly retained their vision through changing political agendas and government granting criteria, a slippery economy, and endless fundraising drives. Finally, over a decade later, in 1994, a 21,000-square-foot (1,890 sq m) facility was opened in a park overlooking Discovery Passage.

The Friends of the Tidemark Theatre, 1989, celebrating the third anniversary of the performing arts facility, which was converted from the old Van Isle Theatre. Left to right: Kim Patrick-Hoff, Linda Osing, Jacquie Gordon, Bill Ritchie, Irene Plato, Margo Cormack, Faye Skuse, Joyce McMann (back), Mary Murphy, Sharon Wilson, Penny Liebel and Susan O'Connor. *MCR 18574*

Museum at Campbell River trustees Jocelyn Skrlac (at left edge), Morgan Ostler, Stephanie Tipple, Bob Duncan, Lynn Nash and Joe Painter stand with President Bob Gordon, as he welcomes more than 1,000 guests to the official opening of the new museum at the corner of 5th Avenue and the Island Highway, 1994. *Courtesy MCR*

Pat Martin of Raven Industries, who quietly blended into the crowd of over 1,000 people at the opening ceremonies, played a major role in raising the funds for the new facility. He continued to work behind the scenes to garner the support of generous corporate donors to pay for the installation of sophisticated exhibits portraying the history of the people of north Vancouver Island.

The watercolourist Doris Ritchie played a lead role in nurturing both performing and visual arts associations in Campbell River for decades. In 1994 Ritchie and her fellow Campbell River Arts Council members opened the town's first public art gallery in the Centennial Building on Tyee Plaza.

Sports facilities, always a vital part of the Campbell River scene, were also enhanced in the 1980s and '90s. A 67.8-acre (27 ha) sports park was opened in Willow Point in 1987 and the first phase in the Storey Creek Golf Course was completed in 1989. Two independent loggers, Alex Linton and Henry Norie, began a ski resort on Mt. Washington that would become a major destination for skiers from around the world.

Dan Samson says one of the rewarding traits of Campbell Riverites is their willingness to speak out. "And they have the assurance that they will be listened to." This assertiveness, according to Arthur Mayse, is a holdover from the town's "yeasty" beginnings, which he characterized as having a certain "bounce and spit-in-your-eye hardihood" not always found in more refined towns.

Campbell River's first woman mayor, Mary Ashley, led her council through a barrage of outspoken "spit-in-your-eye" debates through much of her term in office in the early 1990s. The

Jay Stewart (right foreground), sitting across from Jim Henderson, photographed by Grant Patterson in 1985. A Museum at Campbell River group of long-time residents gathered each week to reminisce about the history of the community. Stewart, the dedicated visionary behind the society's campaign for a new museum, also initiated diverse outreach programming, which remains one of the society's most popular services. *MCR 13141*

critical issue was the municipality's long-standing plan to develop the Beaver Lodge Lands direct-ly west of the main residential areas.

However, residents had become very attached to the beautifully reforested acreage with its meandering salmon-bearing streams. When the stalwart band of Campbell River conservationists took issue with the municipality's plans, the editor of the *Mirror* newspaper, Alistair Taylor, toured the lands with Don McIvor of the Environmental Council and Charlie Cornfield of the Fish and Game Club. "What an eye-opener," declared the surprised editor. "One of the most beautiful forests within walking distance of any community lies behind that veil of green holding back the subdivisions rolled up to the land's doorstep...a forest so silent you would think you were a hun-dred miles into the bush..."

From the municipality's perspective the lands were pivotal to their plan to contain the north-south sprawl of the town. They had not completed negotiations with the province to buy the lands, but had begun installing infrastructure in the surrounding area, intending to link it with a combined college/high school, a sports complex, a housing development and the extension of Dogwood Street on Beaver Lodge Lands.

The balance tipped in favour of the Friends of Beaver Lodge Lands when Bruce Murdoch spot-ted a notation on a Forest Service document that suggested the lands had been a gift. Don McIvor and Stan Goodrich went to Victoria on behalf of the Environmental Council and found the deed, confirming that the lands had been given to the province in 1931 for a reforestation demonstration project. But by this time only 750 of the original 1,000 acres (400 ha) remained.

Colin Gabelmann, MLA for the district, was duty-bound as BC's attorney general to honour the terms of the trust. Of his many accomplishments while serving this riding, the resolution of the Beaver Lodge Lands issue is one of his proudest achievements: "We added quite a big parcel to the original Trust and allowed the college and high school, Timberline, to go ahead...one or two of the subdivision areas...along with the Dogwood [Street] extension— while at the same time enlarging the Trust area by purchasing adjacent land.... It will be Campbell River's Stanley Park."[7]

Jim Lornie followed Mary Ashley as mayor of Campbell River in November 1993, coming to the job as a third-generation resident. While Lornie is a man deeply rooted within the traditions and culture of the town's past, he also took office as a man of the present, naming the revitalization of the Campbell River estuary and a positive start on land claims with the First Nations as his paramount concerns. He voiced the opinion that the Campbell River, the vital nursery for the continuing economy of the district, is the heart of the town. Indeed, the municipality played a key role in the 1990s in saving the river, starting with the 1994 purchase of the Campbell River Spit, which was scheduled to be converted to a park in 2004.

By the 1990s the majority of the community stood with conservationists in their drive to restore the Campbell River estuary, a task Roderick Haig-Brown had urged Riverites to undertake decades before. In the early 1970s Haig-Brown had opposed the building of Quinsam Hatchery, preferring to see provincial funds used for a full-scale cleanup of the estuary to preserve natural habitat and genetic stocks. The hatchery project went ahead and the salmon were saved, although now diminished in their genetic diversity.

Some residents point to Jim Van Tine, director of the hatchery, as the river's greatest champion. He has worked closely over decades with conservationists in a slow but tenacious drive to restore the river. An important part of Van Tine's work has been a vigorous public education program, designed to teach everyone, from children to industrialists, the value and importance of regenerating fish stocks and enhancing spawning and rearing watersheds.

By the early 1980s the Campbell River had become toxic to chinook and steelhead. Meanwhile, "the Quinsam Hatchery prevented Campbell River chinook from going extinct," according to Rob Bell-Irving. It was the Tyee Club, under Past President Mike Gage, that precipitated a unique collaborative effort to clean up Campbell River estuary. The club raised a quarter of a million dollars to re-gravel the Second Island channel, creating the required habitat for spawning salmon. No sooner was the work complete than the hydro dam released flood waters, washing out the new gravel bed, right after the salmon spawned. "This led to the Campbell River Watershed Management Committee, which now co-manages all Campbell River flows," explained Bell-Irving. Immediately following the "quarter million washout," Mike Gage and the Tyee Club raised the money from BC Hydro and private companies to start all over again.

Hatchery staff have stocked streams from Sayward to Oyster Bay, replacing salmon runs that had been extinct since the 1970s. Each now has its own steward group, safeguarding stocks and raising funds for continuing rehabilitation.

In 1997 Jim Van Tine took a temporary position with the Department of Fisheries and Oceans to lead a groundbreaking project to restore the Campbell River to a near-natural state. The scale of the program is said to be unique in the province. With many of the sources of industrial pollution removed from the river, the cleanup began. A foul-smelling oil spill from 1947, on the old Elk River Timber Company property, was uncovered and sopped up. The riverbanks have been reshaped and planted with marsh grasses, and new spawning channels created, with the assistance of former estuary occupants like Raven Industries. When the project is complete there will be public trails along the south bank of the river, with bridges to the small islands in the estuary.

The salmon fishery continues to be of vital importance to First Nations groups throughout the district. In 1994, after years of protests and court cases, the Kwakiutl Territorial Fish Commission, representing much of northern Vancouver Island, signed a multi-year agreement with the federal Department of Fisheries and Oceans. Among other things the agreement allows for an annual allocation of salmon to be taken for food, ceremonial and social purposes.

First Nations people took assertive steps toward self-government throughout the 1980s, as well as reclaiming social and economic rights. In 1985 Native women who had married non-Native men (which, through an old proviso in the Indian Act, had robbed them of their status) regained their rights as band members. "There are ... many people of Native ancestry who are not recognized by the federal government but who share the same burden of being different and wanting an equal part in society," said the Kwakwaka'wakw leader Bobby Joseph. Cindy Lou Inrig and her children were the first of hundreds of Native people in the Campbell River district to regain their rightful status.

The Department of Indian Affairs began downsizing in readiness for First Nations bands to move toward self-government, and the easing of paternalistic controls encouraged bands to set up their own businesses. On the Cape Mudge bluffs overlooking the Strait of Georgia the Wewaikai Band opened a first-class tourist lodge named after the ancient village, Tsa-Qua-Luten.

The circumstances of the Homalco Band of Church House went through a radical transformation in this period, sparked by a federal government offer to buy a right-of-way through part of their land at Bute Inlet. Chief Richard Harry turned this government offer into a land swap that allowed his band to relocate to 160 acres (64 ha) near the Campbell River Airport. By 1997, Band members had constructed forty-seven homes and a fine new cultural centre on their newly established reserve, while taking tremendous strides toward regaining a healthy economy and society.

In the early 1980s the Homalco Band logged parts of their remote reserve lands to enormous advantage, and their salmon hatchery on the Orford River in Bute Inlet has had an excellent return rate. They were the first to begin formal land claim negotiations in the 1990s. "This is a very historic day for Homalco First Nations," said Bobby Joseph, as the treaty negotiations process kicked into high gear in 1995. "It is a proud day for all members of the band." Closed-door sessions with band representatives, Mayor Jim Lornie, and federal and provincial delegates are expected to continue through several more years of complex negotiation. Their mutual aim is to deal with a backlog of unfinished business dating back to the removal of allocated band land in 1888.[8]

The Lekwiltok people of the district are also compiling the necessary data to begin negotiations for their claims, complicated by ambiguities in the original reserve allocations to the Wewaikai and Weiwaikum Bands. Legal actions between the two bands have not yet brought about mutually satisfactory clarification of their existing property rights.

Meanwhile the Weiwaikum people have made rapid strides in creating new economic opportunities. After years of negotiating with all levels of government, the band began construction of their marina north of the Quadra ferry dock in 1989. "The original concept was to build a recreational marina, using part of the estuary," recalls the band's business manager, Bob Duncan (a great-great-grandson of Capt. John Kwaksistala). "Negotiations with the Department of Fisheries led to broadening the plan extensively because the area to be filled [on the outside of the Spit] became much larger, 42 acres [16.8 ha]." The deal struck required the band to build new spawning channels to enhance the estuary, prior to designing a planned shopping mall, hotel, casino, convention centre and cruise ship docking facilities.

The band broke new ground for First Nations communities across the country by embracing an equal partnership with the Northwest Group, rather than simply leasing out band land. Their partners determined that Campbell River was "under-retailed" and the end result was a massive open strip mall, with enough major stores to constitute two side-by-side complexes. "The project will stem the flow to the south—namely Courtenay but, mostly, Nanaimo—of a significant amount of retail spending," said Alistair Taylor, editor of the *Mirror*, following the opening of the mall.

Welcome figure created by Bill Henderson, Junior Henderson and Greg Henderson, Discovery Harbour Centre. The Weiwaikum Band purchased foreshore rights and filled a portion of their reserve facing onto Discovery Passage to create a shopping mall and marina complex, opened in 1998. *Courtesy Weiwaikum Band and Northwest Group*

The Campbell River Indian Band Development Corporation (CRIBCO) sees the Discovery Harbour project as both a financial investment for each band member and a source of employment, fostered by the band's employment training counsellor.

The new mall, which has incorporated First Nations designs and motifs created by the Henderson family, has a unique quality. The waterfront walkways, offices, a pub and restaurant overlook the marina and Discovery Passage, while retail businesses front on a giant parking lot. At the heart of the whole is a First Nations gallery shop. Alistair Taylor of the *Mirror* described the opening celebrations in May 1998: "The fireworks that capped Saturday's grand opening of Discovery Harbour Centre celebrated more than just the opening of a shopping mall. Discovery Harbour Centre symbolizes the Campbell River Indian Band fulfilling its role as a major player in Campbell River's modern economy. [The project] makes a statement to Campbell River and the province that the Campbell River Indian Band is not just here and surviving, and not just a quaint cultural entity but a thriving economic powerhouse in the regional economy and a dynamic society in its own right."

Mall developers and First Nations business people from across the country have visited Discovery Harbour Mall to gather inspiration. "There is nothing to compare to this mall in size, scope and nature anywhere else in Canada, maybe in North America," said Bob Duncan, with justifiable pride.

Not everyone in the town of Campbell River views Discovery Harbour Mall with enthusiasm. But for those old salts whose memories stretch back to similar developments of the past, when both the Tyee Plaza and Ironwood Mall shifted the balance of power in the business sector, this is just one more stage in a continuum of change.

"We'll all just have to watch the tide going out on this one and see what's left on the shore when it starts coming back in again," says Thor Peterson. Compounded by yet another bleak recessionary period, the Discovery Harbour complex and the band have become the focus of animosity from merchants whose businesses have been levelled. Others, like Something Special Gifts and Pioneer Hardware on Shoppers Row, are navigating change by enhancing their strengths—specialization and personalized small-town service.

When the late Arthur Mayse reflected upon the period of tremendous growth and change that radicalized the town in the 1980s, it brought to mind one of his wife's childhood memories of a visit to Campbell River in the late 1920s: "[Win] paused by an old man who dozed in the sun on the government wharf. The greybeard opened his eyes, gazed at her owlishly, then delivered himself of a statement that had in it elements of prophecy. 'Y'know, kid,' he said, 'this place'll be a city one day.'"

His sage prediction has not yet been fully realized, but the town has been charting a steady course toward that mark ever since. The old "greybeard" no doubt based his prediction on the wealth of timber and fish in the region, bringing a steady stream of working men stumping past him on the wharf. He may also have recognized the pivotal position of the place as an access point and service hub for the surrounding district. Or maybe it was the excited air of holiday people like Win's family, exclaiming over the fantastic view of the islands and mountains surrounding the town, that inspired his comment. All of these things were enough to lead an old man with time on his hands to forecast a grand future, one that would be pushed and shoved into place with a yeasty, spit-in-your-eye determination handed down from one generation to the next—from Captain John Kwaksistala and Lillie Thulin to Jacquie Gordon and Bob Duncan.

In the spring of 1998 fishing guides and hotel keepers braced themselves for an indifferent, or worse, tourist season. The news that the BC fishery was on the wane had spread far and wide. Their predictions were justified. In spite of endless summer sun, business for many was marginal. But oddly enough, the Tourist Bureau reported a marked increase in visitors, the streets were busy and the ferry lineups to Quadra and Cortes Islands were packed. Something had changed. A new kind of tourism had emerged. Every second vehicle that passed through town sprouted kayaks and camping gear. The baby boomers, with their kids, dogs and hiking gear, had "found" the Discovery Coast.

A few companies read the signs in advance and were prepared. Bob Wright, owner of Painters Lodge, bought the prestigious April Point fishing lodge on Quadra Island and promoted it as a jumping off place for ecotourism. Christine Portmann and John Waibel, a mountaineer and a commercial fisherman turned kayaking outfitters and guides, could barely keep up with the demand for their Rebecca Spit Park sunset tours. The Museum at Campbell River's test run of a kayaking trip to historic and archaeological sites was triple-booked. Rob and Laurie Wood, mountaineers, escorted groups of Europeans through the alpine meadows and icefields at the head of Bute Inlet, where the mountains are recognized as being among the ten best climbing peaks in the world.

It wasn't just a new breed of tourists who discovered the beauties of the district in 1998. A new sort of resident had also arrived. The ability to live in close proximity to a range of outdoor pursuits while residing in a mid-sized town with all the basic amenities has tremendous appeal for people seeking alternatives to urban living. The profile of 1990s residents includes retirees with an

In the 1990s, Spirit of the West Adventures of Quadra Island teamed up with the Museum at Campbell River to offer heritage sites tours by kayak. Seen here, left to right, Catherine Temple, Shirley Philbrook, Peggy Waibel and Christine Portmann. *Courtesy Spirit of the West Adventures*

interest in hiking and boating, and a new generation of "homesteaders" breaking land on the islands while earning a living by telecommuting to their urban jobs. Western Forest Products moved their head office from Vancouver to the Discovery Harbour complex, a cost-saving measure that benefits its employees who want to escape urban traffic.

Looking down Campbell River's main street at the end of that summer of sun 1998, Bruce Baikie questioned how the town would respond to the new lifestyle that was emerging. Can a town wearing the tidy, conventional stamp of its rich industrial basis be restyled as a quaint haven for ecotourism? "Are they going to stick around in a town that has pulp mill smoke blowing down the streets? I don't think so. We've got to rethink what we offer here and get the pulp mill to clean up its act."

Some have questions of another kind. There are benefits from the new trend toward ecotourism that will encourage enriched environmental and cultural values and maintain seasonal jobs—but these advantages come at a price. Ecotourism is dominated by a self-contained

Aerial view of Campbell River in the 1990s. *Courtesy MCR*

type of visit, which injects far fewer dollars into the local economy than was enjoyed in the high-priced sport fishing industry. And some of the natural wonders that act as a draw, such as Robson Bight—where eager whale watchers and other boaters have actually begun to disturb the whale population—are suffering a negative impact as thousands of visitors motor, paddle and tramp through environmentally sensitive areas.

A wise one soaking up the summer sun on the waterfront today might put a slightly different spin on the predictions of the old greybeard from Win Mayse's youth. The forecast might be for a modest continuation of Campbell River's first industries—harvesting the maturing timber in the lush Sayward forest and the hatchery fish returning in Discovery Passage—while at the same time pointing to the mountains, ocean passages and islands at the town's feet. In the new millennium this environment, still rich and unique, will remain Campbell River's trump card in the game of economic survival.

Notes

Chapter 1

1. Dietrich Bertz, trans., "Legend #5, Legend of the Island Comox," excerpt from Franz Boas, *Indian Myths and Legends from the North Pacific Coast*, prepared by Randy Bouchard and Dorothy Kennedy, Museum at Campbell River Archives.

2. Remains of two mosasaurs, two elasmosaurs and a sea turtle have been found in the Puntledge and Trent River areas in the Comox Valley. Some of these remains are on display at the Courtenay and District Museum.

3. David Nagorsen, Grant Keddie and Richard Hebda, "Early Holocene Black Bears, *Ursus americanus*, From Vancouver Island," in *The Canadian Field-Naturalist* 109 (1) (1995), pp. 11–18.

4. Catherine Carlson, "The Early Component at Bear Cove," *Canadian Journal of Archaeology*, 3: 177-194.

5. Edward Curtis, *The North American Indian*, Vol. 10, 3rd ed. (Johnson Reprint Corp., 1978), first published in 1915, p. 137.

6. Lindsay Oliver, "Burial Recovery Report," conducted under the Archaeology and Outdoor Recreation Branch Permit Number 1989–34; May 1989.

7. Homer G. Barnett, *The Coast Salish of British Columbia* (Eugene OR: University of Oregon, 1955), p. 246.

8. Barnett, *The Coast Salish*, pp. 94–95.

9. Barnett, *The Coast Salish*, pp. 25–26.

Chapter 2

1. Ruby (Hovell) Wilson, interviewed by author, notes, fall 1998.

2. Documentation of the first Russian trade activity is scant but it is believed Russians came to this part of the coast as early as 1741. Spanish and British exploration, starting in 1774, was more carefully recorded.

3. Bern Anderson, *The Life and Voyages of Captain George Vancouver* (Seattle: University of Washington Press, 1960), p. 213, quoted in John Frazier Henry, *Early Maritime Artists of the Pacific Northwest Coast, 1741–1841* (Vancouver: Douglas & McIntyre, 1984).

4. Cecil Janes, trans., *A Spanish Voyage to Vancouver and the North-West Coast of America* (London: The Argonaut Press, 1930), p. 68.

5. C.F. Newcombe, ed., *Menzies' Journal of Vancouver's Voyage, April to October, 1792* (Victoria: Province of BC, 1923), pp. 81–82.

6. Robert Galois, *Kwakwaka'wakw Settlements, 1775–1920, A Geographical Analysis and Gazetteer* (Vancouver: UBC Press, 1994), pp. 405–6.

7. W. Kaye Lamb, ed., *The Voyage of George Vancouver, 1791–1795*, Vol. II (London: Hakluyt Society, 1984), p. 623.

8. Robert Galois, *Kwakwaka'wakw Settlements*, pp. 406–7.

9. Cecil Janes, *A Spanish Voyage*, p. 82.

10. Cole Harris, *The Resettlement of British Columbia: Essays on Colonialism and Geographical Change* (Vancouver: UBC Press, 1997), p. 4.

Chapter 3

1. Robert Galois, *Kwakwaka'wakw Settlements* p. 55.

2. George Quocksister, interview by author, notes, Campbell River, spring 1999.

3. Franz Boas, quoted in *Kwakwaka'wakw Settlements*, p. 51.

4. *Ibid.*, pp.266–67.

5. Harry Assu with Joy Inglis, *Assu of Cape Mudge: Recollections of a Coastal Indian Chief* (Vancouver: UBC Press, 1989), p. 5.

6. Homer Barnett, *The Coast Salish of British Columbia* (Eugene OR: University of Oregon, 1955) p. 25.

7. Robert Galois, *Kwakwaka'wakw Settlements*; and Robert Duncan, interview by author, notes, Campbelll River, fall 1998.

8. J.M. Yale, quoted in Duff and Taylor, *A Post-Contact Southward Movement of the Kwakiutl* (Victoria: Government of BC, 1956).

9. James Douglas, diary, 1840, BC Archives AB 40 D75.2.

10. James Douglas, quoted in Duff and Taylor, *A Post-Contact Southward Movement.*

11. Edward Curtis, *The Kwakiutl*, Vol. 2 of *The North American Indian*, pp. 110–12.

12. *Ibid.*

13. Morag Maclachlan, ed., *The Fort Langley Journals, 1827–30* (Vancouver: UBC Press, 1998), p. 202.

14. William Fraser Tolmie, *The Journals of William Fraser Tolmie, Physician and Fur Trader* (Vancouver: Mitchell Press, 1963).

15. James Douglas, diary, 1843, BC Archives AB 40 D75.4A.

16. Robert Galois, *Kwakwaka'wakw Settlements*, quoting rough census data compiled by the HBC and from the first official census records of 1881, pp. 38, 41.

17. Peg Pyner, "Uncle John Manson Laid to Rest on Cortes," *Courier*, January 23, 1957.

18. Robert Galois, *Kwakwaka'wakw Settlements*, p. 235.

19. Robert Galois, *Kwakwaka'wakw Settlements*, p. 235.

20. James Henderson, memoirs, Museum at Campbell River Archives.

Chapter 4

1. Fred Nunns, letter to Ernest Nunns, 1889, BC Archives.

2. David Day, "Eustace Smith: The Last Authority," in *Raincoast Chronicles 6/10* (Madeira Park BC: Harbour Publishing, 1983).

3. Fred Nunns, diary and letters, BC Archives.

4. Michael Manson, "Sketches from the Life of Michael Manson," memoirs, Museum at Campbell River Archives, Etta Byers Collection.

5. Fred Nunns, diary, BC Archives.

6. Richard Somerset Mackie, *The Wilderness Profound: Victorian Life on the Gulf of Georgia* (Victoria: Sono Nis Press, 1995).

7. B.C. Saunders, "Campbell River retrospective," 1954, BC Archives, Museum at Campbell River vertical file.

8. "Comox Lore," *Comox Argus*, March 19, 1931.

9. Arthur Mayse, interviews with Susan Mayse, tape recordings, BC Archives.

10. *Weekly News*, January 29, 1895.

11. Michael Taft, ed. *Tall Tales of British Columbia*, Sound Heritage Series, No. 39, (Victoria: Government of BC, 1983), pp. 54–55.

12. Cecil Smith, obituary, newspaper clipping, n.d., Museum at Campbell River Archives, Smith Family vertical file.

13. Vital Statistics, Schedule B—Deaths, 43160, BC Archives.

14. 1901 Dominion Census.

15. Richard Mackie, *The Wilderness Profound* quoting the *Weekly News*.

16. Edgar Willmot Wylie, will, BC Archives.

17. Doris Andersen, *Evergreen Islands, The Islands of the Inside Passage: Quadra to Malcolm* (Sidney BC: Gray's Publishing, 1979).

18. "Delightful Place is Valdes Island, Article by Resident Gives Charming Picture," *Comox Argus*, January 3, 1924.

19. 1891 Dominion Census.

20. *Weekly News*, January 29, 1892.

21. *Weekly News*, January 29, 1895.

Chapter 5

1. *The Log* (Columbia Coast Mission newsletter), 1906. Hinchy was a massive brute of a man with a fearsome reputation. He died from the effects of alcohol in about 1908.

2. 1901 Dominion Census, Sayward District. The census taker included annotations in the margins, listing the names of the logging camps.

3. John Antle, unpublished memoirs, Vancouver Public Library, Special Collections.

4. Harry Assu, interview, notes, May 6, 1988, Museum at Campbell River Archives.

5. Sir John Rogers, *Sport in Vancouver and Newfoundland* (London: Bell, 1912).

6. Wallace Baikie, memories of Joe Thomson, in *The Truck Logger*, September 1963.

7. *The Log*, October 1906, BC Archives.

8. "Lumber Camps Past and Present," *Daily Colonist*, April 21, 1905. The article is subtitled "from our Correspondent, Rock Bay, Valdes Island," although Rock Bay is not located on Valdes.

9. Fred Thulin, interview, n.d., BC Archives, Fred Thulin vertical file.

10. Charles Thulin's obituary, *Comox Argus*, April 28, 1932.

11. Joe Thomson's story, as related in an unpublished speech by Wallace Baikie, Museum at Campbell River Archives. There are numerous versions of the story of how the Thulins came to purchase the Campbell River site. In a 1933 telephone interview with the Vancouver city archivist, Fred Thulin recalled that a police officer suggested the purchase. In interview notes made in the 1950s by Ed Meade, curator of the Campbell River Museum, an old-timer gave a similar story to Baikie's, but with different names. In this telling the sale price was $600.

12. Thulin Family, oral history interview, 1958, tape recording, Museum at Campbell River Archives. Many different dates are cited for Charlie and Mary's move to Campbell River. Mary's recollection was 1908.

13. Elinor Swain Smith, "The Nine Lives of Cougar Smith," unpublished biography of Cecil Smith, Museum at Campbell River Archives.

14. H. Johnson, unpublished journal of an exploratory survey trip into the Buttle Lake region,

July 7, 1910, Museum at Campbell River Archives.

15. "First Teacher Opens Addition," *Campbell River Courier*, September 9, 1970.

16. Helen Mitchell, *Diamond in the Rough, The Campbell River Story* (Langley BC: Frontier Publishing, 1975).

17. Bill Law, oral history interview, tape recordings, Museum at Campbell River Archives.

Chapter 6

1. Eve (Willson) Eade collection, Museum at Campbell River Archives, 88-22.

2. Mike Andrews, interview by author, Campbell River, 1978, notes; John Perkins Jr., interview by author, Campbell River, fall 1998. Perkins recalls seeing the Quinsam Hotel being constructed around 1924.

3. Robert C. Scott, *My Captain Oliver* (Toronto: United Church, 1947).

4. The exact date when the Hkusam Village was abandoned has not been recorded. It seems to have been in use sporadically for several decades following the World War I influenza epidemic.

5. Helen Mitchell, *Diamond in the Rough*.

6. Letter, 1926, Thomas Hudson Collection, BC Archives.

7. *Comox Argus*, February 28, 1924.

8. Some recall the date of the buyout as 1912, while notes from an interview with Ed Dalby set the date at 1923.

9. "Campbell River," *Comox Argus*, March 15, 1923.

10. *Comox Argus*, May 21, 1925; Francis Dickie oral history interview, 830:1, tape recording, BC Archives; Tom Hall, interview by author.

Chapter 7

1. Letter from the secretary of an unnamed organization, perhaps the Board of Trade, March 11, 1932, Museum at Campbell River Archives.

2. Helen Mitchell, *Diamond in the Rough*.

3. Letter, March 11, 1932.

4. "Canon Alan Greene Welcomes Congregation at Anniversary," *Campbell River Courier*, July 19, 1956.

5. "Double Wedding at Cape Mudge," *Comox Argus*, January 3, 1935.

6. Thulin Family, oral history interview, n.d., 829:1, tape recording, BC Archives.

7. Roderick Haig-Brown, interview by Imbert Orchard, Campbell River, 1969, tape recording, BC Archives.

8. Dr. Richard Murphy, notes to author, December 1998.

9. Ayako (Atagi) Higashi, memoirs, October 1989, Museum at Campbell River Archives.

10. Roderick Haig-Brown, "Japanese in Canada," letter to the editor, *Comox Argus*, 1947.

11. Roderick Haig-Brown, *Measure of the Year* (Toronto: William Collins and Sons, 1950).

12. Martin Fossum, memoirs, Museum at Campbell River Archives.

13. John Shaw, "The Iron River Story," manuscript, 1985, 91-6, Museum of Campbell River Archives.

14. "H.R. MacMillan Gets Timber," *Comox Argus*, February 9, 1939.

15. Ruby (Hovell) Wilson, oral history interview, A 202, tape recording, Museum at Campbell River Archives.

16. *Campbell River Courier*, October 28, 1970.

Chapter 8

1. Richard Mackie, e-mail to author, April 30, 1998.

2. Roderick Haig-Brown, *Measure of the Year*.

3. "81-Year-Old Lady Fights Battle of the Buttle Lake," *Courier*, May 28, 1952.

4. Roderick Haig-Brown, *Vancouver Province*, n.d.

5. Roderick Haig-Brown, "The Fight for Strathcona Park," n.d., University of BC Library, Special Collections, B53.

6. Bob Langdon, oral history interview, tape recording, Museum at Campbell River Archives A59-1.

7. Bob Langdon, scrapbook, private collection.

8. Helen Mitchell, *Diamond in the Rough*.

9. Alan Haig-Brown, e-mail to author, November 1998.

10. *Comox Argus*, February 21, 1951.

11. Arthur Mayse, "Tough As Rawhide, He Was," *Upper Islander*, February 15, 1986.

12. *Courier*, May 6, 1953.

13. Renny Englebert, "River Slave to Vancouver Island," *Vancouver Sun* magazine supplement, January 31, 1948.

14. *Mirror*, November 21, 1990.

15. Dr. Dick Murphy, oral history interview, tape recording, Museum at Campbell River Archives A155.

16. *Ibid.*

17. Helen Mitchell, *Diamond in the Rough*.

18. "Through our Files: 8 Years Ago, Taken From Our Files Dec. 20, 1950," *Courier*, December 20, 1950.

19. T.W. Paterson, "Indian Chief Billy Assu Civilized the White Man," *Daily Colonist*, November 5, 1967.

20. Estelle Rose, letter to the editor, *Courier*, December 5, 1956.

21. Tom Barnett, conversation with author, notes, winter 1998.

22. *Courier*, March 27, 1963.

23. *Upper Islander*, May 18, 1966.

24. "Eric Sismey Helped Survey Strathcona Park in 1912," *Victoria Colonist*, 1965.

25. Ray Williston, oral history interview, October 1975, tape recording, BC Archives 1375:24.

26. Roderick Haig-Brown, *Vancouver Sun*, March 5, 1966.

27. *Vancouver Sun*, March 5, 1966.

Chapter 9

1. Roderick Haig-Brown, *From the World of Rod Haig-Brown, Writings and Reflections* (Toronto: McClelland and Stewart, 1982).

2. Peggy Rowand, "Hippies Find Haven In An Island Refuge," *Courier*, August 5, 1970.

3. Ken Drushka, interview by author, October 23, 1998, Vancouver, tape recording, Museum at Campbell River Archives.

4. Peggy Rowand, "LeDain Report Adds Confusion As Society Goes to 'Pot'," *Courier*, September 2, 1970.

5. Dick Isenor et al., *Edge of Discovery: A History of the Campbell River District* (Campbell River: Ptarmigan Press, 1989).

6. John Young, interview, October 25, 1998, tape recording, Museum at Campbell River Archives.

7. May Tunningly, interview by author, notes, fall 1998; and John Young, interview by author, tape recording, fall 1998, Museum at Campbell River Archives.

8. Michael Hanlon, "Go ahead, kids—cut all the classes you want," from *The Canadian*, n.d., Carihi scrapbooks, Tunningly Collection, Museum at Campbell River Archives.

9. John Young, letter to the editor, *Courier*, December 1966.

10. Bruce Saunders, memo to W.J. Logie, superintendent, September 2, 1970, Museum at Campbell River Archives, Saunders Collection, 87-97.

11. "No Compromise By School Board Head," *Courier*, September 16, 1970.

12. Ed Olive, memoirs, spring 1999, Museum at Campbell River Archives.

13. Paul Williamson, "It Costs Only 10% More To Be First Class," *Victoria Daily Times*, June 21, 1967.

14. "Say Their Peace, Principal John Young," *Campbell River Courier*, September 9, 1970.

15. John Young, interview by author.

16. *Courier*, August 30, 1972.

17. Homalco Indian Band, "Homalco Indian Band Community Development Plan, First Update," November 1985, Museum at Campbell River Archives.

18. Canada Department of Fisheries and Oceans, "Quinsam River Hatchery" pamphlet (n.d.), Museum at Campbell River Archives.

19. Haig-Brown Education Centre, World Wide Web site, quoting a 1950 source.

20. Valerie Haig-Brown, *Deep Currents: Roderick and Ann Haig-Brown* (Victoria: Orca Book Publishers, 1997), p. 196.

21. *Courier*, October 8, 1973.

22. Harry Assu with Joy Inglis, *Assu of Cape Mudge*, pp. 106–7.

Chapter 10

1. Rob Wood, *Towards the Unknown Mountains: An Autobiography from the Canadian Wilderness Frontier* (Campbell River BC: Ptarmigan Press, 1991).

2. Thor Peterson, interview by author, November 1998, tape recording, Museum at Campbell River Archives.

3. *Upper Islander*, August 6, 1985.

4. *Upper Islander*, June 9, 1987.

5. Rob Wood, *Towards the Unknown Mountains*.

6. *Courier-Islander*, May 9, 1989.

7. Colin Gabelmann, interview by author, August 1998, tape recording, Museum at Campbell River Archives.

8. Homalco Indian Band, "Homalco Indian Band Community Development Plan."

Selected Bibliography

Andersen, Doris. *Evergreen Islands, The Islands of the Inside Passage: Quadra to Malcolm.* Sidney: Gray's Publishing, 1979.

Assu, Harry, with Inglis, Joy. *Assu of Cape Mudge, Recollections of a Coastal Indian Chief.* Vancouver: UBC Press, 1989.

Baikie, Wallace. *Rolling with the Times.* Campbell River: Kask Graphics, 1985.

Barman, Jean. *The West Beyond the West.* Toronto: University of Toronto Press, 1996.

Barnett, Homer G. *The Coast Salish of British Columbia.* Eugene OR: University of Oregon, 1955.

Curtis, Edward. *The North American Indian.* New York: Johnson Reprint Corporation, 1978.

Drushka, Ken. *Working in the Woods, A History of Logging on the West Coast.* Madeira Park BC: Harbour Publishing, 1992.

Duff, Wilson. *The Indian History of British Columbia.* Victoria: BC Provincial Museum, 1977.

Egan, Van Gorman. *Tyee: The Story of the Tyee Club of British Columbia.* Campbell River: Ptarmigan Press, 1988.

Galois, Robert. *Kwakwaka'wakw Settlements, 1775–1920, A Geographical Analysis and Gazetteer.* Vancouver: UBC Press, 1994.

Haig-Brown, Roderick. *Measure of the Year.* Toronto: William Collins and Sons, 1950.

Haig-Brown, Valerie. *Deep Currents: Roderick and Ann Haig-Brown.* Victoria: Orca Book Publishers, 1997.

Harris, Cole. *The Resettlement of British Columbia: Essays on Colonialism and Geographical Change.* Vancouver: UBC Press, 1997.

Henry, John Frazier. *Early Maritime Artists of the Pacific Northwest Coast, 1741–1841.* Vancouver: Douglas & McIntyre, 1984.

Hill, Beth. *Upcoast Summers.* Ganges: Horsdal & Schubart, 1985.

Inglis, Joy. *Spirit in Stone.* Victoria: Horsdal & Schubart, 1998.

Isenor, D.E., E.G. Stephens and D.E. Watson. *Edge of Discovery: A History of the Campbell River District.* Campbell River: Ptarmigan Press, 1989.

Janes, Cecil, ed. *A Spanish Voyage to Vancouver and the North-West Coast of America.* London: The Argonaut Press, 1930.

Kennedy, Dorothy and Randy Bouchard. *Sliammon Life, Sliammon Lands.* Vancouver: Talonbooks, 1983.

Lamb, W. Kaye, ed. *The Voyage of George Vancouver, 1791–1795*, Vol. 2. London: The Hakluyt Society, 1984.

Mackie, Richard Somerset. *The Wilderness Profound, Victorian Life on the Gulf of Georgia.* Victoria: Sono Nis Press, 1995.

Meade, Edward F. *The Biography of Dr. Samuel Campbell, R.N., Surgeon & Surveyer, including The Naming and Early History of the Campbell River.* Campbell River, 1980.

Mitchell, Helen. *Diamond in the Rough, The Campbell River Story.* Langley BC: Frontier Publishing, 1975.

Newcombe, M.D., ed. *Menzies' Journal of Vancouver's Voyage, April to October, 1792*. Victoria: Province of BC, 1923.

Reekie, Jocelyn and Annette Yourk, ed. *Shorelines, Memoirs & Tales of the Discovery Islands*. Quathiaski Cove: Kingfisher Publishing, 1995.

Silkens, Thelma. *Campbell River, a modern history of a coastal community*. Campbell River: Museum at Campbell River, 1997.

Walbran, Captain John T. *British Columbia Coast Names: Their Origin and History*. Vancouver: Douglas & McIntyre, 1971.

Index